Traces of Bygone Biospheres

А.В. Лапо

Следы былых биосфер

Издательство «Знание», Москва

Traces
of
Bygone Biospheres

by

Andrey V. Lapo

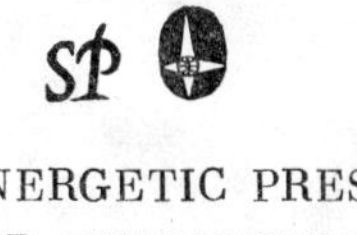

SYNERGETIC PRESS
MIR PUBLISHERS

Co-published by

Mir Publishers
2 Pervy Rizhsky Pereulok, I-110, GSP,
Moscow, 129820, USSR

and

Synergetic Press, Inc.
Post Office Box 689, Oracle, Arizona
85623
24 Old Gloucester Street, London WC1
3AL

Translated from the revised version of *Sledy Bylykh
Biosfer*, Znanie, Moscow, 1987, by V.A. Purto

For distribution in Great Britain, USA, Canada, British
Commonwealth (excluding India), and Nepal

ISBN 0 907791 069

Printed in the Union of Soviet Socialist Republics

Preface

At present our knowledge about the phenomena and processes occurring in the surrounding world has vastly expanded. At the same time it is only now that humanity has begun to understand both the scope of its activities and its dependence on the state of the biosphere. Understandably, the universal interconnection and interdependence of natural phenomena have become the focus of attention of modern natural sciences, and a synthesis of achievements in particular fields has become the dominant trend in the development of science as a whole.

This trend towards synthesis has found its most dramatic manifestation in the interpenetration of sciences concerned with animate and inanimate nature. A science of the biosphere has developed — a science which stands in its own right and cannot be reduced either to geography or biology, but makes use of their advances and results, and, in turn, influences the development of geology. The founder of this science was the Russian scientist Vladimir Ivanovich Vernadsky (1863-1945).

Present-day scientists acknowledge that "Vernadsky did more than simply enrich that vast field known as the Earth Sciences. He so greatly transformed their theoretical base that today we cannot imagine these sciences without his theories about the biosphere, biogeochemical processes and the role that living matter plays in the evolution of our planet"*.

This book will describe the biosphere and the

---

* A. Yanshin, S. Mikulinsky, I. Mochalov, "Speaking of Vernadsky", *Science in USSR*, 6, 3 (1983),

role of life in geological processes. You will learn about the scientists who dealt with these problems and, above all, about V.I. Vernadsky himself. His name is connected to the problems treated in this book, just as the name of Albert Einstein is connected to the theory of relativity. The high moral qualities of Vernadsky and Einstein also link them together. And, evidently, it is not by chance that the greatest scientific discoveries of the twentieth century were made by such irreproachable personalities as Vernadsky and Einstein. "To all who knew him, even slightly, he will remain an ideal of a man of high purity and beauty of character and a scientist who never lost his interest in the search for knowledge"*, one of Vernadsky's contemporaries wrote about him.

Vernadsky's name was famous already during his lifetime. His works were published not only in Russian, but also in Ukrainian, English, French, German, Czech, and Japanese. (The term "biogeochemistry" was first used by Vernadsky** in his article published in English.) In 1889, when quite a young man, he was elected a corresponding member of the British Association for the Advancement of Science. Later, the National Academies of France, Czechoslovakia and Yugoslavia, the Geological Societies of France and Belgium, the Biochemical Society of India, and the American Mineralogical Society elected Vernadsky their foreign member.

---

* T.M. Stadnichenko, "Memorial of Vladimir Ivanovich Vernadsky", *American Mineralogist*, 32, 3-4, 184 (1947).
** V.I. Vernadsky, "A plea for the establishment of a biogeochemical laboratory", *The Marine Biol. Station at Port Erin*, Annual Rep., 37, 38-43 (1923).

Every year since 1959, to commemorate Vernadsky's birthday, Vernadsky Readings have been conducted at the Institute named after him in Moscow. N.V. Belov, D.S. Korzhinsky, A.B. Ronov, A.V. Sidorenko, V.S. Sobolev, B.S. Sokolov, N.B. Vassoyevich, A.P. Vinogradov, and other prominent Soviet scientists, as well as their foreign colleagues T.F.W. Barth, B.R. Doe, R.M. Garrels, T. Owen, A.E. Ringwood, and J. Wyard have paid their homage to Vernadsky.

Among contemporary scientists writing in English, G.E. Hutchinson and H.A. Lowenstam can be said to have contributed most to the development of the ideas considered in this book. Hutchinson is an active propagandist of Vernadsky's ideas in the United States, a well-known biogeochemist, limnologist and ecologist, and a winner of the Franklin medal, the highest award from the Franklin Institute in Philadelphia (which was also conferred upon Thomas Edison, Niels Bohr, Max Planck, Albert Einstein, Enrico Fermi, and Theodosius Dobzhansky). He became interested in the problems of biogeochemistry by the early forties, under the influence of his friendship with Vernadsky's son Georgii Vladimirovich. It was on Hutchinson's initiative that the two most important works of V.I. Vernadsky on the biosphere, translated into English by G.V. Vernadsky and edited by Hutchinson, were published in the United States in the forties. Hutchinson earned his reputation from studies in the biogeochemistry of atmospheric gases, aluminium and phosphorus, from the discovery of the "plankton paradox", from his monographs on ecology and limnology, and from the programmatic work "Biosphere", which, in turn, has been translated into Russian.

Much credit for investigations into the role of life in geological processes is also due to Lowenstam, an outstanding scientist who was forced to leave his native Germany during the time of fascism and is now working in the United States. Lowenstam is well known mainly for his contributions to the study of biomineralization and biosedimentation phenomena, as well as to the investigation of fossil reefs.

The book now includes the most recent findings in the field. The 27th International Geological Congress held in Moscow in August 1984 proved to yield abundant new data on the subject. I have also tried to draw on the comments made by my colleagues in their reviews of the previous editions of the book, in correspondence, and in oral discussions. I am particularly indebted to Doctor Betsey Dexter of the USA, who has painstakingly read through the first English edition of the book and made most valuable comments.

I am not able to enumerate and give special thanks to all who have taken part in discussions about the book, but I do wish to express my deepest gratitude to all of them.

Since references in this text are often made to sources published in the Russian language, with which English-speaking readers may not be familiar, a bibliography for further readings in some European languages has been included.

In conclusion I wish to express the hope that they who open this book will not be disappointed after having read it to the end.

The author

Contents

Portrait of Vladimir Ivanovich Vernadsky by E.S. Za-
rudnaya-Kavos. (Oil on canvas. AN SSR Pushkin House.
First publication.)

A Strange Fate (Foreword)

Father could understand everything.
N.V. Toll-Vernadskaya

"When he was elected an honorary member of scientific institutions, it was an honour both to Vernadsky and, in no smaller measure, to the institutions that elected him. These institutions took pride in avowing: 'Academician Vernadsky has consented to be our honorary member'...

"More than half a century has passed since the time when his scientific creativity was in its prime, a very long period indeed, but during this period there was no scientist to match him...

"It is very difficult to become another Vernadsky, but young scientists ought not to lose hope. Way is open wide to them... If we pose the question whether anyone of them will be a second Vernadsky, it is difficult to give a positive answer. Certainly, anything is possible in nature, and one should not lose hope.

"What matters most is that everyone of us can improve the quality of our work and can attain new essential results if we follow the examples laid down by Vernadsky, study the principles and apply the specific features of his work."

This is what an outstanding geologist of our time, the Lenin prize winner Academician D.V. Nalivkin*, said at the centenary of Vernadsky in 1963.

This book is about Vernadsky's theories, about the biosphere, and the aim with which this book was written is that each of us will be able, as Nalivkin put it, "to improve the quality of his work".

Vernadsky was an astounding figure in the natural sciences of the twentieth century. It seemed as if he had no awareness that science was partitioned into fields (and in the modern natural sciences their number is over a thousand).

Vernadsky was a naturalist in the broad sense of this word, possibly, the last one in the history of science. Though he was neither a biologist nor a geographer by education, biologists rank him with Darwin and Pavlov, and geographers consider him to be one of the originators of modern geography. Vernadsky's works are not merely fundamental in some particular field: Vernadsky also founded new sciences. There are at least three such sciences: radiogeology, biogeochemistry, and the study of the biosphere (recently it was suggested that the latter science should be called biospherology**).

Although biochemistry and the teaching of the biosphere are new branches of science, they

---

* D.V. Nalivkin, "In memory of the world's greatest geochemist". In: *Materials for the Scientific Session of the All-Union Geographical Society,* Leningrad, 3-5 (1963).
** G.V. Guegamian, "About the biospherology of V.I. Vernadsky", *Journal of General Biology*, 41, 4, 581 595 (1980).

actively influence long-standing areas of natural sciences. Recently the article "Vital Forms of Plants Relating to the Teaching of the Biosphere" was published in *The Botanical Journal*. Also, at a recent scientific conference, G.G. Vinberg, a well-known Soviet biologist, President of the All-Union Hydrobiological Society and Corresponding Member of the USSR Academy of Sciences, read a paper entitled, "Vernadsky's Ideas in Modern Limnology". Limnology is the scientific study of lakes and Vernadsky was never scientifically involved in it.

It is a strange fate: Vernadsky's ideas have contributed to the development of those allied areas, in which he did not work. Evidently, Vernadsky not only laid foundations and formulated fruitful ideas in the sciences. Albert Einstein once said: "Science is an attempt to bring the chaotic diversity of our sensory experience in correspondence with a certain unified system of thinking". Vernadsky created such a system. This system of thinking, or, if you like, global conception, is based on the leading role of life in geological processes. It was created by Vernadsky for the geological past, but—strange fate!—it became actual, even topical for us, who live in the end of the second millennium. Vernadsky's conceptions are the methodological basis for developing environmental control programs today.

"It is a strange fate", wrote Vernadsky*, then at the age of twenty five, to his wife, "Most of all I was attracted, on the one hand, by the problems

---

* "From Vernadsky's Correspondence", *Priroda*, 9, 76 (1948).

of the historical life of mankind, and, on the other hand, by the philosophical aspects of mathematical sciences. But I did not go in for either of these fields. I did not go in for history, because I wanted first to receive training in natural history and then to cross over to history; nor did I go in for mathematics, since I did not believe in my mathematical abilities..."

Yet Vernadsky had decided upon the path to follow quite early. On his seventeenth birthday Volodya Vernadsky asked his father for an English edition of one of Darwin's books (by that time he could already read in several languages). His father presented him with something else—evidently, being of the opinion that it was too early for his son to read such serious books—and Volodya was so upset that his father had to give in. This book with the inscription "To my beloved son", is kept in Vernadsky's study in Moscow which is now a museum.

In his early years Vernadsky had already formulated questions about which he cogitated all his life. The manuscript of the report which he read at a conference of the Student Scientific and Literary Society of Petersburg University in December of 1884 has survived, and there we find the following words: "But what is life? And matter—which is in perpetual continuous and lawful motion, where endless destruction and creation occurs, where there is no rest—is it dead? Can it be that only the hardly noticeable film on an infinitely small dot in the universe—on the Earth—possesses radical, specific properties, and that death is reigning all over beyond it?... For the time being one can only raise these questions.

Their solution will be sooner or later given by science."

The "Vernadskian phenomenon" was moulded by the encyclopaedic character of his interests. His closest friends were people of various professions. Those who knew Vernadsky well could not help wondering at his conduct in conversations: he was not only a fine listener, but could easily "get his companion to talk", as one would say today. And those were not idle conversations. With D.S. Rozhdestvensky Vernadsky talked about nuclear physics; with N.Ya. Marr, about the Japhetic theory; with D.D. Pletnev, about theoretical fundamentals of cardiology; with N.I. Vavilov, about the colouration of plants and about the varieties of wheat.

In his eightieth year, in answer to the question in a questionnaire: "What do you regard as most characteristic and most valuable in the way you organize your labour as a scientist: a plan, accuracy, a systematic approach, or something else?" Vernadsky wrote, "I think that, most probably, it is a systematic approach and the striving for understanding the world around me. In addition, I attach extreme importance to matters of ethics*."

If we open Vernadsky's "Biogeochemical Essays", a collection of his papers published in 1940, we shall see the following dedication about the author's preface: "I dedicate these 'Biochemical Essays' to my wife Natalia Yegorovna, née Staritskaya, with whom I have been for more than fifty years, to my helpmate in work, never

---

* *Priroda*, 9, 97 (1967).

failing in her belief that to live is to love people and to search freely for truth". Is there any need in saying that such an understanding of the import of life was the guiding ethical principle for Vernadsky himself?

Vernadsky would not have been Vernadsky, were it not for his ability to organize his work to the maximum possible extent. Many of his contemporaries noted his ability to take advantage of, as he used to say, the smallest "bits of time". Vernadsky attached great importance to this and passed on the skill of time saving to his son Georgii and daughter Nina.

And there is one more characteristic detail: in answer to another question from the questionnaire we have already mentioned, Vernadsky wrote: "I have a reading knowledge of all Slavonic, Romance and Germanic languages."*

Strange fate! "We consult him now no less frequently, perhaps, even more frequently than during his lifetime; particularly in the course of our scientific work, where his thoughts and evaluations always attend us", one of Vernadsky's contemporaries wrote about him. His work is striking not only because of his profound knowledge of the subject, but also because of the wealth of factual material and (now we know why!) excurtions into history. Some of Vernadsky's works are such that, one would think, only a whole body of authors could have the power to write them. But they were written by one man, rather advanced in years: Vernadsky wrote all his main works about the biosphere when he was already

---

* *Priroda*, **9, 96 (1967).**

over sixty. Not always did it come easily to him.

"If you observe persons engaged in scientific work, you notice how often they are irritated because of the course taken by, and the essence of their work, or how often they cannot make themselves work, because all their will has been used in petty, strenuous tasks and they have to summon up their strength again..."—this is a quotation from another letter Vernadsky wrote to his wife in the same year of 1889*.

These qualities of Vernadsky—the encyclopac dic character of his interests and his outstanding capacity for work—provide, I think, a clue to the understanding of the "Vernadskian phenomenon". And, as Academician Nalivkin says, though one may not become a second Vernadsky, it is necessary that one should learn from his example.

The first thing that strikes one is the integrity of Vernadsky's world outlook. I cannot refrain from citing one more of his letters, written in 1892**:

"I generally do not understand the division of love into some kind of 'sensual', or animal, and some kind of lofty, or 'ideal', type. It seems to me that, in general, the conception about the sensual or animal entertained by us is something really comical. Only one thing matters here: how high in general is the personality of each of the two who are in love and to what extent are they equal. We see absolutely the same thing everywhere: in friendship, in common conversation,

---

* "From Vernadsky's Correspondence", *Priroda*, 9, 76 (1948).
** *Russian Literature*, 3, 198-199 (1979).

in the way of spending time together, etc. The baseness of nature or low culture will put the same stamp of vulgarity anywhere. I think, the time has come for us to stop regarding the 'body' as something despicable and to get rid of the narrow Christian (or monkish) division into the spirit and the body. Real spiritual life, the real highly principled side of life consists simply in using the best sides of both the body and the spirit".

The expression of his lucid eyes was that of a philosopher and a child; his gait was fast, his figure was well-proportioned, a little stooped only in his old age. Vernadsky did not like to be photographed, and only a few of his photographs are left. For some reason, descriptions of his appearance in the memoirs of his contemporaries are also few. The best description was given by Nalivkin*. It is dated 1914.

"... A narrow, chiselled face, high prominent forehead of a scientist, dark hair streaked with grey running in cascades above it caused wonder and surprise. But even these features were merely a background for eyes of unparalleled clarity, lucidity and profundity. It seemed that the entire cast, the entire soul of this extraordinary man was gleaming in them."

Vernadsky died in 1945, in the eighty-second year of his life.

Vernadsky is not easy to read: his mode of thinking was in abstract philosophical categories.

---

* D.V. Nalivkin, "Preparation of expeditions to Central Asia", *Contributions to the History of Geological Sciences*, Issue 11, 30 (1963).

His works are rich in factual material and tabulated numerical data, but there are few illustrative charts, effective images and colourful comparisons. Sometimes this resulted in him not being understood. The approach to Vernadsky, from the historical perspective, has been reversed: one need only compare the evolution of his creative legacy, given in different years. The fiftieth anniversary of the publication of Vernadsky's monograph about the biosphere was marked by holding special conferences; yet in 1927 it had been appraised by his reviewer in the following manner:

"Geologists calmly listened to Academician Vernadsky before, and they now listen taciturnly to yet another of his antihistorical communications. The rather interesting book of Vernadsky requires, however, a critical approach. The style of exposition is somewhat heavy. The book suffers also because the main, most important ideas are inadequately underscored and concentrated. Nevertheless, the interest which the book presents must motivate its study notwithstanding."

Indeed, geologists "calmly listened" to Academician Vernadsky. Vernadsky's works about the role of life in geological processes were rarely cited in the thirties, and in the obituary no mention at all was made that he had created the science of the biosphere. At that time only the Biogeochemical Laboratory (BIOGEL) organized by Vernadsky was concerned with problems of biogeochemistry (his laboratory has now become the Institute of Geochemistry and Analytical Chemistry, bearing Vernadsky's name).

The grandeur of Vernadsky's ideas was recog-

Martian surface. Photograph taken from the **lander module** of the US spaceship "Viking-2" in September, 1976. **(From:** *Priroda*, 1977, 2, p. 134.)

nized only after his death. In 1945 Academician A.E. Fersman*, one of the most convinced disciples of Vernadsky, called by his friends "ball lightning" for his tremendous energy (and for his figure), wrote the following about the creative legacy of Vernadsky:

"For decades, for whole centuries will these brilliant ideas be extended and studied, will new

---

* A.E. Fersman, "Vladimir Ivanovich Vernadsky", *Bull. of MSN*, Geol. section, **21**, 1, 53-54 (in Russian with English summary) (1946).

Sea cucumber, a characteristic representative of abyssal fauna. The Atlantic Ocean at a depth of 2120 m. (From: B.C. Heezen, C.D. Hollister, *The Face of the Deep*, N.Y. a.o., 1971, p. 135.)

pages, providing a source for new strivings, be opened... It is not yet time for delving deeply into his vast archives and numerous records of his biography; it will take many years of work for his disciples and historians of natural sciences to reveal the main trends in his scientific creativity, to unriddle the complicated compositions of his text, still not clear to us. This task lies with the generations to come..."

Vernadsky was already worshipped, but not yet understood. Now the time of understanding has come. At the 27th International Geological Congress I happened to witness a curious event

Г.А. Zavarzin, a well-known Soviet microbiologist and Corresponding Member of the USSR
Academy of Sciences, started reading his paper
by showing a slide with a quotation from Vernadsky's book "The Biosphere". Then, after present-
ing his own factual material for about 40 minutes, Zavarzin concluded the report by saying
(I quote from my notes): "I am very sorry that I
could not add anything new to Vernadsky's
words published in 1926". Vernadsky's books
which were not published during his lifetime are
now published: two volumes of "Reflections of
Naturalist" (1975, 1977), "Living Matter" (1978),
a third issue of "Problems of Biogeochemistry"
(1980), works on the history of science (1981),
"Pages of Autobiography" (1981), Vernadsky's
correspondence with B.L. Lichkov (1979, 1980)
and A.E. Fersman (1985)... Written 50 to 70 years
ago, these materials in a strange way turn out to
be new in their ideas, in the depth with which
the scientific material is treated and in the
breadth with which it is generalized. In the modern
natural sciences Vernadsky remains the leader.
It is a fate to be envied...

1. The Biosphere

Ages and millennia had passed before human thought could note the traits of a single consistent mechanism in the seemingly chaotic picture of nature.

V.I. Vernadsky, 1926

In 1926 in Leningrad a book was issued in two thousand copies, with nothing showy in its design. This book, however, was to become one of the greatest events in the history of natural sciences of the twentieth century. It came from the pen of Vernadsky and its title was "The Biosphere". It was in this very thin book, which contained only one hundred and fifty pages, that the biosphere of the Earth was for the first time shown to be an integral dynamic system controlled by life. Three years later the book was reissued in Paris in French.*

After the appearance of "The Biosphere" the general ideas about the world, entertained by naturalists, changed. One must agree with Aldo Leopold that the greatest discovery of the 20th century is not radio or television, but the recognition that the Earth is organized as an extremely com-

---

* W. Vernadsky, *La biospfère*, Alcan, Paris, 1929. The first English edition appeared only in 1986, when the present book was being prepared for publication (V. Vernadsky, *The Biosphere*, Synergetic Press, 1986).

Eduard Suess. (From: K. Bogdanovich. *Eduard Suess* (obituary), 1914.)

plex system. Vernadsky was the founder of this new approach.

More than half a century has passed since "The Biosphere" appeared. Extensive data have been collected providing evidence for the determining role of life in geological processes, and concerning the deposits dating back to the biospheres of bygone epochs.

It is this compass of problems that we shall consider in our book. But, as V.I. Lenin said, "... anyone who tackles partial problems without previously settled general problems will inevitably and at every step 'come up against' those general problems without himself realizing it."*

Bearing this in mind, we devote the first chapter of the book to the theory of the biosphere.

This term appeared in the scientific literature in 1875 in a monograph devoted to the geological structure of the Alps. The author of the monograph was Eduard Suess (1831-1914), a Gold Medal winner of the Russian Geographical Society, an eminent Austrian geologist, "a generalizer of geological facts", as Academician V.A. Obruchev

---

* V. I. Lenin, *Collected works*, v. 12, p. 489, Foreign Languages Publishing House, Moscow, 1962.

used to call him. Suess wrote, "One thing seems to be foreign on this large celestial body consisting of spheres, namely—organic life... On the surface of continents it is possible to single out a self-contained biosphere..."*

Thus, inconspicuously for contemporaries, the word "biosphere" had come into use. Suess coined it concurrently with two other similar terms: "hydrosphere" and "lithosphere", by analogy with the term "atmosphere" already current in the literature. Having coined a new term for which such a brilliant future was in store, and actually introducing a new concept into science, Suess gave no definition of it. In their euphonious Latin, biologists call such terms *nomen nudum*, which means "naked name". The term "biosphere" began to be used occasionally in the scientific literature: it can be found, for instance, in the works of J. Murray and J. Walther, published at the turn of the century, but each author understood the term in his own way.

In the scientific and popular literature, and even in textbooks the term "biosphere" is sometimes ascribed to the famous French naturalist Jean Baptiste Lamarck (1744-1829). This is not correct; Lamarck is to be credited for having introduced the term "biology" (but not "biosphere") to science and for having been the first to estimate the scope of activity of the living organisms found on Earth. The confusion over the origin of the term "biosphere" may be due to the fact that Vernadsky (who always had a profound re-

---

* E. Suess, *Die Enstehung der Alpen*, Wein, 1875, S. 159.

spect for the works of his predecessors) quoted Lamarck's works many times but never mentioned that the term "biosphere" was not used there.

Lamarck lived at the time when the natural sciences did not suffer yet from specialization. Along with the treatises which we now classify as biological (using Lamarck's own term), Lamarck wrote the voluminous work "Hydrogeology", published in 1802. Chapter Four of this work is entitled, in the intricate style of that time, "What is the influence of living bodies on the substances found on the surface of the Earth and constituting its crust and what are the results of this influence?" Here Lamarck was more than half a century ahead of his time and, as Vernadsky put it, came close to the concept of the biosphere and to the realization of the planetary role of life: *"Complex mineral substances* of all kinds that constitute the external crust of the Earth occurring in the form of individual accumulations, ore bodies, parallel strata, etc., and forming lowlands, hills, valleys, and mountains, are exclusively products of the animals and plants that existed within these areas of the Earth's surface"* (Lamarck's italics). These words sound surprisingly modern, though they were written at the time when there was no, and could not be any, factual material to substantiate them: geologists began doing microscopic studies of rocks a good half a century later. And without knowing the microscopic structure of rocks, what can one say about the structure of the Earth's crust? It

---

* J. Lamarck, *Hydrogeologie*, Paris, 1802, pp. 167–168.

is no wonder that the prophetic words of Lamarck were forgotten for a long time.

A fundamentally important contribution to the development of our present-day understanding of the biosphere was also made by the famous German naturalist, a person of encyclopaedic learning, honorary member of the St. Petersburg Academy of Sciences and of the Russian Geographical Society, Alexander von Humboldt (1769-1859). It is not without reason that Humboldt is called the Aristotle of the nineteenth century. He is credited not for extending the knowledge in any particular field of natural science, but for being the first to view the Earth (even if on the level of natural philosophy) as a single whole. Humboldt developed this global approach (as we now term it) in his fundamental work "Kosmos", on which he had been working his whole life. An idea developed in "Kosmos" was that life was present everywhere ("all-animateness" of the Earth), and that it was inseparately connected with the inorganic world (an idea which was absolutely new for the nineteenth century!). The author even used the term "living sphere" (die Lebensphäre), though only once and without any comments. Vernadsky rated Humboldt's works very highly. He wrote: "His posing of the problems... approaches the geochemical conceptions of our time. To him living matter is an indissoluble and regular part of the planet, inseparable from its chemical medium."*

Finally, Vernadsky's direct predecessor and teacher was the founder of contemporary genetic

---

* V.I. Vernadsky, *Works*, v. 1, p. 19 (in Russian)

soil science V.V. Dockuchaev (1846-1903), who is to be credited for having been the first among naturalists to understand the danger of fractionating the science about nature into a plurality of particular disciplines. In his work "Concerning the Teaching of the Zones of Nature" (1898) Dokuchaev wrote that natural sciences had made great advances in the study of such natural objects as living organisms, minerals, rocks, and so forth. But at that time investigations concentrated on individual objects "rather than on their relationships, the genetic, everlasting and always regular connection which exists between forces, bodies and phenomena, between inanimate and living nature... Meanwhile, these relationships, these regular interactions constitute the essence of cognition of nature, the core of real nature philosophy—the best and highest charm of natural sciences."*

Dokuchaev had focussed his attention on the soil, i.e., a natural body where the interaction of the three "natural kingdoms" singled out at that time occurs: minerals, plants, and animals. Dokuchaev had singled out the soil as an autonomous—the fourth—natural kingdom and showed that the properties of soil are determined by interaction of biogenic and abiogenic factors.

Vernadsky picked up and brilliantly developed the ideas of his teacher. If Dokuchaev's works on soils may be likened to a spark, then the works of Vernadsky on the biosphere, no doubt, were the flame which flared up from that spark. And

---

* V.V. Dokuchaev, *Works*, v. 6, Moscow, Publishing House of USSR Academy of Sciences, 1951, p. 399 (in Russian).

though the term "biosphere" was introduced into the literature not by Dokuchaev but by Suess, it is Dokuchaev alone who is regarded as the harbinger of the contemporary teaching of the biosphere. It is not without reason that already in our time, in the book "Fundamentals of Ecology" by the American scientist E. Odum, Dokuchaev was called the "pioneer of ecology."*

Having creatively developed the ideas of his predecessors—Lamarck, Humboldt, and Dokuchaev—and having used the actually "ownerless" term of Suess, Vernadsky created a principally new approach to the phenomena of life. Therefore, as was justly noted by A.M. Gilyarov, a contemporary methodologist in ecology, although the theory of the biosphere can be traced back to concepts originating in nineteenth century science, "the formation of an integrative approach to the biosphere, as well as the very introduction of this level of organization of living matter, are due entirely to Vernadsky"**. The thesis, "Everything is connected with everything", which was later set forth by Barry Commoner*** as the "First Law of Ecology" had already been realized with respect to biology in the fundamental works of Vernadsky.

In simple terms, the biosphere is our environment, the "nature" in which we live. In his various works Vernadsky gave several definitions of

---

* E.P. Odum, *Fundamentals of Ecology*, III ed., W.B. Saunders Co., Philadelphia, 1971.

** A.M. Gilyarov, "Methodological Problems of Modern Ecology. Changing of Leading Conceptions", *Priroda*, 9, 101 (1981).

*** B. Commoner, *The Closing Circle*, New York, 1971

the biosphere, always emphasizing its two distinctive features: the first feature is that "the biosphere is the envelope of life, i.e., the area of existence of living matter"*; and the second feature is that "the biosphere can be regarded as the area of the Earth's crust occupied by transformers which convert cosmic radiation into effective terrestrial energy, i.e., electric, chemical, mechanical, thermal, etc."**

In his works Vernadsky emphasized the ubiquity of life (recall the "all-animateness" of the Earth as Humboldt understood it). And, indeed, the most improbable localities prove to be inhabited: thermal springs, in which the temperature of water reaches the boiling point and, in some cases, even exceeds it; perennial snow in the Himalayas, where at a height of 8300 m at least nine species of bacteria can be found***; arid deserts (in African deserts, famed for their aridity, there live, for example, more than 500 species of insects); and supersaline lakes****, where cyanophyceae, archebacteria, and one species of shrimps flourish, while flagellates and di-

---

* V.I. Vernadsky, *Works*, v. 1, Moscow, Publishing House of USSR Academy of Sciences, 1954, p. 178 (in Russian). (Further on references to this edition will be abbreviated as *Works*.)

** W. Vernadsky, *La biosphère*, 1929, Alcan, Paris, p. 12.

*** G.E. Hutchinson, *The Ecological Theater and the Evolutionary Play*, New Haven and London, Yale Univ. Press, 1965.

**** T.D. Brock, "Ecology of Saline Lakes". In: *Strategies of Microbial Life in Extreme Environments* (ed. M. Shilo), *Life Sci. Res. Rep.*, 13, 29-47 (1973).

atoms drag out a miserable existence, but, nevertheless, exist! Strange as it may seem, but even the Dead Sea is populated by organisms: several species of archebacteria and algae dwell there (perhaps we had better put its name in quotation marks—the so-called "Dead Sea"?).

Vernadsky's teacher Dokuchaev regarded the biotic and abiotic factors as being partners that enjoyed equal rights in the formation of soil. Vernadsky, having passed over to the global level, showed that the leading factor which transforms the face of the Earth is life. Its specific feature resides not only in that it accelerates chemical reactions, but also in that some reactions outside of organisms, at normal temperatures and pressures, do not proceed at all. For example, fats and carbohydrates are oxidized in an organism at a temperature of about 37 °C, whereas outside it they can be oxidized only when heated to 450-500 °C. Microorganisms synthesize ammonia from molecular nitrogen at normal temperature and under normal pressure, but under industrial conditions this reaction can occur only at 500 °C and 300-350 atm. This means that in living organisms some specific catalysts must develop, which accelerate the rate of chemical processes.

Such protein catalysts actually produced by the protoplasm have been found in living organisms and have been named "enzymes". Extremely small quantities of these enzymes are sufficient for the chemical processes to proceed in living organisms. In the whole world hardly a dozen kilograms of nitrogenase can be collected, but nitrogenase is a wonderful enzyme which organisms use for the synthesis of nitrogenous compounds from atmospheric nitrogen. Academician I.P. Pavlov called enzymes "instigators of life". In recent years the leading role of enzymes in life processes has become all the more apparent. For instance, there is an opinion that "life is nothing else but the strictly ordered interaction of enzymatic processes" (Willstätter, 1929), and in Professor Yermolaev's recent manual of physical geography* "the biosphere is understood as being that part of the geographical envelope of the Earth, within the boundaries of which the physico-geographical conditions ensure the normal functioning of enzymes". First attempts have been made to reveal the role of enzymes in geological processes as well.**

The biosphere of the Earth, as we understand it today, is a global open system having its own "inputs" and its own "outputs". Its "input" is the flux of solar energy coming from space; its "output" comprises those substances formed in the process of the vital activity of organisms, which for some reason have escaped from the biological cycle (sometimes for many millions of years). Figuratively speaking, this is an output to "geology".

At present the biosphere of the Earth is considered to be a cybernetic system possessing the properties of self-regulation. Fifty years before

---

* M.M. **Yermolaev**, *Introduction to Physical Geography*, Leningrad, Leningrad State University Press, 1975, p. 229 (in Russian).
** G.I. Bushinski, "Inhibitors and stimulators in lithogenesis", *Lithology and Miner. Resources*, 4, 495-497 (1967).

such terms did not exist, and Vernadsky spoke in this sense about the "orderliness of the biosphere" (and in earlier works, about its "mechanism").

Vernadsky saw one of the most characteristic manifestations of the orderliness of the biosphere in the presence of an ozone shield which is located above the biosphere and absorbs ultra-violet radiation deleterious to life (for us this is a most dramatic manifestation of self-regulation of the Earth's biosphere as a cybernetic system). The composition of the gaseous envelope of our planet is fully regulated by life.

Another example of self-regulation is the World Ocean. Every year rivers introduce 1.5 million tons of calcium carbonate into the ocean, but the salt composition of oceanic water remains substantially unchanged. Why? Organisms use these carbonates for building their skeletons, and after their death these carbonates go down to the oceanic floor. Thus, through the creation of "calcium covers" of our planet the composition of oceanic water is stabilized. This mechanism has been working in the biosphere for millions of years.

Consequently, self-regulation of the Earth's biosphere is ensured by living organisms. This allows one to regard the biosphere as a *centralized* cybernetic system. This name is used to denote systems in which one element, or sub-system, plays a dominant role in the functioning of the system as a whole. This element is called the *leading part* of the system, or its *centre**. Liv-

---

* A.D. Hall, R.E. Fagen, "Definition of system", *General Systems*, 1956, v. 1, pp. 18-28.

ing organisms in the biosphere play the role of such a centre.

According to the diversity law of Ashby*, a cybernetic system possesses stability for blocking external and internal disturbances only when it has sufficient *internal diversity*.

The Earth as a planet is characterized by considerable diversity of *natural conditions*. This is determined by its spherical shape, by its revolution around the Sun and rotation about its own axis, which, in turn, conditions latitudinal and seasonal changes in the intensity of the solar energy input; considerable diversity of natural conditions is also created by the dissected relief of the Earth. The range of the absolute data of the Earth's surface is over 19 km: from $+8848$ m (Mount Chomolungma, Everest) to $-11\,022$ m (Mariana Trench in the Pacific Ocean). But the main diversity of the Earth's biosphere is created by living organisms.

A most interesting (so far underestimated) generalization about the creation of nonuniform medium by organisms was made in the beginning of this century by the Russian microbiologist, Professor M.A. Yegunov (1864-1937): "Any medium populated by living organisms is a bioanisotropic medium. Bio-anisotropy is a general phenomenon; there is no bio-isotropy. This follows from the fact that between the medium and every organism a continuous metabolism takes place, and therefore at any given moment different points of the medium differ from each other

---

* W.R. Ashby, *An Introduction of Cybernetics*, New York, Wiley, 1958.

in their physico-chemical composition. Diffusion can never completely level out these differences as long as the cause that brings them about exists"*.

It is believed that about two million species of living organisms are represented in the present-state biosphere (there have been about a billion of them during the entire period of its existence). Each of the species includes millions and billions of individuals distributed in the space. Recently it has been calculated that on the territory near the Angara river, within an area of 0.23 square kilometres, there live 535 (!) species of invertebrates, each of these species, naturally, interacting with the environment in its own way. It is the activity of living organisms that creates the extraordinary diversity of the "nature" around us, the extraordinary diversity of the biosphere. Perhaps, until recently we could not appreciate this diversity: we simply had nothing to compare our biosphere with. Only now, after we have seen on the screens of our television sets and on the pages of illustrated editions the landscapes of other planets, deprived of life, only now can we fully appreciate the "internal diversity" of the biosphere. This provides a definite guarantee for the preservation of life on our planet.

It is difficult for us now to imagine the real scale of those geological catastrophes which have occurred in the history of the Earth. The most dreadful earthquakes which occurred within the

---

* M.A. Yegunov, "Bio-anisotropic basins". In: *Yearbook of Geology and Mineralogy of Russia*, 1900-1901, 4, 42.

memory of mankind were accompanied by faults with an amplitude of 4 to 6 m. Tectonic phenomena of such dimensions are considered to be a national disaster: let us recall the dreadful Peruvian earthquake of 1970, which took about 100 thousand lives. Geological deposit faults are known which have an amplitude of several kilometres. No doubt, the subsidence did not come about all at once, but went to a depth of several kilometres!

The most terrible form of volcanic activity is lava flows. Eruptions of such a type have been rather rare occasions within the memory of mankind. The largest of them took place at the beginning of this century on a sparcely populated territory in Alaska. The hight of the cliff formed there by solidified lava reaches 100 m. In the 1883 eruption of the Krakatoa volcano (in the Sunda Strait, Indonesia) the fallout of volcanic ash formed 2 to 60 m layer on the island.

How frequent have geological catastrophes been in the history of the biosphere? Nevertheless, all the great catastrophes that have occurred in the biosphere (including the glaciations) were always local rather than global in character. In other words, such a catastrophe has not yet occurred which could destroy all life on the Earth. The theories of catastrophism are sometimes discussed, but, as a rule, they are not substantiated by factual data. These ideas were first formulated by the famous French zoologist Georges Cuvier (1769-1832), who explained changes in the fauna of the Earth by periodic natural calamities. Cuvier did not explain the causes of the catastrophes —they were "miracles". Due to his reputation his doctrine of catastrophism was at one time rather widespread and acquired numerous followers. For example, the French paleontologist A.D. d'Orbigny (1802-1857) held that there had been 27 catastrophes in the history of the Earth, while the Swiss naturalist J.L.R. Agassiz (1807-1873) suggested as many as 50 to 80.

These views, one would think, could be shelved by now, but the idea of geological catastrophe has again become the subject of extensive discussions in the press. The reason for this was the finding of a thin (only a few centimetres thick) intermediate layer between the Cretaceous and Paleogene layers, greatly enriched with iridium, one of the elements of the Platinum Group. Such layers were found in several regions of the globe (Denmark, Italy, Spain, New Zealand, and in depressions in the Pacific and Atlantic Oceans)*. The concentration of iridium in the intermediate layer was one or even two orders of magnitude higher than usual. Since iridium is one of the elements characteristic of meteorites, it was suggested that this element may have been brought into the intermediate layer by an asteroid (about 10 km in diameter) which exploded upon collision with our planet, dispersing asteroidal material in the atmosphere which then gradually precipitated over the territory of the Earth. Scientists began to associate mass extinctions of numerous groups of organisms (first of all, of dinosaurs), corresponding to that interval of geological history, with this event.

---

* L.W. Alvarez, W. Alvarez, F. Asaro, H.V. Michel, "Extraterrestrial cause for the Cretaceous—tertiary extinction", *Science*, 208, 4448, 1095-1108 (1980).

In recent years a fundamental and detailed analysis of the changes in fauna between the Mesozoic and Cenozoic was carried out at the Paleontological Institute of the USSR Academy of Sciences in cooperation with other agencies. Different groups of organisms were studied, and the changes in their class, order, and family were traced within the period of interest. This comprehensive investigation demonstrated that the extinction of different groups of the organic world had occurred gradually and not simultaneously. Also, the extinction of dinosaurs had taken place *prior to* the appearance of the iridium layer. Academician L.P. Tatarinov, Director of the Paleontological Institute, proceeding from the results of these investigations, has come to the conclusion that in general "the hypothesis about the global catastrophe as the main cause for the change of the biota in the history of the Earth has not in any case been substantiated by sufficiently reliable paleontological data".

And what about the iridium? Scientists from the University of Maryland (USA) recently demonstrated* that iridium can be of terrestrial origin as well. Studying the products of the explosion of the Kilauea volcano on the Hawaiian Islands, they found an extremely high concentration of iridium. In addition, the iridium did not accumulate in the lava, but entered the atmosphere along with volcanic ash and gases. This ensured a wide dispersion of iridium in the

---

* W.H. Zoller, J.R. Parrington, J.M. Phelan Korta, "Iridium enrichment in airborne particles from Kilauea volcano: January, 1983", *Science*, **222**, 4628, 1118-1121 (1983).

biosphere. True, in this case, the iridium supply was not great. But at the end of the Mesozoic period, gigantic outflows of basalts took place (and formed, in particular, the basalt traps of the Deccan Plateau in India). They could have led to a sharply pronounced accumulation of iridium in the atmosphere and then to its accumulation in a definite clear-cut interbed. Incidentally, this interbed is not present everywhere: for example, it is absent in the boundary deposits of the Cretaceous and Paleogene, which have been studied in detail in the Crimea by the scientists of the Paleontological Institute of the USSR Academy of Sciences.

Thus, the entire geological material accumulated demonstrates the continuity in the development of the organic world of the Earth throughout geological history and demonstrates the correctness of Vernadsky's conclusion about the absence of azoic deposits (i.e., deposits formed in the absence of life) in the Earth's crust. The internal diversity of the biosphere has ensured its stability even to the most significant catastrophic shocks. This stability is determined by the exclusive diversity and almost unlimited number of living organisms inhabiting the biosphere, by the interchangeability of the ecosystems constituting the biosphere, by duplication of the individual links of the biogeochemical cycles, by the vital resilience and activity of individuals, etc.

Professor O.P. Fisunenko, a paleobotanist of Voroshilovgrad, has calculated that the number of genera of higher plants found in different periods was: in the Silurian, 1; in the Devonian,

Charles Lyell. (From: M.A. Engelgardt. *Charles Lyell*, St. Petersburg, 1982.)

36; within the interval from the Carboniferous to the Triassic 150 to 200; from the Jurassic to the Neogene, 250 to 330. These figures refer only to a small interval of the geological history, but even they demonstrate a definite tendency towards an increase in the internal diversity of the biosphere in the case of higher plants. It may be assumed that this tendency has been steadily strengthening the "noise immunity" of the biosphere.

Thus, the Earth's biosphere is a self-regulated cybernetic system with an ever-increasing noise immunity, possessing the properties of homeostasis. The development of this idea, which originated in the last century, was recently traced by H.T. Odum*. The homeostasis of the biosphere is determined by the activity of living matter.**

A characteristic feature of the biosphere is the indissoluble connection and all-penetrating interaction of living and nonliving (or, as Vernadsky preferred to call it, "inert") substance.

---

* H.T. Odym, *Systems Ecology: An Introduction*, New York, J. Wiley and Sons, 1983, p. 577.
** J.E. Lovelock, M. Whitfield, "Life span of the biosphere", *Nature*, **296**, 5857, 561-563 (1982).

Charles Lyell* in his "Principles of Geology", evidently, was the first to introduce a special concept for the interaction of the organic factors (community of living organisms) and inorganic factors (climate, soil, relief, etc.) of the environment. Lyell called it "station". Later the British ecologist A. Tansley** (1871-1955), discussing the interaction of living and nonliving substances, introduced the concept of ecosystem now widely employed in the world literature. According to the definition given by D.V. Panfilov, "an ecosystem is a complex of interconnected organisms of different species and of the abiotic medium that is changed by them, which is capable of self-regulation and complete self-renewal of the biota". Ecosystems may be of any size. For instance, on land they can vary from several metres (sand dunes, microdepressions in steppes and semideserts, small lakes in tundras) to several kilometres (solonchaks, homogeneous stretches of steppes, forests, etc.). The biosphere of the Earth is a global-scale ecosystem. Underscoring this, Professor Heinrich Walter, the well-known geobotanist of the FRG, writes: "The Earth is one large entity, and events taking place in the Earth's environments, in the biosphere, exert a mutual influence upon each other. Climate, soil, vegetation, and animal life should not, therefore, be considered simply as isolated branches of sciences. It is impossible to separate the phenomena associated with life from environmental

---

* Ch. Lyell, *Principles of Geology*, v. II, London, 1832; 2nd ed., 1833.
** A.G. Tansley, "The use and abuse of vegetational concepts and terms", *Ecology*, 16, 284-307 (1935).

factors, and the task of the ecologist is to understand these interconnections. The biosphere is a vast ecosystem within which the continuous cycling of material and flow of energy takes place (certain smaller portions of the biosphere also constitute ecosystems)"*. In the contemporary literature such an approach is becoming more widespread**.

In the Soviet scientific literature the term "biogeocoenosis" is also sometimes used. This term was suggested by Academician V.N. Sukachev in 1942. Biogeocoenosis is now understood to be an area of the biosphere through which not a single essential biocoenotic, microclimatic, hydrological, soil, geomorphological, or geochemical boundary does pass.

In essence, both these concepts are close and differ mainly in details. Since the concept of ecosystem is "non-dimensional", we shall adhere to this term.

Ecosystems, like the biosphere as a whole, are "biocentric" and in most cases have a sufficiently complicated structure. Nevertheless, no matter how complicated this structure may be, there prevails the law discovered in 1935 by G.F. Gauze, at that time one of the closest collaborators of Vernadsky and now an Academician of the USSR Academy of Medical Sciences. The theorem of Gauze reads: "Two kinds of animals with

---

* H. Walter, *Vegetation of the Earth and Ecological Systems of the Geo-biosphere*, New York, Springer-Verlag, 1979, p. 1.
** J.D. Miller, J.L. Miller, "The earth as a system", *Behavioral Science*, 27, 4, 303-322 (1982).

a very similar way of life cannot exist in one and the same ecological niche."*

Due to their complicated structure, the ecosystems possess the properties of homeostasis, which finds expression in minimization of the negative effect of changes in the environments through rearrangement of the structure of the biota. The "homeostaticity margin" of the ecosystems can be measured in terms of the maximum load they are capable of withstanding without passing over to a new qualitative state. This homeostaticity margin can be measured in units of concrete effects, e.g., the amount of contaminants, temperature variations, humidity variations, etc. The stability of the biosphere as a whole is equal to at least the sum of the homeostaticity margins of the ecosystems constituting it.

Although the ecosystems are relatively closed, they are intimately interconnected. Their interaction manifests itself in the mutual exchange of the products of metabolism of living organisms, of the living organisms themselves, of various mineral and organic substances. In order to pass over from studying innumerable and quite diverse ecosystems to a more extensive comprehension of the functioning of the biosphere as a whole, Yu.P. Byallovich** has suggested that specific complexes of ecosystems—biogeosystems—should

---

* G.F. Gauze, "Investigation of the struggle for existence in mixed populations", *Zool. Journ.*, 14, 2, 243 (1935).

** Yu.P. Byallovich, "Systems of Biogeocoenoses". In: *Problems of Biocoenology*, Moscow, Nauka, 1973, pp. 37-47 (in Russian).

be singled out. According to the definition given by D.V. Panfilov*, "a biogeosystem is a part of the biosphere with a directed abiotic transfer of substances and energy that are transformed by the biota of specific ecosystems. The main forms of such a transfer are river runoffs on land, horizontal circulation flows in oceans and seas, and also wind transfer of substances and energy". The interaction of biogeosystems ensures the functioning of a unified gigantic cycle of substances within the entire biosphere. There are many proofs of the case in hand. The simplest proof is that we consume oxygen all the year round, whereas oxygen is produced by plants only during the vegetation period which may last throughout the year only in the tropical zone. This means that when it is not the vegetation period in our hemisphere we consume oxygen produced by the plants of the opposite hemisphere. There is also more dismal evidence of the global integration of the biospheric cycling: DDT has been found in the bodies of Antarctic penguins (this preparation, naturally, was never used in the Antarctic); radioactive strontium appeared in the milk of European women four months after each successive test of atomic weapons on the atolls of the Pacific Ocean.

The main elements participating in the biospheric cycling are hydrogen, oxygen, carbon, nitrogen, calcium, potassium, silicon, phosphorus,

---

* D.V. Panfilov, "Ecosystemic and Biogeosystemic Structure of the Biosphere". In: *Modern Problems of the Geography of Ecosystems*, Moscow, 1984, p. 27 (in Russian).

sulphur, strontium, barium, iron, manganese, zinc, molybdenum, copper, and nickel. The cyclings of chemical elements in which living matter participates have been given the name of biogeochemical cyclings.* At present greater attention has been given to their study in connection with environmental control.

The heterogeneity of the structure of the biosphere, its "mosaicism", is determined by the presence of regions in it which differ in their biogeochemical specialization, or biogeochemical provinces, as they were initially called. This concept was first introduced by Vernadsky in co-authorship with A.P. Vinogradov and further elaborated by the latter. The biogeochemical provinces were understood to be areas on the surface of the Earth, differing from the adjacent areas in the concentration of chemical elements or compounds in them and, as a result, causing different biological reactions of the local flora and fauna. Studies on the biogeochemical zoning of the Soviet Union were started in 1944. The map compiled by V.V. Kovalsky (1899-1984), Corresponding Member of the All-Union Lenin Academy of Agricultural Sciences, on the basis of those studies is considered to be one of the best in the world.

The global biogeochemical cycling in the biosphere is not closed. The reproducibility of separate cycles reaches 90-98 per cent.

---

* P.A. Trudinger, D.J. Swaine, G.W. Skyring, "Biogeochemical Cycling of Elements—General Considerations". In: *Biogeochemical Cycling of Mineral-Forming Elements*, Amsterdam, Elsevier, 1979, pp. 1-27.

In the geologic time-scale incomplete closure of the biogeochemical cycles leads to differentiation of the elements and to their accumulation in the atmosphere, hydrosphere, or in the sedimentary envelope of the Earth. These several per cent of substance not involved in the biotic cycle, constitute the "output to geology" which we have already mentioned.

But "geology" is found not only at the "output", but also at the "input" of the biotic cycle of the biosphere. Iohannes Walther (1860-1937), the famous German geologist, was one of the first to pay attention to this fact. He wrote: "The biosphere constitutes a peculiar transition zone between the atmosphere, hydrosphere, and lithosphere. Carbon dioxide of the air in the form of hard fossil coals could participate in the composition of the Earth crust in the same manner as lime dissolved in water once did, and, if we take into consideration that carbon dioxide can be delivered by way of volcanic processes from the pyrosphere, then even the hot Earth's core enters into reaction with living matter." Elaborating on this approach with a tremendous corpus of present-day data, the well-known Soviet geochemist, winner of the golden medal named after Vernadsky and Corresponding Member of the USSR Academy of Sciences, A.B. Ronov has come to the conclusion that the biotic cycle is to a considerable extent "open" and that constant supply of carbon dioxide to this cycle from the bowels of the Earth is required. Ronov has formulated the following "geochemical principle of preservation of life": "Life on the Earth and other planets, all other things being equal, is possible only so long as these planets are active and the interchange of energy and matter between their inside core and surface takes place."*

Only *substances* are involved in the continuous cycle in the biosphere; concerning energy one can speak only about a *directed flux*. E.P. Odum called the cycling of substances and unidirectional flux of energy two great principles or laws of general biology and ecology, which follow directly from the laws of thermodynamics. Solar energy coming into the biosphere is partly consumed for the synthesis of organic matter. The biosphere is a "factory producing macromolecules": at this factory photoautotrophic organisms, absorbing solar energy, convert inorganic matter that consists of small molecules and is poor in energy into organic compounds which consist of large molecules and are rich in energy, and thereby supply all living matter with them. This process is called photosynthesis. When these compounds are transferred from one trophic level to another, energy is gradually dissipated. After final decomposition of organic residues, energy is partially accumulated in the Earth's crust in the form of aluminosilicates, "geochemical storage batteries" as they are called. When discussing the penetration of the outer envelope of the Earth by solar energy, the Soviet crystallographer Academician N.V. Belov (1891-1982), who formulated the idea about geochemical storage batteries, drew a parallel with a diamond. When light falls on a diamond, part of the light is reflected from the

---

* A.B. Ronov, "Vulcanism, accumulation of carbonates, life," *Geochemistry*, 8, 1274 (1976).

faces of the precious stone, a significant part gets inside the diamond and can emerge from it only after having indergone multiple reflections from the inner faces of the diamond. Solar energy accumulated by living matter is subject to similar wanderings (in the geologic time-scale).

To illustrate the differences in transformations of energy and matter in the biosphere, the Soviet investigators and popularizers of science P.P. Vtorov (1938-1979) and N.N. Drozdov used a graphic example: a water mill. Its wheel rotates ceaselessly, remaining in the same place, and symbolizes the stock of matter in the biosphere. However, in order that the wheel can rotate, a constant inflow of water is required. In an analogous manner, the flux of solar energy incoming from space "rotates" the wheel of life on our planet.

How fast does this wheel rotate? In Vernadsky's time it was not known, but now we can answer this question.

Renovation of the entire living matter of the Earth's biosphere is accomplished every 8 years on average. The matter of land plants (the phytomass of land) is renewed approximately every 14 years. In the ocean the circulation of matter proceeds many times faster: the entire mass of the living matter is renewed in 33 days, whereas the phytomass of the ocean is renewed every day! The process of the complete substitution of water in the hydrosphere takes 2800 years. In the atmosphere, the substitution of oxygen takes several thousand years, and the substitution of carbon dioxide gas, 6.3 years.

These figures show that the geochemical effect of the activity of living matter in the biosphere manifests itself not only during the geologic time (millions and billions of years), but is clearly evident even within the historic time (thousands of years and less).

At the same time, some other substances participating in the biogeochemical cycle have considerably lower migration rates. Thus, the time required for the photosynthetic decomposition of the water mass of the World Ocean amounts to 5 or 6 million years (above we spoke about the water cycle without the chemical decomposition of water). The duration of the global cycles of carbon, nitrogen, and phosphorus also comes to millions of years.

As early as 1926 Vernadsky had brought up the question of the boundaries of the biosphere; he returned to it in a special article in 1937.* At that time, however, it was difficult to give a definite answer. It is still not easy to do now.

N.B. Vassoyevich, a prominent Soviet geologist and Corresponding Member of the USSR Academy of Sciences, has brought attention to an important feature of the structure of the biosphere, which Vernadsky has emphasized: the existence of a "life stability field" and a "life existence field" in the biosphere. In the first case (the "stability field") there exist "conditions which life withstands without ceasing its functions, i.e., conditions under which an organism suffers, but survives"; in the second case (the "existence field") there exist "conditions under which an organism can produce progeny, i.e.,

---

* V.I. Vernadsky, "About the limits of the biosphere", *Izv. AN SSSR*, geol. series, 1, 3-24 (1937).

increase the living mass, increase the effective energy of the planet... The limits of the biosphere are conditioned first of all by the life existence field"*. Such an approach to the definition of the boundaries of the biosphere is in complete agreement with the present-day understanding of the biosphere as a global ecosystem (recall the definition given by Panfilov, cited above).

We now consider the problem of which physico-chemical conditions actually existing on the Earth limit the development of life and, consequently, determine the boundaries of the biosphere.

The first condition is a sufficient quantity of carbon dioxide gas and oxygen. It has been established that in the Himalayas the green vegetation zone is limited to an altitude of 6200 m where the partial pressure of carbon dioxide gas is one half that at sea level. But even at a greater altitude life does not vanish completely. Certain species of spiders and insects are still found and they feed on organic residues brought by the wind.

The second condition is a sufficient quantity of water (necessarily in the liquid phase) which ensures the normal course of enzymatic processes. Areas of the Earth's surface, where life would be limited by this factor are extremely seldom encountered.

Third, there are favourable thermal conditions which preclude both too high temperatures (which cause coagulation of proteins) and too low temperatures (which stop the work of enzymes).

---

* V.I. Vernadsky, *Works*, v. 5, pp. 72, 63 (in Russian).

Record-holders in survival are procaryotic organisms: bacteria and cyanobacteria. (We shall discuss them later.) Some species live in the snow, in small pools of fresh water on the ice floes drifting in the Arctic, in rock formations of the Antarctic; others live in hot springs at a temperature above 100 °C.*

A fourth condition is the presence of a "subsistence wage" of the elements of a mineral diet—a factor which to a considerable extent limits life within large areas in oceans, but very rarely reduces it to zero.

And fifth, is the hypersalinity of the aqueous medium, which when approximately ten times higher than the concentration of salts in sea water limits life. Artificial mats, in which evaporation of brines is carried out, are sterile.** Subterranean waters with a concentration of salts exceeding 270 g/litre are also deprived of life.

The above-stated factors limit the development of life only within very small areas. The prominent American ecologist Robert E. Ricklefs*** cites the following examples: the slopes of Mount McKinley in Alaska, where water exists only in the solid phase because of year-round below-zero temperatures, and is, therefore, inac-

---

* T.D. Rock, *Thermophilic Microorganisms and Life at High Temperature*, New York, Springer-Verlag, 1978.

** G. Gerdes, W.E. Krumbein, "Animal Communities in Recent Potential Stromatolites of Hypersaline Origin". In *Microbian Mats: Stromatolites. MBL Lectures in Biology*, New York, Alan R. Liss, Inc., 1984, pp. 59-83.

*** R.E. Ricklefs, *The Economy of Nature. A Textbook on Basic Ecology*, Portland, Chiron Press Inc., 1976.

4*

cessible for living organisms; White Sands (N. Mex., USA), where pure gypsum sands (whence the name—the White Sands National Monument) are altogether deprived of mineral elements required in a diet. Yet, lifelessness of these areas is questionable and, in any case, ephemeral. For example, other areas that Ricklefs considers to be lifeless—Death Valley (Calif., USA) and the volcanic island Surtsey, which was formed in 1963 near Iceland—are already populated with cyanobacteria.

But, perhaps, the oceanic abyss is lifeless? The history of studies on this problem is quite instructive.

At the beginning of the nineteenth century the conviction reigning supreme was that at a considerable depth of the ocean life was absent, because ... it was cold and dark there. Such weighty arguments were sufficient grounds for not carrying out any direct observations. The first who decided to check the problem experimentally was one of the founders of oceanology and professor of the Edinburgh University, Edward Forbes (1815-1854). In 1842, while taking samples in the Aegean Sea at a depth to 400 m, he found that organisms were distributed there vertically (corresponding to the depth) and were encountered less frequently at greater depths. By extrapolation of his data, Forbes came to the conclusion that at a depth of 540 m there was the "zero of animal life", i.e., below that depth there was no life. Forbes called the zone azoic (from the Greek *azoos*: *a-*, without and *zoe*, life). Nevertheless, when the Norwegian biologist Michael Sars collected invertebrates from a depth of about 1000 m, the "zero of animal life" had to be shifted down to more considerable depths. The one-kilometre depth proved to be no limit either: a piece of damaged transatlantic telegraph cable lifted in 1860 from a depth of 2160 m turned out to be overgrown with representatives of the most diverse groups of animals: hydroids, corals, bryozoans, mollusci, and other bottom dwellers. At approximately the same time, Charles W. Thomson, a graduate of the Edinburgh University, started investigating deep Norwegian fjords and also water areas between Scotland and the Faeroes Islands. To the east of the Wesan Island at depths of about 3700 m he found numerous kinds of sea animals. In 1872 Thomson directed an oceanographic expedition on the steam corvette "Challenger". Present-day scientists hold that this expedition which lasted three and a half years yielded more information than the ocean studies of all the preceding centuries. This expedition proved that life existed everywhere at all the depths accessible to investigation at that time. During the 1940s and 50s the results from expeditions on the "Vityaz'" (USSR) and "Galatea" (Denmark) demonstrated that the ocean is inhabited down to its maximal depths. Yet no one had seen these inhabitants alive until the moment the bathyscaphe "Trieste", with the Swiss scientist Jacques Piccard (the son of Auguste Piccard who invented the bathyscaphe) and US lieutenant Donald Walsh on board, touched the bottom of the Mariana Trench on January 23, 1960 at 13:06. At the point of submersion the depth reached 10 919 m, the temperature of water was 2.4 °C, and the pressure was approximately 1100 atm.

Jacques Piccard reports:* "The bottom was absolutely smooth, with only a few small clumps. But—the most important thing!—just an instant before we touched the bottom a fish floated up into the light circle... In one second, which accommodated years of work and preparation, we solved the problem that had tormented oceanographers for decades... We got proof that neither pressure, nor darkness or cold taken together have the power to stop life." The myth about the "zero of animal life" finally sunk into oblivion. Yet, the most common inhabitants of maximal oceanic depths proved to be not fish but holothurians. These are original, rather primitive invertebrates. Gerald Durrell described them as most disagreeable among all the sea dwellers. Holothurians are called "sea cucumbers", although some of them look more like pumpkins or swollen sausages covered with thick reddish-brown warty skin. One may share Durrell's opinion that these animals are not the most beautiful inhabitants of our planet, but life in eternal darkness at a pressure above 1000 atmospheres is not at all sweet either...

And what about polar seas? Is their mass of water, isolated from the external world by a thick armour of ice, inhabited? Until 1937 it was believed that this body of water was either altogether uninhabited or very scarcely populated. But the investigations carried out during the drift of the Soviet polar station "North Pole" by one of the members of Papanin's team—P.P. Shirshov (1905-1953), who later became an

---

* J. Piccard, *Profondeur 11 000 Metres*, Paris, 1961.

academician—revealed that the waters of the Arctic Ocean were populated even at the highest latitudes. The upper layers of the oceanic waters were found to be rich in shell-less pteropode mollusci, small crustaceans, and medusae. Plankton nets brought catches even from a depth of 3000 m. A still more striking discovery was made forty years later by American scientists in quite different quarters: in the coastal waters of the Antarctic, covered with permanent ice.*

Investigations were carried out in the Ross Sea, where the thickness of the ice reached 420 m. The sea water there proved to have been isolated from sunlight and from the direct effect of the atmosphere by an ice armour which formed at least 120 thousand years ago. It was natural to assume that under such conditions life could not exist in the sea. But contrary to expectations, the ice dungeon proved to be inhabited! Television cameras and other research instruments lowered into an ice-hole detected a rather diverse community of organisms in the vast volume of water; this community consisted of diatoms, foraminifera, anthropods, crustaceans, and bacteria. Among them some absolutely unusual, hitherto unknown species were encountered.

Thus, both the entire land surface (with the exception of very limited areas) and the ocean depths correspond to the "life existence field" as Vernadsky understood it and, consequently, pertain to the biosphere. As regards the atmosphere, the only inhabitant there is the so-called "aeroplankton": bacteria, yeast fungi, spores of mould

---

* *Science News*, **112**, 19, 292-293; 26/27, 421 (1977).

fungi, of mosses and lichens, as well as viruses, algae, cysts of protozoans, and so on.* Viable microorganisms have been found at an altitude of up to 77 km. The majority of microorganisms, however, die in a few minutes or even seconds after they get (not on their own accord!) into air. For the surviving microorganisms the air medium is also not favourable, and they sink into a state of anabiosis. True, it is assumed that some microorganisms can propagate in low-level storm clouds, but this has not yet been proved. Therefore, the atmosphere on the whole does not essentially satisfy the definition of an ecosystem: neither self-regulation of the system, nor self-renovation of the organisms takes place there. This is exactly the case of a "life stability field" according to Vernadsky—a zone overlaying the biosphere. Hutchinson has called it parabiosphere (from the Greek root 'para', at the side of, alongside of), in which are included the major part of the territory of the glacial shields of the Antarctic and most arid areas of deserts.**

Where then are the real confines of the biosphere?

Rendering the definition given by Vernadsky more concrete, one can attribute to the biosphere those zones of the Earth, where aborigenic communities of living organisms exist. Do the lowest atmospheric layers meet this condition? Evi-

---

* V.V. Vlodavets, "Microflora of atmospheric air". In: *The Role of Microorganisms in the Cycle of Gases in Nature*, Nauka, Moscow, 1979, pp. 50-64 (in Russian).
** G.E. Hutchinson, *The Ecological Theater and the Evolutionary Play*. New Haven and London, Yale Univ. Press, 1965.

dently, yes, since insects and birds dwell there. Among insects there are active predators which live by hunting in the air and come down to earth only from time to time and for spending the night. Many birds, in their turn, are insectivorous and prey in flight. Thus, the lowest atmospheric layers are the native element for many insects and birds, and therefore should be included in the biosphere. The upper boundary of the biosphere should be drawn judging from the highest active flights made by flying organisms (the record-breakers among them being, naturally, birds). So far the record has been held by a prematurely perished griffon vulture which collided with an aircraft at a height of 12.5 km. Above this boundary the parabiosphere is located.

The situation with the lower boundary of the biosphere is more complicated. Vernadsky believed* that the entire sedimentary envelope of the Earth was populated by bacteria. The data available at that time about the occurrence of bacteria in the Earth's crust were insufficient. Only individual observations had been made. In 1901, for the first time, the engineer V. Sheiko found bacteria in the deep subterranean waters of the Baku oil fields; a quarter of a century later the American scientist B. Bastin and the Soviet researcher T.L. Ginzburg-Karagicheva published descriptions of the microorganisms found in the subterranean waters of oil fields. Later, in the course of well-drilling operations on the Apshe-

---

* V.I. Vernadsky, "About the limits of the biosphere", *Izv. AN SSSR*, geol. series, 1, 16 (1937).

ron Peninsular bacteria were encountered at a depth of 1700 m.

However, further investigations did not confirm Vernadsky's supposition that the *entire sedimentary envelope* of the Earth is populated with bacterial life. The distribution of microorganisms in subterranean water, and, hence, the lower boundary of the biosphere between the continents, proved to be determined by the temperature of the water, its circulation conditions, and the concentration of mineral salts. Live bacteria are found in subterranean waters at a temperature of up to 100 °C, though their maximum vital activity is limited to "only" 80 °C. The critical concentration of mineral salts has already been mentioned—270 g/litre. In the course of deep-drilling operations in the Volga region and in West Siberia anaerobic microflora, both active and diverse in composition, were found at a depth of 1 to 3 km and sometimes even deeper. However, bacteria are not found at appreciably smaller depths if the mineralization of water exceeds the specified limit or if the deposit is "sealed". Such zones, devoid of life (or "azoic") were found in the Angara-Lena Basin at a depth of about 500 m, and in the Volga-Kama Basin, at a depth of about 1200 m.*

As regards the bottom sediments of the World Ocean and inland waters, here the oxygen concentration determines lower boundary of living organisms. It has been shown, for example, that in the zone of hydrogen sulphide poisoning of the Black

---

* L.E. Kramarenko, *The Geochemical and Prospecting Importance of the Microorganisms of Subterranean Waters*, Leningrad, Nedra, 1983 (in Russian).

Sea the sediments are sterile already at a depth of 5 cm from the surface of the bottom.* In the Pacific and Indian Oceans microflora dwell in the bottom sediments to a depth of 10-12 m, while in the Caspian Sea they are found at no less than 114 m below the surface of the sea bottom. It has been suggested (though without proof so far) that a layer of bottom sediments down to a depth of 200-250 m from the surface of the sea bed may still be populated.

Thus, the vertical width of the biosphere in the ocean covers the entire depth of oceanic waters and includes the bottom film of life, which varies markedly in thickness; the biosphere on continents comprises a thin superficial layer and a thick underground layer. All the daylight surface of our planet belongs to the zone of the biosphere. The only exceptions (doubtful as they are) are those rare cases which we have already mentioned. The distribution of living organisms in the biosphere is shown in Fig. 1.

These are, according to the present-day conceptions, the boundaries of the Earth's biosphere. The title chosen by Vernadsky for the major book of his life was: "The Chemical Structure of the Earth's Biosphere and of Its Surroundings", but Vernadsky had not defined what he implied by the "surroundings" of the biosphere. A contemporary interpretation is given by Vassoyevich.

Vassoyevich** suggests that one should single

---

* Yu.I. Sorokin, *The Black Sea*, Moscow, Nauka, 1982 (in Russian).

** N.B. Vassoyevich, "Various interpretations of the concept of the biosphere". In: *Investigations of Organic Matter of Contemporary and Fossil Sediments*. Nauka, Moscow, 1976, pp. 381-399 (in Russian).

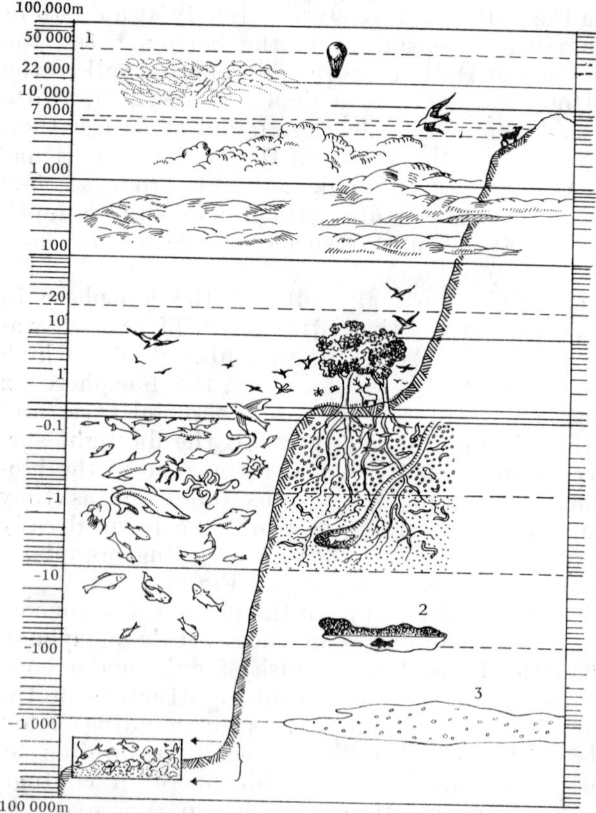

Fig. 1. Distribution of living organisms in the Earth's biosphere (after Kadar, 1965):

1—ultraviolet radiation; *2*—burrowing organisms; *3*—petroleum bacteria

out a "megobiosphere" (from the Greek word "megos", great, mighty), i.e., a multilayered envelope of the Earth, formed as a result of the activity of living matter. Its upper boundary is defined by the limit to which the biogenic atmosphere extends; its lower boundary is the envelope of the Earth, not subject to the influence of life. The megobiosphere includes:

(a) The apobiosphere, i.e., the upper portion of the Earth's atmosphere which is beyond the boundary to which abiotic life forms extend;

(b) The parabiosphere;

(c) The biosphere, which corresponds to the enbiosphere as understood by Hutchinson;[*]

(d) The metabiosphere, which corresponds to "the area of bygone biospheres" as defined by Vernadsky.

Vernadsky defined "the area of bygone biospheres" as an envelope of the Earth, that had at any time been subject to the influence of life. He wrote that the Earth's crust "encompasses within the range of several dozen kilometres a number of geological envelopes which some time in the past were biospheres on the surface of the Earth. There are the biosphere, the stratisphere, the metamorphic (upper and lower) envelope, and the granitic envelope. It is only now evident that they all originated from the biosphere. There are bygone biospheres".[**]

---

* G.E. Hutchinson, *The Ecological Theater and the Evolutionary Play*, New Haven and London, Yale Univ. Press, 1965, p. 27.
** V.I. Vernadsky, *The Chemical Structure of the Earth's Biosphere and of Its Surroundings*, Nauka, Moscow, 1965, p. 35 (in Russian).

Thus, owing to the constant influx of solar energy, the intensive work of living matter which is the recipient of this energy, and the incomplete closure of the biotic cycle, the biosphere had been continually creating concentric planetary envelopes around itself: the parabiosphere and the apobiosphere (towards its exterior), and the metabiosphere (towards its interior).

A characteristic feature of the biosphere as a dynamic system is its nonequilibrium which is a consequence of the work of living matter and of the influx of solar energy. As early as 1935 a junior contemporary of Vernadsky, the prominent biologist Erwin Bauer (1890-1942), who spent the last 7 years of his life in the Soviet Union, wrote: "Living systems are never in equilibrium; at the expense of their free energy they constantly perform work to avoid the equilibrium required by the laws of physics and chemistry under existing external conditions... We shall call this principle of ours the 'principle of the stable nonequilibrium state' of living systems".* Now it is called the principle of Bauer.

This principle is valid for the biosphere as a whole. The gaseous composition of the atmosphere and the salt composition of the ocean are not in equilibrium. Another example is provided by A.I. Perelman, a prominent Soviet geochemist: the river water of the taiga and the humid tropics contain both oxygen and humic substances in a dissolved state. At equilibrium humic sub-

---

* E.S. Bauer, *Theoretical Biology*, Académiai Kiadó, Budapest, 1982, p. 238.

stances would have been oxidized by the oxygen present in the system; but such an equilibrium is never reached, since, though oxidation does proceed, new portions of both humic substances and oxygen constantly enter the system.

A distinctive feature of the biosphere is that it is "watered". "Water without life is not known in the biosphere; negligible in weight, such occurrences of it are rare—and temporary, like the water of crystallization in minerals; such are the waters of volcanoes, reach in free sulphuric or hydrochloric acid, perhaps, some brines—and that is all."* At the same time, water is the medium for practically all the chemical processes occurring in the biosphere. This is exactly the reason why chemically pure water in the biosphere is as rare an occurrence as water devoid of life. Vernadsky liked very much the definition of life as "animated water", which had been given by the nineteenth century French zoologist R. Dubois, and he repeatedly quoted it in his works. Poetic lines about water also belong to Antoine de Saint-Exupery: "Water, you have neither taste, nor colour or odour, they delight in you, without knowing what you are. One cannot say that you are necessary for life; you are life itself..."

Water has a rare property, invaluable for living organisms: it is an inert solvent, i.e., it does not change chemically under the effect of the substances it dissolves. Due to this fact water can be used repeatedly by organisms. A. Szent-Györgyi called water "the matrix of life".

----

* V.I. Vernadsky, *Works*, v. 4, Book 2, p. 75 (in Russian).

The total content of water in all the tissues of all the living organisms is approximately 5 times greater than in all the rivers of the globe. Recent investigations have shown that half of the water contained in the roots of plants is renewed within several minutes. As a result, the water cycle on land is determined almost exclusively by the transpiration of the plants: they evaporate most of the water which has fallen to land in the form of atmospheric precipitation. In the ocean the entire volume of water is filtered through by the crustacea of the plankton within half a year; however, the upper layer alone (0 to 500 m) is filtered in such a manner within 20 days*.

Finally, one more characteristic feature of the biosphere resides in its indissoluble ties with space, to the greatest extent, with the Sun. The connection of solar activity with terrestrial phenomena was noted already in the last century. In 1852 Rudolf Wolf (1816-1896), a Swiss astronomer of Bern, calculated the dependence of the Earth's magnetism on the periodicity with which spots are formed on the Sun.

However, heliobiology (the science about the influence of the Sun on biological processes) is considered to have originated only in 1915, when the report "Periodic Influence of the Sun on the Biosphere of the Earth" was read at the Moscow Archaeological Institute. In this report, the author A.L. Tzhijevsky (1897-1964), who later became an eminent scientist, formulated a concept, to

---

* V.G. Bogorov, *"Plankton of the World Ocean"*, Nauka, Moscow, 1974, p. 320 (in Russian).

which he then devoted the rest of his life*. The concept may seem even trivial. Really, is there anything surprising in that life on the Earth is determined by the Sun? At the present time a tremendous range of phenomena have been discovered that are controlled by the "rhythm of the Sun", ranging from the outbreaks of massive proliferations of locusts to the average academic performance of school children. Tzhijevsky was the pioneer, but he did not live to see his ideas recognized...

Now, let us bring some ideas together.

The biosphere is perceived as an external envelope of the Earth, permeated with and formed by life, its development being determined by the constant influx of energy from space (mainly solar energy). The biosphere of the Earth is characterized by the presence of liquid water and extensive low-temperature reactions which proceed in the aqueous medium and are to a considerable degree regulated by the action of enzymes. The biosphere produces a gaseous envelope towards its outer edge, and an envelope of sedimentary rocks ("the area of bygone biospheres" or "the metabiosphere") towards the interior of the planet. The cycle of substances in the biosphere is shown diagrammatically in Fig. 2.

Man occupies a specific place in the biosphere. Emphasizing this circumstance, Prof. Heinrich Walter writes: "Man was placed in a whole and natural world, which, thanks to his mental capacities, he is able to regard objectively, thus rais-

---

* A.L. Tzhijevsky, *Les epidèmies et perturbations electromagnètiques du milieu extèrieur*, Paris, 1938.

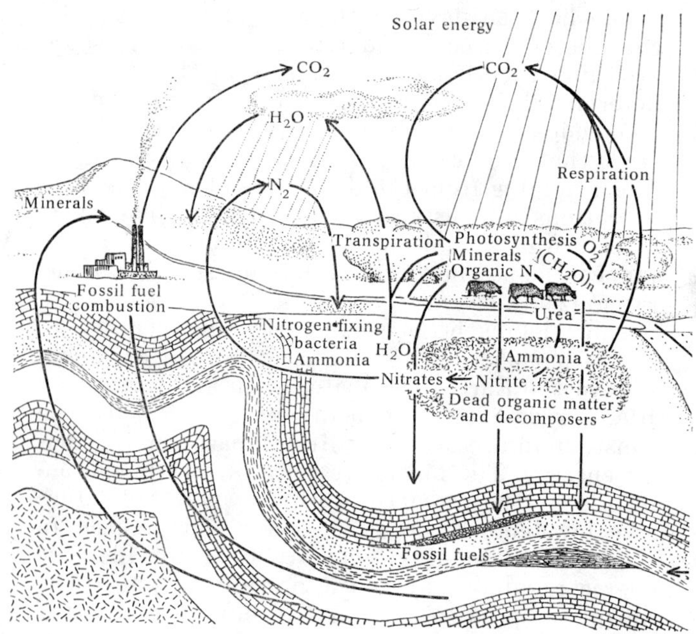

Fig. 2. Cycle of main substances in the biosphere (after Hutchinson, 1970)

ing himself above it. On the one hand, he is a child of this outer, apparent world, and dependent upon nature, but on the other hand, through the world within, he has access to the godly."*

* H. Walter, *Vegetation of the Earth and Ecological Systems of the Geo-biosphere*, New York, Springer-Verlag, 1979, p. 1.

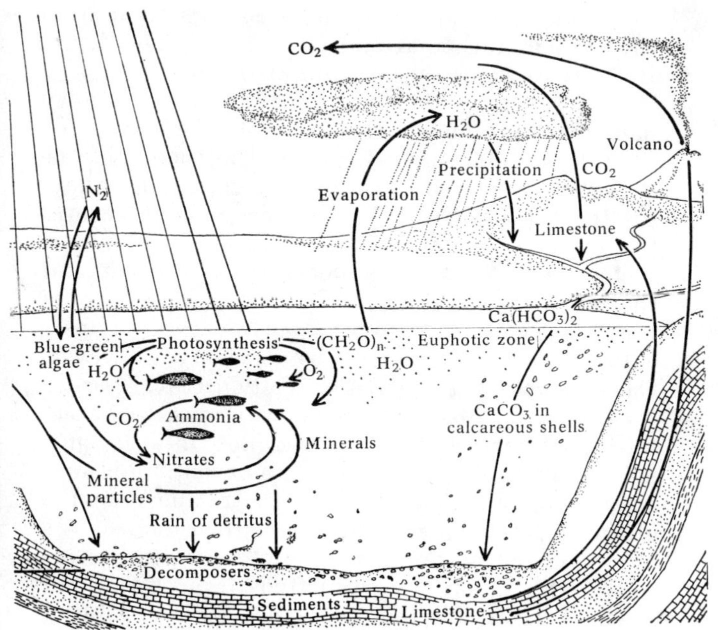

Recently "UNESCO Courier" (1981, No. 5) published a chart illustrating the way in which man came to realize the overall interconnectedness of natural phenomena and of his role in it, or of how, quoting the journal, "the formation of the modern concept of ecology" came about. Vernadsky made a decisive contribution to the development of this concept with his theory of the noosphere and of the leading role of mankind in modern geological processes.

Vernadsky called the biosphere controlled by the mind of man the noosphere (from the Greek

root 'noos', mind). He borrowed this term from
the French mathematician and philosopher E. Le-
Roy (1870-1954) who formulated the concept of
the noosphere* with his friend, the well-known
paleontologist and anthropologist P. Teilhard de
Chardin (1881-1955). However, the theory of the
noosphere occurred to the French colleagues under
the influence of Vernadsky's ideas, whose lectures
in geochemistry they had attended at the Sor-
bonne in 1922-1923. Incidentally, still earlier, at
the turn of the century, J. Murray had in passing
used the neologism "psychosphere", which, apparently was not picked up by anybody. However,
the concept of LeRoy and Teilhard de Chardin
was strongly idealistic, even religious in character. (Teilhard de Chardin was not only an eminent paleontologist, but also a catholic mission-
ary, although at odds with the ruling doctrine
of Catholicism.) Teilhard de Chardin defined the
noosphere as "a new canopy", "a thinking stratum", which, having originated towards the end
of the Tertiary period, has since been unfolding
over the world of plants and animals, outside of
the biosphere and above it**.

Vernadsky's attitude towards the noosphere was
altogether different. "I know Marx but little,"
he confessed to Professor B.L. Lichkov, "but I
think that the noosphere will be fully in concor-
dance with his basic conclusions."*** Vernadsky's

-----

* E. LeRoy, *L'exidence idéaliste et le fait de l'èvolut-
ion*, Paris, 1927, p. 27.
** P. Teilhard de Chardin, *Le phénomène humain*,
Paris, 1959.
*** *Correspondence of V.I. Vernadsky with B.L. Lich-
kov (1940-1944)*, Nauka, Moscow, 1980, p. 40 (in Russian).

article "Some Words About the Noosphere" was published in Russian in 1944 and proved to be his last publication to appear during his lifetime; some months later, already after Vernadsky's death, the article was reissued in the USA. In effect, it was Vernadsky's scientific bequest. In this article ideas were formulated that Vernadsky had come to by degrees, through the logic of his creative work: "The historical process is being radically changed under our very eyes. For the first time in the history of mankind the interest of the masses on the one hand, and the free thought of individuals on the other, determine the course of life of mankind and provide standards for men's ideas of justice. Mankind taken as a whole is becoming a mighty geological force. There arises the problem of the *reconstruction of the biosphere in the interests of freely thinking humanity as a single totality.* This new state of the biosphere, which we approach without our noticing it, is the *noösphere*"* (italics are Vernadsky's —*A.L.*).

The noosphere is characterized, above all, by the global colonization of the Earth by mankind. Indeed, as Vernadsky emphasized, the history of human society is not only, and even not mainly, the history of wars, changes of dynasties, palace revolutions, etc.; it is, first and foremost, *the history of man's mastering of the planet.* It was already after Vernadsky's death that mankind began to conquer outer space. A grandiose picture of the future development of the noosphere was presented by the prominent Soviet astronomer,

---

* V.I. Vernadsky, "The biosphere and the noösphere", *American Scientist,* **33,** **1,** 8-9 (1945).

I.S. Shklovsky in his book "The Universe, Life, and Reason" (1962).

In the middle of the last century Charles Lyell compared the abilities of the men of that time with the action of terrestrial elements. If all the people living on the Earth, Lyell wrote, tried to break up the lava which have effused from Icelandic volcanoes in the course of only three years and tried to transfer it to the depths of the ocean, they could work for several millennia and still fail to complete the task. The conclusion drawn by Lyell is not very comforting—man is small and miserable in the face of the geological elements.

In the twentieth century the situation has changed. As early as thirty years ago Vernadsky observed that mankind *was becoming* a powerful geological force. Today man *has* indeed *become* that geological force which transforms the face of the planet. Man is growing new varieties of plants, he is developing new breeds of farm animals. Selection and domestication are examples of the transition of the biosphere into the noosphere. Man extracts billions of tons of raw materials from the bowels of the Earth and introduces these materials into the biotic cycle (in 1970, the world's extraction of mineral ores per capita reached 20 tons). At present mankind produces 10 times as much energy as is absorbed by living matter.* Man transforms the landscapes which surround him (see Fig. 3). It is common practice to distinguish two varieties of cultural landscapes,

------

* E.V. Girusov, S. S. Lappo, "Limits of potentials of the biosphere", *Priroda*, 12, 4 (1974).

which exemplify the noosphere: the agrosphere and the technosphere. The first comprises various plantations, fields, gardens, greenhouses, pastures, groves, parks, piscicultural grounds, and so forth. The technosphere is an aggregation of all the items of material culture, as it were, "built into" nature by mankind. There are plants and factories, air fields, stadiums, motorways, architectural structures, and so on. Yet, no matter how grand technology may be, man remains the motive force of the noosphere. And if the "primordial" biosphere is *biocentric*, the noosphere is, in its essence, doubtlessly, *anthropocentric*.

Emphasizing the humanistic purpose of the concept of the noosphere, Vernadsky wrote:* "The problem of planned, consistent activities which will aid us in mastering nature and accomplishing the correct distribution of wealth, connected with the comprehension of the unity and equality of all people, of the unity of the noosphere, is now on the agenda." The optimization of the conditions of man's existence—this is how the main trend of development of the noosphere may be expressed. Vernadsky developed the same idea**: "It has become clear, and is more deeply penetrating the consciousness of mankind, that we now have a real opportunity to obliterate malnutrition, starvation and poverty, to greatly diminish the incidence of diseases, and prolong

---

* V.I. Vernadsky, *Reflections of a Naturalist*, Book 2, Moscow, Nauka, 1977, p. 109 (in Russian).
** V.I. Vernadsky, *Chemical Structure of the Biosphere of the Earth and Its Environment*, Moscow, Nauka, 1965, p. 271 (in Russian).

Fig. 3. Changes in the landscapes of the forest zone in the course of development of human society:

A—landscape of 9000-3000 years B.C.; *B*—landscape of 5000-3000 years B.C.; *C*—landscape of 700-1850 years A.D.; *D*—modern landscape

human life to the maximum."

"I am the most alive among the living", writes the poet A. Tarkovsky. In Vernadsky's recently

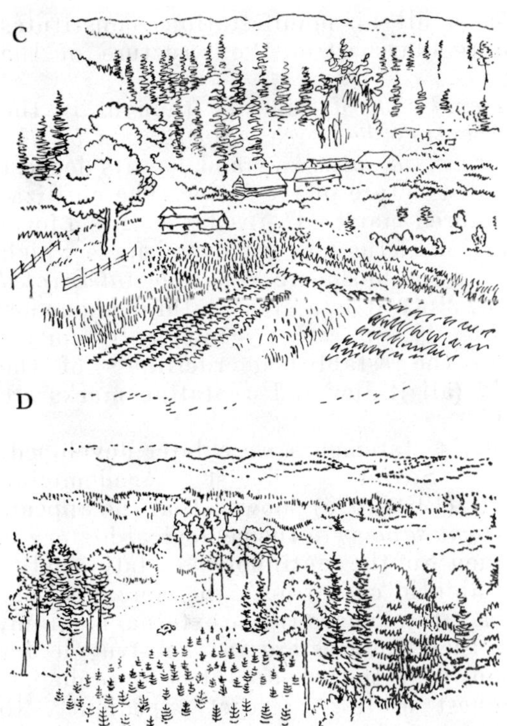

published book "Scientific Thought As a Planetary Phenomenon" the following three conclusions about the place of man in the biosphere are formulated:

"1. Man, as observed in nature, like all living organisms, like any living matter, is a specific *function of the biosphere*, within its specific definite space-time.

"2. Man in all his manifestations constitutes a definite regular part of the structure of the biosphere.

"3. The *explosion* of scientific thought in the twentieth century *has been prepared for by the entire history of the biosphere* and has its deepest roots in the structure of the latter. The civilization of "cultured mankind", insofar as it is a form of organization of the new geological force which has formed in the biosphere, *cannot be interrupted or destroyed*, since it is a great natural phenomenon, historically, or, rather, geologically corresponding to the established orderliness of the biosphere"* (all italics and quotation marks are Vernadsky's).

Vernadsky's statements were later developed. Thus, the Soviet biologist Academician S.S. Shvarts (1919-1976) showed that the appearance of *Homo sapiens* in the geological history is the consequence of the continuous adaptation of life to diverse abiotic conditions: the more precisely animals react to changes in the external medium, the higher their chances are in the struggle for life. Reason, from the standpoint of an ecologist, is the highest ability to react expediently to changes in external conditions. Furthermore, the origin of the mind in the human species has led to the formation of the noosphere. This was vividly sketched by the Soviet writer B. Agapov: "Naked, hairless, thin-skinned, small-mouthed, with unsteady small teeth, with musculature far weaker than that of his enemies, running and leaping

---

* V.I. Vernadsky, "*Reflections of a Naturalist*", Book 2, Nauka, Moscow, 1977, pp. 32-33 (in Russian).

much worse than they, man has created a second nature around him, from the shirt on his body to sputniks in space. And in this second nature, and because of it, he has become the most powerful being on the planet."

Vernadsky was convinced that the history of mankind is not something accidental and that it is connected by adamantine ties with the development of the biosphere. Vernadsky revealed this connection more fully (recall that he once thought of becoming a historian!) in his most profound work "Thoughts About the Contemporary Significance of the History of Knowledge". Vernadsky wrote: "Throughout the centuries periods recur when within one generation or a few generations, in one country or in a few countries, many richly endowed personalities appear, whose intellects create the force that alters the biosphere."*

Vernadsky's ideas about the noosphere are still far from being completely incorporated. In its relationship with nature mankind is not yet always guided by the ancient maxim formulated by Hippocrates: "Primum ne noceas" ("First of all, do not harm"). While, on the one hand, extremely productive cultural coenoses of the agrosphere are being created, on the other hand, the impoverishment and extermination of natural ecosystems are taking place. "Thus, the noosphere, so dear to Vernadsky ... is running the risk in reality of turning into the technosphere, or rather, into 'the sphere of avidity', governed by the spirit of fortune-hunting, by mediocrity, by

____

* V.I. Vernadsky, *Selected Works on History of Science*, Nauka, Moscow, 1981, p. 233.

P. Duvigneaud at the tribune of the XIIth International Botanical Congress (1975). (From: *XII IBC, Proceedings,* Nauka, Leningrad, 1979, p. 73.)

the absence of social consciousness, by the ideal of destruction and by the egotistic doctrine of 'after me, the deluge'", said the outstanding Belgian ecologist P. Duvigneaud addressing the XIIth International Botanical Congress.* He considers that in the present situation agriculture must constitute a single whole with modern technology, which is reduced to a minimum in biological and ecological processes and produces no deleterious effect on biogeocoenoses. There is no other way.

The eminent American botanist Frits W. Went, whom this author had the good fortune to meet in Leningrad at the same Congress, once calculated that the present-day population on the globe consumes 1000 times as much food and raw materials as the virgin nature of our planet can give. In other words, should people have to return to using only natural resources, only one in every thousand of those now living would survive. The same idea was set forth by Hutchinson in 1970:

* P. Duvigneaud, *"Noosphere et l'avenir de la végétation du globe"*, XII Int. bot. congr., Proc., Nauka, Leningrad, 1979, p. 78.

"By noosphere Vernadsky meant the envelope of the mind that was to supersede the biosphere, the envelope of life. Unfortunately the quarter-century since those words were written has demonstrated how mindless most of the changes wrought by man on the biosphere have been. Nonetheless, Vernadsky's transition in this deepest sense is the only alternative to mankind shortening its life-time by millions of years."[*]

Vernadsky was an optimist. In 1932 he wrote in answer to his opponents: "What we are now living through is not a crisis which disturbs weak souls, but the greatest change in the scientific thought of mankind, which is accomplished only once in millennia; we are experiencing scientific advances, never witnessed by the long generations of our ancestors... Standing at this turning-point, surveying the future opening up, we should be happy that we have been destined to experience this, to participate in the creation of such a future."[**]

Vernadsky's optimism is not unfounded. It is precisely the teaching of the biosphere and noosphere that allows for the development of a complex of ecological measures which can enhance the biological productivity of the Earth. As Shvarts said in his report to the session of the USSR Academy of Sciences dedicated to its 250th anniversary, any prognosis about the development of science in the next decades includes the following: substantial changes in the structure

---

[*] G.E. Hutchinson, "The biosphere", *Scient. American*, **223**, 3, 53 (1970).

[**] V.I. Vernadsky, "The problem of time in modern science", *Izv. AN SSSR*, OMEN, 4, 541 (1932).

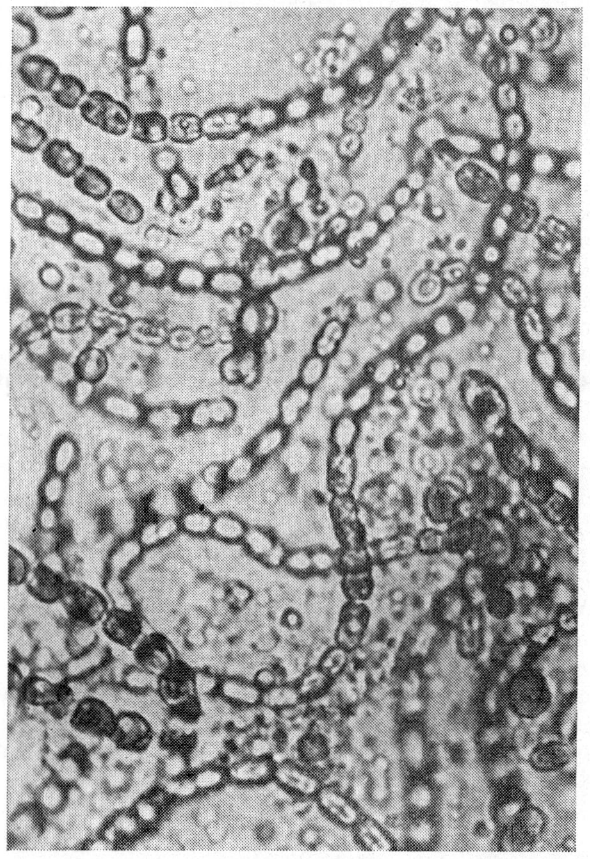

Filamentous cyanobacteria Nostoc. (From: *Scient. Amer.*,
1970, Sept., p. 136.)

of the biocoenoses of the Earth; the creation of specific biocoenoses capable of self-renovation and self-regulation; anthropogenic landscapes featuring an increased stability and an enhanced capacity for biological purification; and the maintenance of the overall balance of the biosphere at a level ensuring optimal development of human society.

In the world's press nowadays one sometimes encounters three interwoven letters "MAB" in combination with a maximally simplified representation of the human figure, the symbol of life in ancient Egypt. This is the emblem of the international programme "Man and Biosphere" adopted at the XVI General Conference of UNESCO in 1970. In 1980 about 100 countries were already participating in the activities envisioned by this programme.

The objective pursued by MAB is to undertake long-term investigations on the effect of man's activities on the natural processes occurring in the biosphere. As the programme states, "MAB aspires to destroy obsolete barriers between scientists—naturalists, sociologists, decision-makers—and suggests instead an interdisciplinary approach directed towards solving the problems of controlling both natural ecosystems and those modified by man."

Vernadsky's concept of the biosphere is essentially the theoretical basis of this international programme. In addition, philosophical aspects of his concept of the noosphere have also had a considerable international effect.*

---

* S. Tagliagambe, *Scientia*, **118**, 505-535 (in Italian and English) (1983).

2. Living Matter

We glibly talk
 of nature's laws
but do things have
 a nature cause?
Black earth turned into
 yellow crocus
is undiluted
 hocus-pocuc.

Piet Hein. 1966

In his book "The Chemical Structure of the Earth's Biosphere and of Its Surroundings" Vernadsky raised the question about types of matter of which the biosphere is composed*:

"Its matter (i.e., the matter of the biosphere.— *A.L.*) consists of seven fundamentally dissimilar natural parts that are not geologically accidental.

"First, it consists of an aggregation of living organisms, of *living matter*, scattered in myriads of individuals...

"Second, we deal with matter which has been created and processed by life, with *biogenic matter*, which is a source of extremely powerful potential energy (coal, bitumen, limestone, petroleum, etc.). After its formation geological activity of living organisms in this matter is low.

"Third, we have the matter created by processes in which living matter does not participate, that is, *inert matter*—solid, liquid, and gaseous...

---

* V.I. Vernadsky, *The Chemical Structure of the Earth's Biosphere and of Its Surroundings*, Nauka, Moscow, 1965, pp. 58-60.

"The fourth component is *bio-inert matter*, which is created simultaneously by living organisms and inert processes, and which represents the dynamic equilibrium systems of them both. This includes the oceanic, and almost all other, waters of the biosphere, petroleum, soil, weathered crust of the Earth, etc. Organisms play the leading role in their formation.

"Fifth, there is *matter*, which is in a state of *radioactive decay* in the form of a few relatively stable radioactive elements... Here we are dealing with chemical elements of complex isotopic composition, which penetrate all substances of the biosphere and go down to an unknown depth...

"On the other hand, all the matter of the biosphere and, evidently, of the biosphere alone, is permeated by a sixth form of matter—*scattered atoms*, which are continually created from all kinds of terrestrial matter under the influence of cosmic radiation...

"Finally, the seventh type of terrestrial matter is *matter of cosmic origin*..." (italics are Vernadsky's everywhere.—*A.L.*).

In this chapter we shall consider the types of matter found in the biosphere, paying particular attention to living matter.

Vassoyevich, considering the classification of matter suggested by Vernadsky, noted that from the logical standpoint it is not flawless, since the differentiated categories partly overlap (for instance, matter of cosmic origin is at the same time inert). Another example, the dismal experience of mankind since Vernadsky's death has taught us that radioactive isotopes (e.g., strontium-90) accumulate in living organisms and, consequently, can enter into the composition of both living and inert matter. As regards "biologically inert matter", it cannot be regarded as a specific type of matter, since, according to the definition given by Vernadsky, it consists of two matters (both living and inert). In its character it is not matter but a dynamic system, the fact emphasized by Vernadsky himself (we shall discuss this problem in Chapter 5).

Vernadsky constructed this classification of the types of matter in the biosphere according to several parameters:

(a) The character of matter (living or inert);

(b) The character of the initial matter (biogenic matter and inert matter are differentiated, life not taking part in the formation of the latter);

(c) The radioactivity of matter (matter is distinguished, which is in a state of radioactive decay);

(d) The degree of dispersion of the molecular structure (matter is distinguished, which is represented by scattered atoms);

(e) The terrestrial or extraterrestrial origin (matter of cosmic origin is distinguished).

We shall try to represent the genetic classification of the types of matter of the biosphere in matrix form. We shall choose the following three main parameters: (a) the character of matter: living or nonliving; (b) classification according to the initial material: formed from living matter, biogenic; and formed from nonliving matter, abiogenic; and (c) its terrestrial or extraterrestrial origin (Table 1). Radioactivity and the degree of dispersion of the molecular structure as classification parameters are omitted.

Table 1. Types of Matter of the Earth's Biosphere

Character of matter	Classification according to initial material	Types of matter of terrestrial origin	Types of matter of extraterrestrial origin
Living	Biogenic	Living matter. Synonyms: bios, biota	Not known
Living	Abiogenic	Not known	Not known
Nonliving	Biogenic	Biogenic matter: (a) neobiogenic; (b) paleobiogenic. Synonym: organogenic matter	Not known
Nonliving	Abiogenic	Abiogenic matter of terrestrial origin. Synonym: inert matter	Abiogenic matter of extraterrestrial origin. Synonym: matter of cosmic origin

Matter of terrestrial origin in the biosphere may be both living and nonliving. According to Vernadsky, all living organisms of the biosphere belong to the category of living matter. Contemporary living matter is biogenic, since it is formed exclusively by propagation of the already existing living matter.

Over the ages there has existed a belief in the possibility of the spontaneous origination of living matter from nonliving.

Aristotle (384-322 BC), who was called the "Father of All Sciences", believed that plants originated spontaneously from the earth, fish from ooze, and worms from rotting corpses of dead animals. Due to his unshakeable authority these views became generally adopted. In an encyclopaedia of ancient natural science, the poem "On the Nature of Things" written by Lucretius Carus (first century BC) contains the following lines about putrefying substances:

Though the dull clod, or sapless root as dull,
When the moist shower the putrid strife has roused.
Themselves the vermin race in crowds create:
Changed, then, their nature from arrangements new,
And full empowered perceptive life to rear.

An opposite thesis, "omne vivum e vivo" ("all the living from the living"), which Vernadsky called "the principle of Redi"* developed later. Francesco Redi (1626—1697) was a naturalist, physician, and poet who worked in Florence. In 1668 he ran a series of famous experiments investigating the spontaneous generation of life from decaying meat which went down in the history of science. Redi made the correct conclusion that maggots developed not through spontaneous generation but from eggs laid in the decaying meat by flies. In 1674 Redi was accused of heresy for such views, but he did not abandon them.

-----

* W. Vernadsky, *La géochimie*, Alcan, Paris, 1924, pp. 331-334.

Redi was ahead of his time for centuries. It was two hundred years after Redi that the great French scientist Louis Pasteur (1822-1895) performed a series of classical experiments with bacteria (1860-1861) providing experimental proof that there can be no spontaneous generation of life.

Vernadsky did not consider "the principle of Redi" to be absolute. In 1931 he wrote: "The Redi principle does not deny abiogenesis: it only indicates the limits within which abiogenesis does not occur. In the Earth's history it is possible that at one time there was no biosphere, and physico-chemical conditions or states existed on the Earth's crust, which are now absent, but which then were sufficient for abiogenesis."

Florentine naturalist, physician, and poet Francesco Redi. (From: W.A. Locy, *Biology and its Makers*, N.Y., 1915, p. 280.)

Nonliving matter present in the biosphere can be either biogenic or abiogenic. Biogenic matter is created as a byproduct of the vital activity of organisms. Constituents of biogenic matter are the remains of dead organisms, products of their shedding and fall-off such as the following: chitinous integuments of arthropods, hair and teeth lost by mammals, horns shed by deer, feathers lost by birds, fallen leaves (and also bark) of trees, ripe fruits separated from plants, pollen, etc. This mass can be considerable; for example, during the 20 years of its life a crayfish sheds 50 carapaces; by the end of their life the dead organic matter of woody plants exceeds the weight of living matter by 3 to 4 times—recall the resilient carpets of conifer needles around fir-trees or of shed bark around eucalipti. Constituents of biogenic matter are also the excrement of animals and external products of the metabolism of living organisms (recent investigations have shown that in aquatic ecosystems 10 to 40% of the primary products of planktonic algae is, evidently, secreted into the medium and may serve as a source of carbon and energy for other organisms). The role of external metabolism products is very important in bacteria. Higher plants also secrete specific substances into the environment and they are called phytoncides. Other biogenic matter are such various substances as urinary and biliary calculi, pearl, galipot (resin), milk, honey, wax, filament secreted by silkworm, web, and so on.

Biogenic matter falls into two categories:

(a) Neobiogenic matter which is formed by living matter extant in the given geological epoch;

(b) Paleobiogenic matter formed by living matter of past geological epochs.

A distinctive feature of neobiogenic matter is its extreme instability in the biosphere, mainly because it is actively processed by living organisms. Only an insignificant part of neobiogenic matter becomes fossilized (and thus falls into the category of paleobiogenic matter). However, curious things sometimes happen. For example, a web was found, which had been woven millions of years ago! It was preserved by a lucky chance: as soon as this small web had been woven by the eight-legged ancestor of our spiders, resin somehow covered it; the resin solidified, deposited into sediments, and after millions of years a piece of amber was found with the web enclosed in it. In some gem shops in the United States one can buy such coprolites for 5 dollars apiece. These coprolites sometimes contain another paleobiogenic substance, namely, fossil excrement of dinosaurs.

The first paleobiogenic substance whose organic origin was proved were enigmatic triangular stones, known since antiquity. They were called "stone tongues", in Latin—glossopetrae, and were considered to be "freaks of nature". They were abundant on the island of Malta, and every owner of a more or less large collection of rarities in Europe could boast of one or several pieces of glossopetrae. It was established only in the 17th century by the great Danish naturalist Nikolaus Steno (1638—1686) that these were the fossil teeth of sharks. Thus, the first principles of paleontology were laid down.

Living matter is studied by the biological sciences; however, biogenic matter is not specially studied by any of the natural sciences. Therefore, as stated in a conference document, "geologists should pay the greatest attention to the material products of the vital activity of organisms... This is one of the important specific features in the approach of geologists to the vital activity of the organism, and should always be

Fossil shark tooth (in times of old they were called glossopetrae) in phosphorite of the Paleogene Period. Lifesize. Algeria. Photo by Ya.V. Samoilov (From: Ya.V. Samoilov, *Deposits of Phosphorites in Algeria and Tunisia*, 1912, Table II, Fig. I.)

remembered*." One cannot but agree with this statement.

Finally, the last type of matter of terrestrial origin is nonliving abiogenic matter. Examples of such substances are products of volcanic eruptions and gases evolving from the interior of the Earth. According to present-day estimates,

---

* "*Materials for Discussion and Conference on Sedimentary Rocks*", Publishing House of the USSR Academy of Sciences, Moscow, 1951, p. 50 (in Russian).

about 3 billion tons of abiogenic matter annually enter the biosphere.

It has not been scientifically established whether the matter of extraterrestrial origin contains either living or biogenic matter. So far signs of either have appeared only in science fiction novels and films, although it is true that in 1961 the British journal "Nature" published a paper by G. Claus and B. Nagy*, in which unusual formations found in meteorites were described. The authors called them "organized elements" and defined them as the remains of extraterrestrial microorganisms. Later, similar microscopic formations were found in other meteorites, sometimes in appreciable quantities, but the biogenic nature of the "organized elements" was not confirmed.

However, according to the conclusions drawn by the cosmochemist G.P. Vdovykin**, the "organized elements" are silicates, surrounded by a shell of abiogenic carbonaceous substance.

Thus, in spite of extensive searches, no traces of either living or biogenic matter of extraterrestrial origin have yet been found. Abiogenic matter of extraterrestrial origin is, however, quite a real thing.

Certainly, everyone knows about meteorites, although their appearance is a rather rare natural phenomenon. Since the 15th century only several hundred meteorites have been observed to fall

---

* G. Claus, B. Nagy, "Microbiological examination of some carbonaceous chondrites", *Nature*, **192**, 4803, 594-596 (1961).
** G. P. Vdovykin, "Organized elements in carbonaceous chondrites", *Geochemistry*, 7, 678-682 (1964).

and collect on the Earth. There have been only 5 cases of a man being hit by a meteorite, i.e., one per century, and one person has been killed.

Meteorites are the best known but far from the most widespread form of abiogenic matter of extraterrestrial origin. They are primarily composed of meteoric dust, with the diameter of particles ranging from dozens of microns to smaller particles of almost molecular size. The total amount of abiogenic matter of extraterrestrial origin, arriving annually from space to the biosphere of the Earth, varies considerably, according to estimates given by different authors. Most experts, however, estimate it at 10^4 to 10^6 tons a year. This is not much of course, but during the 4.5 billion years of the Earth's existence, the thickness of the layer of matter of extraterrestrial origin has accumulated and reached a depth of few hundred metres. This layer is, however, nowhere encountered in pure form. The Earth's crust is a complex composition of matter, of both terrestrial and extraterrestrial origin.

Living matter, however, constitutes only a very small part of the biosphere. If this matter were distributed over the surface of our planet, it would cover it with a film as thin as 2 cm. Nevertheless, it is precisely living matter that, in Vernadsky's opinion, plays the leading role in the formation of the Earth's crust. Vernadsky wrote: "If the amount of living matter fails to attract attention in comparison to the inert and bio-inert masses of the biosphere, *biogenic rocks* (i.e., those created by living matter) constitute a tremendous part of its mass and go far beyond the limits of the biosphere" (italics are Vernad-

Abiogenic matter of extraterrestrial origin: cosmic dust isolated from Devonian rocks of the Urals. 30-fold magn. (Published in the Russ. ed. of "TBB")

sky's—*A.L.*). Vernadsky made this statement half a century ago, but it is supported by geological data and realized fully only now.*

We have already used the term "living matter", but have not given a comprehensive definition to this concept. Definitions were provided by Vernadsky several times in somewhat different wordings, but the basic meaning did not change: "The living matter of the biosphere is the sum of its living organisms"**. The concept of living matter existed in the natural sciences and philosophy of the nineteenth century, but Vernadsky applied this concept to science in a completely new way. When first encountered it may have

---

* A.V. Sidorenko, V.A. Tenyakov, Sv.A. Sidorenko, "On the biological nature of the Earth sialic crust". In: *Pre-Cambrian*, Nauka, Moscow, 1980, pp. 5-11.
** V.I. Vernadsky, "Problems of biogeochemistry", Part 2, *Trans. Connec. Acad. Arts a. Sci.*, **35**, 487 (1944).

seemed that the concept "living matter" did not introduce anything new and was simply unnecessary: such terms as "life" and "organic world" already existed. As if anticipating these arguments, Vernadsky emphasized that the word "life" has a lot of meanings and nuances.

We are accustomed to the word "life" going beyond the concept of substance and sometimes referring to philosophy, folklore, and artistic creativity (one need only recall the titles of novels, collections of poems, magazines, and motion pictures). The concept "living matter" introduced by Vernadsky is, however, unequivocal and requires quantitative characterization.

"I shall refer to the aggregate of organisms reduced to their weight, chemical composition and energy, as living matter", Vernadsky wrote. In other words, this is the sum total of matter comprised in the living organisms of the Earth. In this interpretation it is important to note that a living organism acts only with its energy, and quantity and composition of its matter; individual organisms retreat before the grandeur of the phenomena being studied. An indispensable attribute of living matter is the cycling of matter and accumulation of free energy in the biosphere that ensures its evolution and an increase in the degree of its organization.

It is significant that Vernadsky, usually extremely modest in self-appraisals and not subject to the pathetic element, considered the creation of the teaching about living matter to be his *calling* in the highest sense of the word. In 1920, having scarcely recovered from a severe illness that nearly brought him to the grave, Vernadsky wrote in his diary: "I have begun to realize clearly that I am to tell new things to mankind in the teaching about living matter, which I am creating, and that this is my calling, my duty, imposed upon me, which I am to carry into effect, like a prophet who hears a voice inside him, that summons him to act".

Vernadsky fulfilled his mission honorably. Perelman writes: "The development of science in the second half of the twentieth century and especially of its practical requirements have demonstrated that, having created the concept of living matter, Vernadsky made a brilliant discovery which has been of tremendous importance to the natural sciences."

Of course, when he introduced the term "living matter", Vernadsky did not consider this matter to be uniform; and furthermore, he did not consider any single compound (or group of compounds) definitive for living matter. In "Essays of Geochemistry", published several times during his lifetime in Russian, French, German, and Japanese, Vernadsky wrote: "An idea, rather widespread some years ago (published in 1924— A.L.), that life phenomena can be explained by the existence of complex carbonaceous compounds (living proteins) is irrevocably disproved by the body of empirical geochemical facts, since neither proteins, nor other carbonaceous compounds, nor protoplasm (consisting of a mixture of the two) can lead to an understanding of living matter. Living matter is an aggregate of all organisms. Its behaviour is the result of its entire matter as a whole. To say that manifestations of organisms are first of all concentrated in proteins rather than in carbonates, or in free atmospheric oxygen generated by them, is to contradict reality."*

Vernadsky considered living matter to be "a form of activated matter", emphasizing that the "energy is greater, the greater the mass of the living matter". From time to time its energy sharply increases, and colossal accumulations of living matter are formed. Outbreaks of such mass proliferations of "our smaller brethren" are described in scientific literature and in fictional works. Thus, Lawrence G. Green, in his excellent book "Old Africa's Secrets", describes mile-long herds of South African gazelles (*Antidorcas marsuplalis*) that migrated over Africa in the last century. Once such herd took 3 days to pass through a village, and gazelles can cover 100 or even more miles a day.

Medieval chronicles describe hordes of mice and rats which from time to time overran towns. Invasions of locusts, causing famine and disaster, have been known since ancient times: in the year 125 BC more than 800 thousand people died from starvation in North Africa because of the mass proliferation of locusts. The greatest invasion of the Colorado potato beetle occurred in the United States in 1874. In that year, in some areas of the Atlantic coast, beetles made up a layer 50 cm thick. The situation became so serious that Bostonians had to abandon their town for a period of time.

Vernadsky used the data of the British natur-

---

* W. Vernadsky, *La géochimie*, Alcan, Paris, 1924, pp. 263-264.

alist G. Carruthers*, who observed the annual flight of locusts over the Red Sea, to illustrate his ideas about temporary accumulations of living matter. The flight of this swarm of insects took a whole day. The swarm occupied a space of 6 thousand km³, and its weight was $4.4 \cdot 10^7$ tons, the weight of all the copper, lead and zinc that man had extracted throughout the last century. Unfortunately, swarms of such dimensions are encountered even today. For instance, according to recent observations in Argentina the flight of a swarm of desert locusts lasted 5 days. Swarms of locusts of up to 120 km in length and 20 km in width are described.

"It can cover all the Earth and devour all that is on the Earth. When it breaks loose, the sun darkens and stars lose their glitter. It has the head of a lion, the neck of an ox, the breast of a steed, the wings of an eagle, the belly of a scorpion, the hips of a camel, the legs of an ostrich, the tail of a serpent"—this passage from an ancient Arab manuscript seems to have been written specially to illustrate in artistic form Vernadsky's idea about living matter as activated matter.

"What is a swarm of locusts from the biogeochemical point of view?", Vernadsky asks and concludes: "It is, like dispersed rock, extremely active chemically, and found in motion"**. No researcher before Vernadsky approached living matter from such a point of view. Living organisms were

---

* G.T. Carruthers, "Locusts in the Red Sea", *Nature*, 41, 153 (1890).

** V.I. Vernadsky, *Works*, v. 4, Book 1, p. 92 (in Russian).

under the jurisdiction of the "biological department", and it never occurred to anyone that living matter could be regarded as rock. The explanation lies in the fact that this rock is of a specific kind.

Let us consider in brief the specific properties of living matter.

1. Living matter of the biosphere is characterized by tremendous free energy. In the inorganic world only unsolidified lava streams are comparable to living matter in the quantity of free energy they contain. They are, perhaps, even richer in energy, but quite short-lived.

2. A sharp contrast between the living and nonliving matter of the biosphere is observed in the rates of chemical reactions: in living matter reactions proceed thousands, and sometimes even millions of times faster (in Chapter One we have already explained this as due to the action of enzymes). Alexander Todd, President of the Royal Society of London, awarded the 1957 Nobel Prize and the 1978 Gold Medal of Lomonosov writes: "One of the specific features of living matter lies in that it carries out chemical reactions with a remarkable accuracy and orderliness and under much less severe conditions than in the production of substances by purely chemical methods." For life processes it is characteristic that to obtain small masses or portions of energy causes much greater energies and masses to be transferred and processed: for example, the weight of insects eaten by a tomtit during one day is equal to the weight of the bird itself; some caterpillars consume and process daily 200 times their own weight.

3. A distinctive feature of living matter is that the individual chemical compounds of which it is composed—proteins, enzymes, etc.—are stable only in living organisms (to a considerable extent this is also characteristic of mineral compounds which are part of living matter). As Friedrich Engels wrote, "death is... the decomposition of an organic body which leaves no trace, except the chemical components of which it was formed"*.

Sometimes one must be "skillful" in order to preserve the external skeleton. Thus, mollusks living in acidic waters in which the substance of their lime shell may be easily dissolved, coat it from the outside with chitin. "We know of only one state of mineral substance completely protected against dissolution in water: this is the state of living organic matter", Academician V.R. Williams emphasized.

4. "Spontaneous movement, to a great extent self-regulated, is a common property of every living natural body in the biosphere."** Vernadsky distinguished two specific forms of motion of living matter: (a) passive, stimulated by their proliferation and inherent to both animal and vegetable organisms; and (b) active, engendered for the purposeful transference of organisms (characteristic of animals and, to a lesser extent, plants).

The passive form of motion of living substance was aptly characterized by N.V. Timofeev-

---

* K. Marx and F. Engels, *Works*, v. 20, p. 610.
** V.I. Vernadsky, "Problems of biogeochemistry". Part 2, *Trans. Conn. Acad. Arts a. Sci*, **35**, 502-503 (1944).

Resovsky: "One of the major manifestations of life resides not in the growing up of the living organism, but in the multiplication of the number of elementary individuals. In this case a certain elementary entity creates another entity similar to itself and separates it from itself, thus giving rise to a new individual." Here the dispersal of individuals or of their germ cells (e.g., spores, seeds) is effected by the forces of nonliving nature (wind, flowing water) or by other actively moving organisms.

Living matter tends to fill all available space (within the limits of the globe, and, as regards man, even farther). The property of maximum expansion is inherent to living matter in the same manner as it is characteristic of heat to transfer from more heated to less heated bodies, of a soluble substance to dissolve in a solvent, and of a gas, to dissipate in space.

Vernadsky called this process "pressure of life" and calculated its velocity by specific formulas. Apparently, the greatest intensity of multiplication, among the organisms existing on the Earth, is displayed by the giant puffball. Each such fungus produces 7.6 milliard spores. Should all the spores survive, already in the second generation the volume of puffballs would exceed the dimensions of our planet by 800 times.

The second form of motion of living substance, distinguished by Vernadsky, is the active form. It is characterized by the self-transference of organisms which disperse in locations favourable to their existence. Dispersal of dioecious animals is effected by the females which produce progeny on new territories. The males settled there ensure an encounter between the sexes and reproduction of the species.

5. Living matter displays considerably greater morphological and chemical diversity than non-living matter. The difference between a virus and, say, an African elephant, is much greater than between any of the most contrasting representatives of nonliving matter. The chemical composition of living matter is strikingly diverse. More than 2 million organic compounds are known to enter into the composition of living matter, while the number of natural compounds (minerals) of nonliving matter is only about 2 thousand that is, three orders of magnitude smaller. Moreover, in contrast to nonliving abiogenic matter, living matter is not represented by the liquid or gaseous phase exclusively. Bodies of organisms are built from substances that are in all three phase states. However, despite all the diversity of the composition of living matter, the entire organic world of the Earth is noted for a surprising biochemical unity. All modern living organisms are built up mainly of proteins comprising the same amino acids, transfer hereditary information along one and the same route (DNA $\rightarrow$ $\rightarrow$ RNA $\rightarrow$ protein) and, moreover, use one and the same genetic code. The establishment of this unity is one of the most fundamental discoveries of biology in our time. To quote A. Szent-Györgyi, "Man does not differ so much from the grass growing under his feet". From our childhood we remember Mowgli's cry addressed to all the living: "We are of the same blood, you and I!".

6. Living matter is represented in the biosphere in the form of dispersed bodies—individual

organisms. The "living ocean" of Stanislav Lem in his novel "Solaris" remains science fiction. The dimensions of individual organisms vary from 20 nm (the smallest viruses) to 100 m (the range is over 10^9). The largest organisms that have ever existed throughout geological history are encountered today: among the animals these are whales and among the plants these are sequoias. According to Vernadsky, the minimum and maximum dimensions of organisms are determined by the possibilities of their gas exchange with the medium.

7. Being disperse, living matter is never found on the Earth in a morphologically pure form, i.e., as a population of organisms of one kind: it is always represented by biocoenoses. This seems to contradict our everyday experience: we know pure pine tree woods where nothing but pines grow; in films we have seen bird colonies (sometimes birds of one kind, e.g., sea-gulls) or sea lion populations on deserted shores of arctic seas. But this monotony only appears as such. As N.V. Timofeev-Resovsky points out*, "even the most simple biocoenosis of some dry pine forest on sand is a community consisting of approximately a thousand species of living organisms". Pine woods could not exist were it not for the decomposition of the decaying needles, branches and trunks by saprotrophic organisms and for the return of mineral substances to the biological cycle. Sea-gulls and sea lions could not live were it not for their "canteen" located near-

---

* N.V. Timofeev-Resovsky, "Biosphere and man", *Priroda*, 8, 2-9 (1970).

by, i.e., the sea with whose inhabitants they constitute a unified ecosystem.

The great Swedish naturalist Carolus Linnaeus (1707-1778) was, probably, the first scientist who correctly understood the systemic organization of the living on the Earth. He presented his views on the subject in 1749 in his dissertation titled "Oeconomia naturae". Having first drawn a dramatic and, it would seem, chaotic picture of life on our planet, Linnaeus, who was much ahead of his time, managed to put all things in their place with a surprising accuracy: "Having considered the rules of nature, we, in the first place, understand that plants are the first, most numerous and main inhabitants on the Earth, but they are ruled over by insects and other animals, above which other predatory creatures are also placed but less in number, and they in turn are also subordinate to their superiors, which are still less numerous than the former."

8. The principle of Redi, "all the living from the living", about which we have already spoken, is a distinctive feature of living matter. Living matter exists on the Earth in the form of the continuous change of generations. Owing to this, contemporary living matter, which is characterized by continuous renovation, proves to be genetically connected with living matter of all the past geological epochs. In contrast to this, nonliving abiogenic matter comes to the biosphere from outer space or comes out in portions from the lower-lying envelopes of the Earth. These separate portions may be formed as a result of similar processes and, thus, be analogous to each other in composition, although generally they

have no genetic connection with each other.

9. The presence of an evolutionary process is characteristic of living matter. The reproduction of living matter occurs not by way of "stamping", i.e., the absolute copying of, preceding generations, but through morphological and biochemical changes which are sometimes slow and sometimes more rapid (in the geological sense!). In addition a purposeful evolutionary process is characteristic mainly of higher organisms, whereas creatures organized in a more primitive manner—procaryotae—are conservative in their structure. It is in fact the presence of the evolutionary process in the case of higher organisms that makes it possible to determine the organism's geological age from fossil remains.

Nevertheless, among the higher organisms there are such over which time seems to have no power. They are our contemporaries, but their closest ancestors lived in remote geological epochs. In popular science literature they are called "living fossils" and in the scientific literature they are called "persistents". The name was suggested by the German scientist Z. Wilser and derived from the Latin "persisto", to stand firm. At present the best-known persistent is, without a doubt, the lobefin fish Latimeria or Coelacanth, the predecessor of all terrestrial vertebrates. This fish was believed to have become extinct at least 65 million years ago—was believed, until Christmas Eve of 1938, when the nets of South African fishermen for the first time caught a specimen of our ancestor alive, which had stubbornly resisted extinction. Paleontologists should be credited that the fish corresponded to the reconstructions they had made from the fossil skeletal remnants.

Another well-known "living fossil" is the Komodo dragon. The Dutch pilot, who was the first to see this dragon in 1911 during a forced landing by his plane on Komodo Island, was nearly dragged into a lunatic asylum after his return to his native country: so improbable seemed to be the description he gave.

There are persistents among plants too. The most striking example here is the ginkgo tree (from the Japanese "ginkyo", silver apricot). Nowadays one can find ginkgo trees mainly in botanical gardens, whereas at one time its closest relatives made up thick forests in the Jurassic period (which is separated from us by 150 million years!).

Persistents exist in the soil as well. In the upper Jurassic coal measures of the Bureya Basin the paleobotanist V.A. Krasilov and entomologist D.A. Krivolutsky found remnants of loricate mites, many of which proved to be identical to contemporary ones!

10. Academician B.B. Polynov (1877-1952) emphasized yet another specific feature of living matter as follows: "The quantity of the mass of living matter, corresponding to the given moment, cannot give an idea of the enormous amount of it that carried out its work during the entire time of the existence of organisms"*. Essentially, the mass of the biogenic matter of the metabiosphere is the integral of the mass of the living matter of the Earth with respect to geolog-

---

* B.B. Polynov, *Selected Works*, Publishing House of the USSR Academy of Sciences, Moscow, 1956, p. 437 (in Russian).

ical time, while the mass of the nonliving abiogenic matter of terrestrial origin is a constant value in geological history. One gram of Archean granite at present will remain 1 g of the same substance, while an equal mass of living matter, though remaining 1 g, will have existed for billions of years through changes of generations and all this time will have been carrying out geological work. Thus the mass of matter, processed by living organisms, largely exceeds their own mass.

Living matter is a specific kind of rock... an ancient and, at the same time, an eternally young rock. A rock which creates itself and destroys itself to appear again in new generations in one of its innumerable forms. The Phoenix of ancient legends.

As any subject of scientific investigation, living matter should be classified. Vernadsky wrote: "We may differentiate between homogeneous living matter, like a genus or a species, etc., and heterogeneous living matter, like a forest, a steppe, or any biocoenosis at large, consisting of different kinds of homogeneous living matter in specific proportions".* And if heterogeneous living matter, as Vernadsky understood it, corresponds to rock, homogeneous living matter may be regarded as a mineral.**

For characterizing uniform living matter at the level of the species Vernadsky suggested the use of three quantitative indices: (a) chemical com-

---

* V.I. Vernadsky, "Problems of biogeochemistry", Part 2, *Trans. Conn. Acad. Arts a. Sci.*, 35, 488 (1944).
** V.I. Vernadsky, "A plea for the establishment of a biogeochemical laboratory".—*The Marine Biological Station of Port Erin Ann. Rep.*, 1923, **37,** 38-43.

position; (b) average weight of organisms; and (c) average rate with which they populate the entire surface of the globe.

As early as 1918, Vernadsky drew attention to the need for investigating the chemical composition of living matter. To solve this problem, he recruited the biochemist, Professor V.S. Sadikov (1874-1942), his numerous pupils, and also A.P. Vinogradov, (1895-1975), who had only then began his career (their joint works on the investigation of living matter

Vladimir Sergeevich Sadikov (Photograph by courtesy of N.V. Sadikova.)

were published in 1924)*. The technique for the chemical analysis of living matter was elaborated by Sadikov.

More extensive investigations into the chemical composition of living matter were carried out at the Biogeochemical Laboratory of the USSR Academy of Sciences (BIOGEL), set up by Vernadsky in 1927 in Leningrad (in 1934 this Laboratory was transferred to Moscow). Papers such as "Analysis of the Plankton from the Ekaterininsky Pond at Detskoye Selo" by

---

* W.S. Sadikow, A.P. Winogradow, "Untersuchungen über die Zusammensetzung des lebendigen Substrats", *Biochem. Zeit.*, Bd. 150, H5/6, SS. 372-391 (1924).

Young research workers of BIOGEL; the last on the right is A.P. Vinogradov

A.P. Vinogradov, "The Mineral Composition of the Skeletons of Some Contemporary Echinoderms" by K.F. Terentieva, and "Investigation of the Chemical Composition of Red Clover" by T.I. Gorshkova were published in the BIOGEL Transactions. This type of research was further developed by Vinogradov, later an academician, who became Director of BIOGEL after Vernadsky's death.

In the late thirties and early forties Vinogradov published an extensive report "The Elementary Composition of Marine Organisms" (which was translated and published in the United States in 1953)*. Investigations of living matter "by measuring and weighing" are still going on. At present non-uniform rather than uniform living

---

* A. P. Vinogradov, *The Elementary Composition of Marine Organisms*, New Haven, 1953.

matter is the subject of investigation, mainly, the biomass and productivity of various ecosystems and, on the basis of these data, of the biosphere as a whole.

Vernadsky approached the classification of living matter from a geochemical point of view. Moreover, he based the classification of organisms on the difference in type of nutrition, elaborated in the 1880s by the German biologist Wilhelm Pfeffer (1845-1920). Vernadsky wrote: "We shall call autotrophic all organisms which obtain all the chemical elements necessary for their life in the contemporary biosphere from the inert matter surrounding them, and do not require ready organic compounds of another organism for the construction of their body"*. This term is derived from the Greek roots "autos", self and "trophē", nourishment. These are the "nourishers" of the biosphere. They not only eat, but feed others.

Pfeffer called organisms that require for their nourishment living matter formed by other organisms heterotrophic. "Heter" in Greek means "other", "different"; hence, heterotrophic organisms are those feeding on others. Organisms that take in a mixed type of nourishment also exist. Pfeffer called them mixotrophic organisms (from the Greek "mixis", the act of mingling or mixing). Examples of a mixotrophic organism are insectivorous plants.

Autotrophic organisms which use sunlight as the source of energy are called "photoautotrophic" (from the Greek "phōtos", light). In addition to light, carbon dioxide and water, these organisms

---

* W. Vernadsky, *La biosphère*, Alan, Paris, 1929, p. 123.

require other elements of mineral nutrition for carrying out photosynthesis, such as nitrogen, phosphorus, potassium, and silicon. Justus von Liebig (1803-1873), the famous German chemist, founder of agrochemistry, was the first to demonstrate the mineral requirements for plant nourishment. Terrestrial plants obtain these minerals through their roots from the soil, whereas algae and photosynthesizing bacteria (even such types exist!) get them from water.

Yet, photosynthesis turned out not to be the only way that primary organic matter could be formed from inorganic matter. In 1889-90 the great Russian microbiologist S.N. Vinogradsky (1856-1953) demonstrated that there are specific microorganisms capable of obtaining energy from the oxidation of inorganic substances.

Nitrifying organisms—the first autotrophic organisms discovered by Vinogradsky—live on the energy liberated by the oxidation of ammonia to nitric acid, which is carried out by them. Vinogradsky described some surprizing properties of nitrifying organisms in the following manner:

"1. Development in a purely mineral medium in the presence of an inogranic substance, which can be oxidized;

2. All the vital activity is most intimately connected with the presence of this substance, which in the case of nitrification is ammonia;

3. Oxidation of this substance is the only source of energy;

4. No need for organic nutrition as a source of structural material and energy"*.

____

* S. Winogradsky, *Recherches sur les organismes de la nitrification. II.—Ann. Inst. Pasteur*. Paris, 1890, v. 4.

The phenomenon discovered by Vinogradsky received the name chemosynthesis, and organisms that carried it out were called chemoautotrophic organisms. Later, various bacteria were discovered that were capable of obtaining energy from oxidation of the most diverse substances, such as hydrogen, methane, carbon monoxide gas, some compounds of iron, sulphur, and even antimony. Thus, a whole world of chemoautotropic bacteria has already been discovered, which play an essential role in the cycling of matter in the biosphere.

As we shall learn in the next chapter, wonderful ecosystems were recently discovered in the depths of the ocean, where the primary producers of organic matter are bacteria that oxidize abyssal hydrogen sulphide. Moreover, some cyanobacteria (blue algae) are also capable of chemosynthesis*, and considering their contribution, the role of chemosynthesis in the formation of the primary biological products of the World Ocean may be quite significant.

As already stated, heterotrophic and mixotrophic organisms cannot synthesize organic substance on their own, but they use it in its ready form. Among the heterotrophs three categories of organisms can be distinguished: *necrotrophs*, those killing the object they feed on; *biotrophs*, those parasiting on it; and *saprotrophs*, those feeding on dead organic remains**.

---

* E. Broda, *The Evolution of the Bioenergetic Process*, Oxford, Pergamon Press, 1975.

** J.M. Anderson, *Ecology for Environmental Sciences: Biosphere, Ecosystems and Man*, London, Edward Arnold Ltd., 1981.

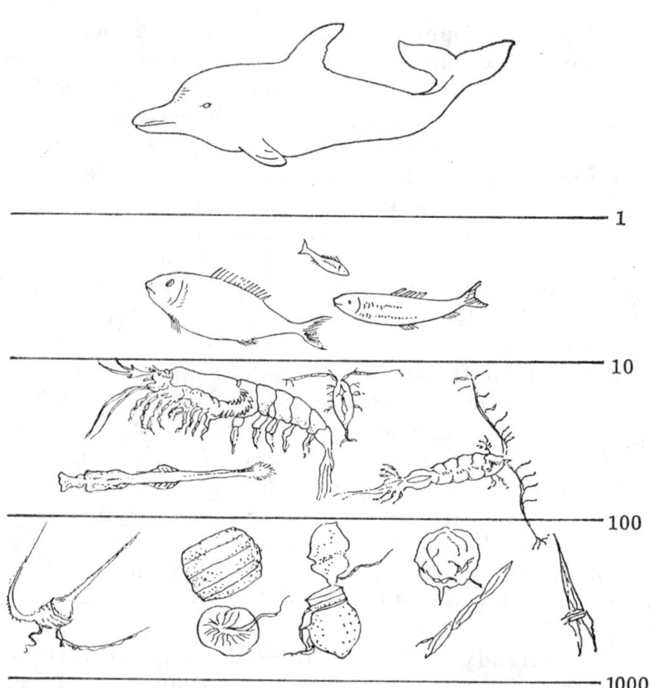

Fig. 4. Trophic pyramid of marine ecosystems (numbers illustrate losses of energy occurring with transition from lower to higher trophic levels)

In developed ecosystems there exists a complicated food chain (otherwise called trophic chain), and consumers of autotrophs, in their turn, become victims. "The beetle ate grass, the bird pecked the beetle, the ferret supped the bird"—such are three links in the food chain of biotrophs, as depicted by N. Zabolotsky.

An aggregate of living organisms dependent on similar nourishment is called a trophic level. Organisms of any level of the trophic pyramid feed on living matter of the lower-lying level. The lowest trophic level (in other words, the base of the trophic pyramid) consists of autotrophic organisms. On the average, only about 10% of energy is transferred from one level to another. (Fig. 4). The rest of the energy is either converted into heat and dissipated, or (most often) is not assimilated at all. The great French physiologist Claude Bernard (1813-1878) wrote: "Life can only exist where there is both synthesis and organic destruction". In the presently existing terrestrial ecosystems, the weight of the living matter of heterotrophs is hundreds and thousands of times less than that of the living matter of autotrophs (in forests, for example, it is 2000 to 5000 times less). As a result, necrotrophs and biotrophs fail to cope with their food resources, and the major part of the products of living matter dies off. The dead organic products and products of the metabolism of biotrophs are consumed by a whole army of various saprotrophs which completely decompose these substances to the following mineral compounds: carbon dioxide gas, water, nitrogen, and mineral salts.

"When the god Anu created heaven, heaven created the earth, the earth created rivers, rivers created ditches, ditches created slime and slime created the worm, the worm looked at the sun and cried, and his tears appeared before the face of the goddess Ei.

"What do you give me as food and drink?" the worm asked.

"I shall give you as food rotten wood and the fruit of trees."

Such is, according to the Babylonian cuneiform text, the origin of saprotrophs on Earth; they not only protect the biosphere from poisoning itself (many of the decomposition products of dead organic remains are extremely toxic) but also, by breaking down organic substances, return carbon and nitrogen to the mineral form, which is the only form of these elements that can be consumed by autotrophs. It is characteristic that while necrotrophs require a mixture of food consisting of various substances (proteins, fats, sugars or starch), saprotrophic bacteria and fungi, in the presence of a source of nitrogen and mineral elements, can be satisfied with a single organic substance, for example, protein or sugar. They easily decompose biogenic organic substances of both vegetable and animal origin. Moreover, they can deal with many organic materials created by man such as plastics or naphthalene. Polyethylene presents great difficulties, but if the polyethylene is exposed to ultraviolet radiation, bacteria can use it as well.

The simplest ecosystem is made up of combination of autotrophs and saprotrophs. Recently an experiment was carried out to elucidate the stability of such ecosystems. Thirty six different combinations of autotrophs (microscopic algae) and saprotrophs (fungi and bacteria) were sealed in test tubes and kept under constant illumination. The experiment lasted for three years. During this period 20 of the ecosystems proved to be incapable of self-maintenance. The remaining 16 developed quite adequately. The biomass of the autotrophs in them ranged from 9 to 99% of the total, and that of the saprotrophs, from 1 to 10%. In the viable ecosystems, the saprotrophic unit consisted up to 90% of some single dominant species; in most cases these species were bacteria from the group of pseudo-monads.

The well-known Soviet physiologist and Academician Ugolev defined the tasks of a new science—trophology. According to his definition, "the subject of trophology is the regularities of assimilation (that is, of the absorption and incorporation of substances necessary for life) at all the levels of organization of biological systems, from the cell, organ and organismic, to the populational and planetary."* In accordance with the basic concept of trophology, each kind of living organism of the biosphere uses definite sources of nutrition and, at the same time, serves as a nutritional object for other kinds of organisms. Living organisms must have a definite phagicity, i.e., be a source of food for another organism, and a definite trophicity, i.e., have nutritional properties and be assimilable. Such an approach leads to the paradoxical conclusion that there exists a mutual adaptation of so-called trophological partners. Figuratively speaking, the victim must not run away too fast from its predator, and the predator must not devour it too easily. Only in this case will predators feed predominantly on ill, defective and ageing members of the population, and the population as

---

* A.M. Ugolev, "Trophology—a new interdisciplinary science". *Vestnik AN SSSR*, **1**, 50 (1980).

a source of nutrition will be maintained at a specific level.

The British ecologist D. Owen* presents the view that in the course of evolution there takes place a mutual adaptation of autotrophs and heterotrophs, and that the traditional view, concerning the perfection of the protective mechanisms of the "one being eaten" against the "eating one" must be radically revised.

Thus, these new approaches confirm the brilliant insight of Vernadsky concerning the universal integration of life within the scope of the biosphere. The concept of interspecific competition, which prevailed in the last century, is being replaced by the concept of the mutual adaptability of species.

We have considered the classification of living matter according to the feeding behaviour of the organisms. The well-known Soviet biologist and biogeographer D.V. Panfilov suggested that living matter should be divided into two categories according to quite a different classification. He distinguished between reproductive living matter and somatic living matter (cells which perform any function except reproduction are called somatic). The mass of reproductive living matter is insignificant as compared with somatic matter, but it is reproductive living matter that determines the continuity of life on our planet. The biospheric role of somatic living matter is to transport the reproductive living matter to all corners of the Earth and thus ensure the ubiquity of life.

____

* D.F. Owen, "How plants may benefit from the animals that eat them", *Oikos*, **35**, 2, 230-235 (1980).

"Who is who" in the biosphere? Let us try to combine two approaches to living matter, the functional and the biological (systematic).

Life in the biosphere exists in cellular and extracellular forms. Viruses are representatives of the extracellular form of living matter. They were discovered in 1892 by the famous Russian scientist D.I. Ivanovsky (1864-1920), who, incidentally, was of the same age as Vernadsky and was his friend at Petersburg University.

Viruses are so original and so different from anything else, that one of the leading paleontologists of our time and Foreign Member of the Academy of Medical Sciences of the USSR André Lvoff gave the following exhaustive definition of viruses: "A virus is a virus".

In contrast to cellular organisms, viruses are devoid of irritability and have no protein-synthesizing apparatus of their own. They are incapable of independent existence and develop only in the cells of other living organisms (cellular ones) such as bacteria, plants, animals, and human beings. In fact, viruses are merely a sub-system in an integrated "virus-cell" system; metabolic functions within the scope of this system are carried out entirely by the cell; consequently, the virus never has direct trophic connections with its environment. It does not feed on anything, in the usual sense of this word, neither does it grow.

One might think that viruses are the most primitive organisms but their genetic apparatus is strikingly diverse. In this cardinal attribute the differences between the poliomyelitis and small-pox viruses, for example, are much more essential than those between bacterium and man. There is a tremendous world of extracellular life! According to the unanimous opinion of scientists, this world was formed by way of a peculiar degeneration of cellular organisms.

Viruses are a scourge to all the living. Settling in living cells, they cause illness and often the death of the host organism. Viruses are responsible for more than half of all human diseases including influenza, measles, mumps, chickenpox, and German measles. The most terrible disseases are also among those caused by viruses, e.g., cancer, AIDS, hydrophobia, infectious hepatitis, and forest-spring encephalitis. It is believed that during the average lifespan of 70 years, man is, on the average, ill with viral diseases for 7 years.

Mankind's struggle against viruses is hindered because of their extremely small dimensions (on the average, viruses are 100 times smaller than bacteria and can be directly visualized only under the electron microscope) and remarkable stability to environmental conditions. Some viruses can withstand boiling for half an hour and short-term treatment with conventional disinfectants, e.g., with alcohol or phenol. Such viruses can only be killed by superheated steam at high pressure or by ultraviolet rays.

Like all other organisms, viruses perform a specific function in the biosphere. By causing severe diseases in living organisms, viruses eliminate the weakest individuals, allowing the most adapted to survive. Viruses, to a great extent, effect natural selection in the biosphere.

Let us now consider cellular forms of life. At present several systems of classification exist.

Table 2. Macrosystem of Cellular Living Organisms* and Their Role in the Biosphere

| Macrosystem of living organisms** | | | Role in biosphere | | | |
| | | | Autotrophs | | Hete-ro-trophs | Mixo-trophs |
Super-king-doms	King-doms	Subkingdoms	Photo-trophs	Chemo-trophs		
Pro-cary-otes	Schi-zophy-tes	Bacteria (eubacteria)	+	+	+	+
		Archaebacteria	+	+	+	+
		Cyanobacteria (Cyanophyceae or "blue-green algae")	+	+	−	+
Eu-cary-otes	Plants	Lower plants (algae)	+	−	+	+
		Higher plants	+	−	+	+
	Fungi	Lower fungi (myxomycetes)	−	−	+	−
		Higher fungi	−	−	+	+
	Ani-mals	Protozoa	−	−	+	+
		Metazoa	−	−	+	−

* Without account of symbiotrophic organisms.
** After A.L. Takhtadzhian (1976) with supplements after V.I. Duda (1984)

We shall mostly use the macrosystem suggested by Academician A.L. Takhtadzhian*, with some refinements in light of the latest achievements (Table 2).

* A.L. Takhtadzhian, *The System of Organic World.— The Large Soviet Encyclopedia*, 3rd ed., 1976, vol. 23, pp. 1386-1391 (in Russian).

According to this system, there are two super-kingdoms of cellular organisms: procaryotes and eucaryotes. The main difference between them is the absence of the karyon (i.e., the cell nucleus)

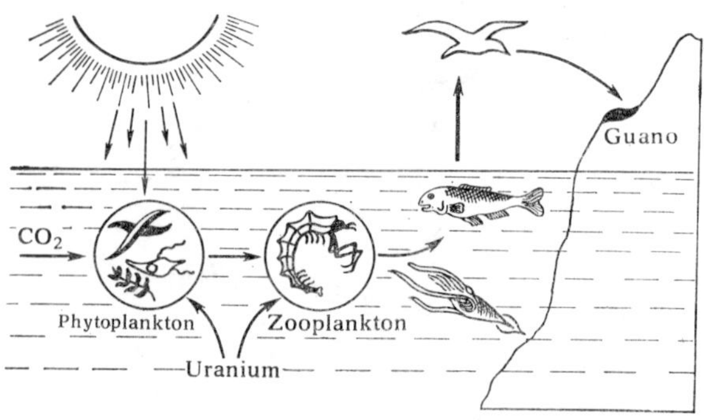

Fig. 5. Diagram of food chain in the ocean, illustrating the possibility of uranium concentration in guano deposits (after Polikarpov, 1976)

in procaryotes (Fig. 5). In procaryotes there is no differentiation between somatic and reproductive living matter.

Bacteria are an example of procaryotic cells. They were discovered in 1683 by Antony van Leeuwenhoek* (1632-1723), also the inventor of the microscope. Half a century later, Carolus Linnaeus in his "Systema Naturae" grouped all the bacteria discovered by that time (as well as all other microorganisms) into the "chaos",

---

* *Letters in Antony van Leeuwenhoek and His Little Animals*, by C. Dobell, New York, Russel and Russel, 1958.

which had been the pleasure of God to create and
the purpose of which was not clear to man. For
contemporary man, bacteria are also associated
with the most unpleasant phenomena—high temperature, chills, swamp fever, etc. However, only
0.1% of all the bacteria existing on the Earth
cause diseases in man (and man battles them
much more successfully than viral diseases).
André Lvoff justly remarked that we should not
be angry with bacteria, since if not for microbes
there would be no life on the Earth and there
would be no microbiologists! There is no exag-
geration in this joke: bacteria perform necessary
functions in the biosphere. Man began making
use of bacteria before even suspecting that they
might exist. Industries based on the vital activity of bacteria such as wine-making, brewing,
bread-baking, and cheese-making date as far as
several millenia BC. A long time passed before
the brilliant discoveries of Louis Pasteur enabled
us to understand the role of bacteria in these
industries so familiar to mankind.

Among all the living on the Earth the subkingdom of bacteria holds the record as to the diversity of its feeding behaviour. It is the only subkingdom which has representatives of all five
types of feeding behaviour.

There are approximately 50 species of photoautotrophic bacteria on the Earth. In contrast to
all other organisms, bacteria do not evolve
oxygen during photosynthesis (but we can pardon
them that!). Bacteria, along with other procaryotes, are the most ancient photoautotrophic
organisms on our planet. Photosynthesis in
bacteria occurs in a fundamentally different way

Nikolai Ivanovich Andrusov (Publ. in the Russ. ed. of "TBB".)

than in plants and with the aid of a different pigment, bacteriochlorin. Photosynthesizing bacteria may sometimes wield a considerable amount of products: according to the data reported by V.M. Gorlenko, in some lakes these bacteria account for up to 75% of all primary products. Photosynthesizing bacteria are found in both fresh and salt water.

The main role of bacteria in the cycling of matter in the biosphere is two-fold: (1) decomposition of dead organic matter, and the return of the constituent elements to the biotic cycle (a considerable part of this work is performed by bacteria in the alimentary tract of metazoans); (2) continuous introduction of new portions of ash elements and nitrogen into the biotic cycle. As early as the end of the last century N.I. Andrusov (1861-1924), an extraordinary Professor of Mineralogy at Yuriev University, who later became an academician, was the first Russian geologist to realize the role of bacteria in the biosphere. "Bacteria, evidently, have existed on the Earth for a long time. The tremendous role they play in the cycle of sulphur, nitrogen and carbon makes the life of the organisms inconceivable without them", he wrote.*

The significance of nitrogen fixation from the atmosphere in the biosphere can be compared only with autotrophic assimilation of carbon dioxide gas. From the general biological standpoint nitrogen is more valuable than the rarest noble metals, but only bacteria (and cyanobacteria considered below) are capable of fixing atmospheric nitrogen in their bodies and thus of introducing it into the biogeochemical cycle.

The functions of bacteria in the biosphere are so diverse that, in principle, ecosystems may exist, in which living matter is represented exclusively by bacteria, part of which may belong to autotrophs and another part, to heterotrophs. Only procaryotes are capable of such an autonomous existence in the biosphere.

Bacteria are ubiquitous in the biosphere. The Dutch microbiologist Martin V. Beijerinck (1851-1931) formulated the following postulate which is now named after him: "Bacteria develop everywhere where there are the conditions for their existence" (of course, they do not develop by spontaneous generation; the principle of Redi is operative here as well). Recently, viable bacteria were even found on the Moon, where they had been brought from the Earth by some previous spaceship.

The world of procaryotes still harbours many secrets, and new methods of research sometimes lead to unexpected discoveries.

---

* N.I. Andrusov, "Bacteriology and geology, their interrelationships", *Sci. Papers of the Imperial Yuriev University*, 1, 19 (1897).

A major event in the modern natural sciences was the discovery of a fundamentally new group of organisms* named archaebacteria (to avoid confusion, all the other previously known bacteria were given the name eubacteria). Without going into detail, the cells of the archaebacteria can be said to relate structurally to the procaryote type, but differ sharply from all other living organisms in their biochemical composition. About 40 species of archaebacteria are known that belong to 25 genera.

The archaebacteria vary in their way of obtaining nutrition. They include chemo- and photoautotrophs (in the latter, light quanta are absorbed not by chlorophyll, as in plants, and not by bacteriochlorin, as in eubacteria, but by another pigment—bacteriorhodopsin). Also, some of the archaebacteria are typical heterotrophs and can develop only at the expense of already produced organic compounds. It is notable that there is a complete absence of plant and animal pathogens among the archaebacteria. Like the other procaryotes, archaebacteria are distinguished by their remarkable unpretensiousness and quite often inhabit environments with extremely unfavourable conditions. They even inhabit solfataras** (vents of sulphurous volcanic gases)—habitats that fit the Christian notion of hell. Temperatures ranging from 85 to 105 °C are optimal for the anaerobic sulphurous archaebacte-

---

* C.R. Woese, "Archaebacteria", *Scientific American*, **244**, 6, 98-122 (1981).

** A. Segerer, K.O. Stetter, and F. Klink, "Two contrary modes of chemolithotrophy in the same archaebacterium", *Nature*, **313**, 6005, 787-789 (1985),

ria. Aerobic sulphurous archaebacteria (discovered in 1981-1983) flourish in a medium with hydrogen ion index (pH) of about 1, while halobacteria prefer dwelling in water in which the sodium chloride concentration reaches 20-30%!

Biochemical data allow us to assume that the archaebacteria are a genetically independent subkingdom (or even kingdom) not related in any way to the eubacteria*. They are evidently very ancient organisms. At any rate, they appeared not later, and perhaps earlier, than the eubacteria (which is exactly why they have been named archaebacteria, from the Greek root "archaeo"—ancient).

Cyanobacteria constitute the third subkingdom of procaryotes. In their viability they can compete only with bacteria and archaebacteria (cyanobacteria are found even in atomic reactors). In 1883 all living matter on Krakatao Island was destroyed by an eruption, but three years later cyanobacteria were found growing on volcanic ash and tuff. Cyanobacteria were the first to return to the ill-famed Bikini atoll after the American atomic weapons tests. Cyanobacteria also were the first settlers on the barren rocks of the Island of Surtsey which came into being in 1963 as a result of the eruption of a submarine volcano to the south of Iceland. Cyanobacteria are encountered everywhere: on land and in the ocean, in hot springs and on the snow. They thrive in the Antarctic, in polluted water bodies or in arid deserts. The olive-coloured slimy film

---

* R.A. Garrett, "The uniqueness of archaebacteria", *Nature*, 318, 6043, 233-235 (1985).

that covers the beach stones washed by waves is home for colonies of cyanobacteria. The small green "leaves" or balls which overcrowd artificial water reservoirs at the time of their "bloom" are also cyanobacteria. Their lavish development in water bodies contaminated with nitrogenous compounds which came from fields is a serious contemporary problem*.

Cyanobacteria are quite diverse in their morphological features. Monocellular, colonial and filamentous representatives are found among them. One of the species of ancient cyanobacteria is named after Vernadsky: Oscillatorites Wernadskii Schep. About a hundred species of cyanobacteria are capable of fixing atmospheric nitrogen. They do not require soil nitrogen; therefore they are able to inhabit such places where there is no soil; such as barren rocks, snow, and the bark of trees.

In his famous "Systema naturae" ("The System of Nature") (1758) Carolus Linnaeus wrote: "Who would believe that such beings as fish can be present in water if we did not see them with our own eyes." These words are no less applicable to cyanobacteria.

What is the biospheric role of cyanobacteria? Evidently, it consists in preparing the previously barren substrate for population by heterogeneous living matter. Cyanobacteria are the pioneers. According to the observations of V.O. Tauson, in the highlands of the Pamirs and of the Caucasus, cyanobacteria along with nitrifying bacteria

---

* G.E. Hutchinson, "Eutrophication", *Amer. Scientist*, **61**, 3, 269-276 (1973).

Indian pipe—a plant which does not trouble itself with photosynthesis (From: F. Went, *In the world of plants*, Moscow, 1972, p. 156.)

form black-coloured thin crust on stones. If one scrapes the crust from the rocks, one can see small insects—Collembola—which process the remains of bacteria and cyanobacteria. This triad creates soil on formerly barren rocks.

It turns out that procaryotes, the most primitive organisms on the Earth, having no proper karyon, are in the vanguard of the conquest of living space and, by their activity, prepare the soil, both in the direct and figurative sense, for more developed ecosystems. They, the procaryotes, can live without us... But we, can we do without them?

Every age creates its own myths. They also appear in our time. Thus, recently the world press made a sensational report on the vital activities of procaryotes (some archaebacteria and eubacteria) at temperatures of 250-300 °C in hot springs in the rift zones of the World Ocean* (we shall tell about these remarkable concentrations of life in Chapter 4). Somewhat later, critical articles appeared** which proved that proteins and nucleic acids cannot function at temperatures of 250-300 °C, and evidently the coacervations formed by the products of thermal destruction of the dead cell matter were erroneously taken to be bacterial cells. There was no sensation... But 105 °C—the authentically established limit to date for the existence of viable procaryotes—is also a record result surpassed by no one in the biosphere.

Thus, procaryotes display a remarkable ability to exist without oxygen in the atmosphere and without nitrogen in the soil. However, the representatives of another superkingdom of living organisms—eucaryotes—do not possess such wonderful properties.

Eucaryotes are morphologically quite diverse, ranging from microscopic fungi to man! Three

---

* A.E. Walsby, "Bacteria that grow at 250 °C", *Nature*, **303**, 5916, 381 (1983).

** R. White, "Hydrolytic stability of biomolecules at high temperatures and its implication for life at 250 °C", *Nature*, **310**, 5976, 430-432 (1984).

main kingdoms are distinguished among them:
plants, fungi and animals. Each kingdom performs
a definite function in the biosphere.

All plants, with rare exceptions, are autotrophs,
in fact, specifically, only photoautotrophs. Photosynthesis takes place due to the presence of
a specific magnesium-containing pigment, chlorophyll, in the cells of the plants.

Proper algae are rather diverse in both their
structure and size (from unicellular Eugleno-
phytae to fifty-metre giants such as Macrocystis
and Pelagophycus). The role of algae in the
biosphere is clear: as autotrophs, algae perform
the function of a green screen on the 70.8% of
our planet covered with water.

Higher plants belong to autotrophs, but
there are unique species among them, which re-
sort to other types of feeding. There are even
predator necrotrophs among them, which feed on
animals procured by way of real hunting, in
order to compensate for the chronic deficiency of
soil nitrogen. Examples to these are sundew,
bladderwort and some other insectivorous exotic
plants such as Nepenthes (a liane of equatorial
forests), Sarracenia and Darlingtonia (growing in
the New World). There are many predatory
plants in Africa. For instance, near Cape Town
Roridula shrubs grow, which capture and devour
small animals up to the size of frogs. The fertile
imaginations of the first African travellers even
created a man-eating tree. It goes without saying
that such a tree is the result of an idle flight of
imagination: plants cannot hold animals larger
than frogs or small fish with their trapping
tools (in the tropics such prey is sometimes even

stolen by dexterous spiders). All in all, there are about 450 species of predatory plants in the biosphere. This is less than 0.2% of 250,000 plants which are known to exist.

Insectivorous plants and some parasitic plants (European mistletoe, dodder) are partial biotrophs, i.e., mixotrophs. Saprotrophs, which are extremely rarely encountered among plants, for example, Hypopitus and Indian pipe, belong to the same category. These small deadly pale plants not troubling themselves with photosynthesis are sometimes encountered in forests. They were considered to exist only on the nutrients obtained from the decomposing forest litter, but they have now been shown to be partial parasites. Evidently, there are no real saprotrophs among plants.*

However, sundew, European mistletoe, Hypopitus are those exceptions which confirm the general rule that plants are photoautotrophs. But while calling the plants autotrophs, we must never forget their complete inability to provide themselves with nitrogen. While literally bathing in a nitrogen atmosphere—there are 80 thousand tons of it over every hectare!—the plants are dependent on the procaryotes for their nitrogen. The leguminous plants which we know from our school days are also no exception here—it is the nitrogen-fixing bacteria dwelling in their tubers that extract nitrogen from the atmosphere, and not the plants! Higher plants feature a predominantly passive form of motion. Reproductive

-----

* T.A. Rabotnov, "Once again about constortia", *Bull. of MSN*, Biol. div., 83, 2, 88-95 (1978).

and somatic parts are differentiated in them, but the possibilities for independent motion of the somatic parts are quite limited. How far can one go using only stems and rootstocks? True, one species of plant does hobble, however clumsily, on its tree feet*, but this species is the creation of science fiction rather than botanical reality. As to the propagation of reproductive matter by itself, plants are altogether incapable of such a thing.

And fungi were fungi.
They're like nobody else on earth.

So laconically has the Japanese poet Jun Takami characterized the fungal kingdom of eucaryotes. The latter have long been attributed to the kingdom of plants, but—the poet is right—fungi are "not like" plants!

Fungi are incapable of synthesizing organic substance by themselves. The majority of fungi are saprotrophs, though necrotrophs are sometimes encountered. These are predatory fungi which capture into their trapping nets small soil inhabitants. But this is a specific case, and while the biospheric function of plants is to create organic matter, the biospheric function of fungi is to decompose dead organic matter and thus prepare it for reutilization by living matter. It has been shown at present that the leading role in the biosphere in this respect belongs exactly to fungi (and not to bacteria, as was thought previously). It is quite unlikely that anybody

---

* J. Wyndham, *The Day of the Triffids*, London, 1951.

now will agree with the eighteenth century
French botanist S. Veillard who exclaimed in a fit
of temper: "Fungi are a cursed tribe, an invention
of the devil, devised by him to disturb the
harmony of the rest of nature created by God."
The "divine harmony" of the biosphere could not
exist without the "cursed tribe" of the fungi.

We have discussed the functions of two kingdoms of eucaryotes, namely, plants and fungi,
in the biosphere. On first examination everything
seems clear: plants play a constructive, creative
role in the biosphere, and fungi play a destructive
role; they close the biological cycle, prepare food
for autotrophs. But then what is the purpose of
animals in the biosphere? What purpose do you
and I serve here?

The heavy body of a cow,
Positioned on four extremities,
Crowned with a temple-like head
And two horns (like the moon in its first quarter),
Will also be not understandable,
Will also be incomprehensible
If we forget about its meaning
*On the map of the living of the whole world.**

Let us try to discover the meaning of animals
"on the map of the living of the whole world".
Let us start with protozoans. Unicellular animal organisms belong to this subkingdom (sometimes they form colonies). They live mostly in an
aqueous medium, in landlocked bodies of water,
ranging from rain pools to the ocean, in the moisture contained in soil and parasitic forms live in
the bodies of other living organisms.

---

* N. Zabolotsky, *Verses and Poems*, Sovetsky Pisatel',
Moscow-Leningrad, 1965, p. 235 (in Russian).

Most protozoans are necrotrophs. They feed on bacteria, unicellular algae and other small organisms, including protozoans. Saprotrophs and biotrophs are also found among them.

Protozoans are a necessary link in the biogeochemical cycling of matter in the biosphere although, perhaps, this link is not as obvious as that of the photoautotrophs. The main function of protozoans is to redistribute living matter in bio-inert systems containing a sufficient quantity of water. For the functioning of the biosphere as a whole, the ability of some marine protozoans to concentrate certain elements in their external skeleton, a feature which is not so clearly manifest in other eucaryotes, is also of great importance.

The second, much more numerous subkingdom of animals consists of metazoans. There are about 1.3 million species in this subkingdom, which is greater than the number of representatives of all other subkingdoms taken together. The majority of metazoans, 7/8 of all the species, live on land. Hutchinson*, addressing the question of why there are so many kinds of animals, came to the conclusion that the extremely high diversity of land fauna is associated with the diversity of land plants. The ample vegetarian diet of the biosphere is almost entirely consumed by the numerous connoisseurs of vegetable food. Predators are considerably less in number. According to the number of species, among the

---

* G.E. Hutchinson, "Homage to Santa Rosalia or why there are so many kinds of animals", *Amer. Naturalist*, 93, 870, 145-159 (1959).

metazoans, insects are in first place, molluscs in second, and vertebrates are third.

Metazoans possess an active form of motion of their living matter. As is correctly stated in an old trustworthy document, "an animal by its nature is a nomadic being". Only rare sedentary forms which attach themselves to a substrate do not feature an active form of motion. The freedom of movement of metazoans determines their main biospheric function. Yu.A. Isakov and D.V. Panfilov write: "In the majority of land-scapes and biocoenoses animals perform an indispensable function by transforming vegetable organic matter into the dispersed state and disseminating it with sufficient uniformity from the living and perished plants to the places of growth and development of subsequent generations of vegetable organisms. This is, if one may say so, the 'cosmic role' of animals"*. However strange this may seem, predators also play an essential role in it. Attacking the flocks of ungulate animals, they drive them from place to place and thus preclude excessive spoiling of pastures.

In addition to plants which extract nutrient substances from soil, animals are the only representatives of the living matter of the biosphere, which transfer cycling matter in a direction contrary to the flow. Should they suddenly disappear from the biosphere, life would be possible only in direct proximity to water bodies. And

---

* Yu.A. Isakov, D.V. Panfilov, "Main aspects of medium-forming activity of animals". In: *Medium-forming Activity of Animals*, Moscow State University Press, Moscow, 1970, p. 4 (in Russian).

while insects transfer various matter over dozens of metres from the plant that has created it, vertebrates transport it over distances measured in kilometres, and seasonal migrations of migratory birds and some fish effect the global transfer of matter in the biosphere.

Metazoans are the only animals in the biosphere, which transport "foreign" reproductive living matter such as spores, pollen and seeds of higher plants, and thus contribute to their settling in the biosphere.

Although primarily necrotrophs, metazoans consume part of the production of autotrophs thereby performing regulatory and stabilizing function in ecosystems. By destroying part of the products, they protect ecosystems against overproduction of nondecomposed dead organic matter which hinders renewal of vegetation. In marine ecosystems animals also perform the function of a regulator of the mass of the autotrophs by eating and thinning the plankton (they also affect them by the excretion of metabolic products into the water). As R.I. Zlotin puts it, losses in the production of autotrophs is the "price" vegetation "pays" to herbivorous animals for the acquisition of homeostasis by the ecosystem.

In the biosphere not affected by man, vegetation, in principle, cannot be overgrazed by herbivorous animals: the population of herbivorous animals will fall before the extent of the "grazing" becomes catastrophic for the vegetation. On average, within an area of the terrestrial portion of the biosphere there live about 10 mass species of vertebrates with a total consumption of about 1 % of the primary production* (in other words, of the annual growth of the vegetation).

By absorbing specific elements and excreting the products of metabolism, animals directly affect their habitat. In this respect the most active are filter-feeding organisms (in aquatic ecosystems) and detritophagous animals (in the soil and bottom sediments of water bodies).

Finally, some of the animals are saprotrophs (worms, some insects and arachnids, carrion-feeding birds and mammals). Observations have shown that the decomposition of dead organic matter proceeds two to five times slower without the participation of animals.

Thus, animals in the biosphere serve as a means of transportation, a control panel, a conditioner, and a sewage disposal system. Evidently, it is not accidental that there are one million three hundred thousand species of them.

We have completed our review of the Earth's organic world and we could stop here if the phenomenon of symbiosis did not exist in the biosphere.

The term "symbiosis" was first proposed in 1879 by the German biologist Anton de Bary (1831-1888) to designate various forms of close cohabitation of two organisms belonging to different species. Back in school we learned about lichens—organisms that are an indivisible composite of algae and fungi. But for a long time lichens were considered to be a strange whim of nature, incomprehensible freaks. It has only

* F.B. Golley, "Impact of small mammals on primary production". In: *Ecological Energetics of Homeotherms* (ed. J.A. Gessaman), US University Press, 1973.

recently begun to be established that symbiosis is a typical form of coexistence for organisms in the biosphere chiefly occurring under conditions unfavourable for vital activities.

Symbiotic relations ensure the functioning of autotrophs and heterotrophs within the confines of a single organism called symbiotrophic.

The marine ciliated worms *Convoluta roscoffensis* are typical representatives of symbiotrophic organisms. They are encountered in enormous numbers on the western shores of France and on the islands of Jersey and Guernsey (Great Britain). After hatching from their eggs, these worms swallow such large amounts of green algae that they acquire a bright green colour. The algae inside the worms remain alive and, as they are supposed to do, occupy themselves with photosynthesis, thus supplying their hosts with food. As a result, the mouth opening and digestive apparatus become superfluous for the worms and gradually atrophy. Taking into account the interests of their "bread-winners" (they cannot live now without photosynthesis!), the worms lead an active life in the water in the daytime, and dig into the sand for the night. Some other metazoans such as the giant bivalve clams *Tridacna gigas**, green hydra, and anthosoan polyps also have built in photoautotrophs.

But this is not yet all. Not without reason is it said that life is stranger than fiction. It has recently been established that some symbiotrophic animals exist at the expense of chemotrophs!

---

* D.S. Jones, D.S. Williams, and C.S. Romanek, "Life history of symbiont-bearing giant clams from stable isotope profiles", *Science*, 231, 4733, 46-48 (1986).

The most vivid example here are rifties, dwelling at the bottom of the ocean where thermal waters rich in hydrogen sulphide emerge. Chemoautotrophic bacteria are also the source of nutrition for some oligochaetes (*Phallodrilus*) encountered at the Bermuda Islands and at the Barrier Reef of Australia, and also for the bivalve mollusk *Solenomyia*.

As pointed out by Academician M.S. Gilyarov (1912-1985), "physiologically, every symbiotrophic animal is in essence not an animal, but a system in which a relatively closed circulation of biogenic elements is ensured... Their example reveals how conditional our notions of an organism are and how complicated it is to define this concept and its limits"*. All the higher organisms are in essence not organisms, but superorganisms, because they include a whole set of microorganisms facilitating digestion (the stomach of a human being contains 400-500 species of them).

Do you remember the butterfly from Ray Bradbury's novel "A Sound of Thunder", that very butterfly that changed the course of history? The famous American science-fiction writer did not exaggerate its importance. The biosphere is a finely balanced system, and there is nothing superfluous and insignificant in it. Both, "an exquisite thing, a small thing that could upset balances", created by Bradbury's imagination, and "the heavy body of a cow" from Zabolotsky's

---

* M.S. Gilyarov, "Ecologically autotrophic animals and their features", *Uspekhi Sovr. Biologii*, **96**, 1 (4), 11 (1983).

Product of biogenic migration of the 2nd type: a ter-
mite nest over 6 m high. North Australia. (From: *Nat.
Geogr.*, **93**, 3, 411 (1948).)

poem, find their place "on the map of the living of the whole world".

I would like to conclude this chapter about the living matter of the biosphere with the words of Vernadsky: "Living matter has always, throughout geological time, been and remains to be an indissoluble regular constituent of the biosphere, a source of energy entrained by it from solar radiations, the matter which is in the active state, which has the main influence on the course and direction of the geochemical processes of the chemical elements in the entire Earth's crust".*

In the next chapter we shall consider the work performed by living matter in the biosphere.

---

* V.I. Vernadsky, *Works*, v. 1, p. 217 (in Russian).

3. The Most Powerful Geological Force

It is impossible to understand the history of sedimentary rocks without taking into account the powerful influence of organisms on the migration of substances in the Earth's crust and on the formation of sediments.

L.S. Berg, 1944

The work of living matter in the biosphere is quite diverse; for a better understanding of the result of this work, some geological concept should first be defined.

Geologists devide the formation of sedimentary rocks into four stages. The first of these, the stage of hypergenesis, is, as it were, preparatory. During this period initial products are formed, which are later transformed into sedimentary rocks. During the second stage, the stage of sedimentogenesis, the transfer of matter and the accumulation of friable noncemented sediments such as sands, clays, coquina, silts, and peat takes place. The third stage is called diagenesis. During this period friable, often loose sediments are transformed into dense strongly cemented rocks such as sandstones, argillites, limestones, and coals. Finally, during the fourth stage, which is called katagenesis, further densification and transformation of the sedimentary rocks takes place. As we shall see later, living matter plays the most important, even decisive

Charles Darwin. (From: *The History of Biology from Ancient Times to the Beginning of the Twentieth Century*, Moscow, 1972, ill. on p. 294.)

role during the stages of hypergenesis, sedimentogenesis and diagenesis.

According to Vernadsky, the work of living matter in the biosphere is manifested in two main forms: (a) chemical (biochemical)—the first type of geological activity; and (b) mechanical—the second type of such activity.

Geological activity of the first type—construction of the body of an organism and digestion of food—is, naturally, more important. The functional definition of life, given by **Friedrich Engels**, is now classic: "Life is the mode of existence of protein bodies, the essential element of which consists in *continual metabolic interchange with the natural environment outside them*, life ending with the ending of this metabolic interchange"* (italics are Engels'.—*A.L.*).

In actual fact, continual metabolic interchange between the living organism and the external environment conditions the manifestations of the majority of functions of living matter in the biosphere. According to the calculations of a biologist, during the lifetime of a man 75 tons of water, 17 tons of carbohydrates, 2.5 tons of proteins, and 1.3 tons of fats pass through his body. However, in terms of the geochemical effect of his physiological activity, man is far from being the most important kind of living matter in the biosphere. The geochemical effect of the physiological activity of organisms is in inverse proportion to their sizes, and the activity of procaryotes—bacteria and cyanobacteria—proves to be the most significant.

The quantity of substance passed through the organism is also of great importance. In this respect the maximum geochemical effect on land is exerted by soil-eaters and in the oceans, by mud-eaters and filter-feeding organisms. Darwin** calculated that the layer of excrement excreted by earthworms on the fertile soils of England was about 5 mm per year! It follows that earthworms pass the entire 1 m thick soil stratum

---

* K. Marx and F. Engels, *Works*, v. 20, p. 616.
** Ch. Darwin, *The Formation of Vegetable Mould Through the Action of Worms*, Murray, London, 1881.

through their intestines every 200 years. In the oceans, polychaetes, representatives of the same phylum of annelid worms and close relatives of the earthworm, compete with the latter in their "throughput capacity"; crustaceans also compete in capacity. A density of 40 polychaetes per square metre is sufficient to annually pass a whole surface layer of bottom sediments, with a thickness of 20 to 30 cm, through the intestines. (The substrate is substantially enriched by this process with calcium, iron, magnesium, potassium and phosphorus.) This, however, is far from being the limit. The Dutch scientist G.S. Cadèe* compiled a cumulative table illustrating the depth of bottom sediments processed by benthos animals. If follows that on the Californian coast living organisms annually process up to 1.5 m of sediments!

Coprolites are found in geological deposits starting from the Ordovician, but it is without doubt that most of them are not taken into account in geological descriptions. This is because of the inadequate study of the problem and because of the absence of diagnostic features for the determination of coprolites.

At the same time, in the bottom sediments of modern water bodies, fecal pellets of invertebrates are quite widespread and often constitute the main component of the sediment. In the South Atlantic, for example, ooze is almost completely composed of the feces of planktonic crustaceans, and along the shores of the North

---

* G.S. Cadèe, "Sediment reworking by *Arenicola marina* on tidal flats in the Dutch Wadden Sea", *Netherl. J. Sea Research*, **10**, 4, 440-460 (1976).

Sea the bottom sediments formed by the feces of mussels are up to 8 m thick.

The second type of biogenic migration of atoms, i.e., mechanical, is definitely manifest in land ecosystems with a well developed soil cover which allows animals to make deep shelters. The outstanding Soviet zoologist A.N. Formosov* (1899-1973) was one of the first to point out that owing to the mounds made by burrowing animals primary unweathered minerals get into the upper layers of the soil and, upon decomposition, are involved in the biotic cycle. The American geologist M. Chaffrey noted that termites and ants may become good assistants for geologists: it will be necessary only to investigate the waste dump around their "mines", which sometimes reach 70 metres!

Mechanical biogenic migration of atoms is widespread not only on land, but also in marine ecosystems, and its role in the latter may prove to be even more significant.

The concepts of a "burrow" and of a "nest" are usually associated in our mind with rodents and birds. But organisms make shelters for themselves on the sea bottom as well, and not only in soft, but also in rocky ground. Oligochaetes and polychaetes burrow as deep as 40 cm or more. Bivalve mollusks usually bury themselves at a shallow depth, but some of them, namely, Solen and Mya, dig burrows that even a marmot would envy: they reach a depth of several metres. However, in the tidal zone and

---

* A.N. Formosov, "Mammalia in the steppe biocenose", *Ecology*, **9**, 4, 449-460 (1928).

Traces of boring of Devonian limestone by the sea worm
Trypanites. Slightly magnified. Photo by R.F. Hekker.
(From: R.F. Hekker, *Introduction to paleoecology*, Moscow,
1957, Table VIII, Fig. 1.)

in the sand washed over by waves neither a burrow can be dug, nor a nest can be built. The
only alternative is to bore rocky formations,
and—drop by drop wears away the stone—such
boring jobs are indeed performed. The rocks are
tackled by algae and sponges, by bacteria and
mollusks, by cyanobacteria, sea-mats, polychaetes, sea urchins and small crustaceans*-**...

Borers appeared in the remote geological past.
Formations bored by them are found even in
Precambrian deposits and they are continuing
their work even today. The boring activity of

---

* J.E. Warme, "Boring as trace fossils, and the
processes of marine bioerosion". In: *The Study of Trace
Fossils* (ed. R.W. Frey), Springer, Berlin a.o., 1975,
pp. 181-227.
** S.A. Smith, C.W. Thayer, C.E. Brett, "Predation
in the Paleozoic: gastropod-like drillholes in Devonian
brachiopods", *Science*, **230**, 4729, 1033-1035 (1985).

pholads (mollusks of the family Pholadidae) sometimes brings about catastrophic results. Recently in the region of Sochi an ill-thought out project caused the shore to be denuded of pebbles, the shore started retreating at a rate of 4 m a year. The main perpetrators of the destruction were pholads. They had occupied every metre of the rocky shore composed of clay shales and had bored underwater burrows. Fortunately, a way out was found. The shore was reinforced with the aid of transverse partitions and the space between the partitions was filled with pebbles. As a result, the borers were destroyed. The pebbles, moving under the impact of the waves, crushed and ground them. In Western Europe, the woolly-handed crab, which was casually brought from China, is carrying out a no less dangerous activity. The crab has got into many rivers and, when building its burrows, it undermines the banks and destroys dams.

Pholad or "sea borer"— an active borer of sea coasts. (From: *The Life of Animals*, v. 2, Moscow, 1968, Table 20, Fig. 13.)

Movement of living matter as such can also be regarded as mechanical biogenic migration. Seasonal migrations of birds, movements of animals in search of food and mass migrations of animals are forms of such movement. Naturally, all these diverse forms of motion of living matter cause the transport of abiogenic matter as well.

As we have seen, Vernadsky classified the processes carried out in the biosphere by living matter according to the character of the processes themselves. N.I. Andrusov, Vernadsky's contemporary, approached this problem in a somewhat different manner. In his work, which we have already cited, he wrote: "The chemical activity of the organism in general, which has geological importance, can be reduced to two categories: first, to the formation of preservable secretions on the external surface or internally; and second, to the formation of liquid and gaseous secretions, capable of entering into various chemical reactions with the surrounding inorganic world". In essence, the same idea on the basis of present-day data was developed by the microbiologist T.V. Aristovskaya. She has pointed out that the migration of the atoms of chemical elements can be both a direct and an indirect result of the vital activity of organisms (first of all, of bacteria). In Table 3 the classification approaches of Vernadsky (horizontal rows) are combined with those of Andrusov-Aristovskaya (vertical columns).

For an understanding of the work performed by living matter in the biosphere, three basic statements, which Vernadsky called "biogeochemical principles", are of great importance. In Vernadsky's formulation* these principles are as follows:

---

* V.I. Vernadsky, *The Chemical Structure of the Earth's Biosphere and of Its Surroundings*. Nauka, Moscow, 1965, pp. 283, 286; *Biogeochemical Essays*, Izd. AN SSSR, Moscow-Leningrad, 1940, p. 185 (in Russian).

Table 3. Character and Localization of Processes Carried out by Living Matter

Geological activity	Type of process	Process occurs: within the organism	Process occurs: outside of the organism
I	Chemical (biochemical)	Digestion of food, construction of body of organism	Secretion of metabolic products and excreta into external environment; extracellular digestion
II	Mechanical	Passing of inorganic components of food through alimentary tract of soil- and mud-eaters	Transfer of nonliving matter by organisms in the course of activity

Principle I: "Biogenic migration of the atoms of chemical elements in the biosphere always tends to its maximum manifestation".

Principle II: "The evolution of species in the course of geological time, leading to the creation of life forms that are stable in the biosphere, proceeds in a direction which increases the biogenic migration of the atoms in the biosphere", or, in another wording: "In the evolution of species, those organisms survive, which by their existence increase the biogenic geochemical energy".

Principle III: "During the entire geological history, since the Cryptozoic*, the population of the planet was the maximum possible for the entire living matter then existing".

For Vernadsky, biogeochemical Principle I is closely associated with the capability of living matter for unlimited proliferation under optimal conditions. "The whirl of atoms", which is life, according to the definition given by Georges Cuvier, tends to unlimited expansion. This results in the maximum biogenic migration of atoms in the biosphere.

Biogeochemical Principle II in essence touches upon the cardinal problem in modern biological theory—the question about the purposeful character of the evolution of organisms. Vernadsky held that in the course of evolution, advantages are obtained by those organisms which have acquired an ability to assimilate new forms of energy or "learned" to utilize the chemical energy stored in other organisms. Thus, in the course of biological evolution the "efficiency" of the biosphere as a whole increases. This has been recently demonstrated in purely mathematical terms by V.V. Alexeyev who, proceeding from calculations, came to the following conclusion: "Evolution must develop in the direction of an increase in the matter exchange rate in the system." And further: "It becomes clear why enzymes were formed, whose role resides in drasti-

----

* The *Cryptozoic period* is the term suggested by the American geologist Ch. Schuhert (1858-1942) for "the era of latent life" (i.e., the Precambrian period).

cally increasing the rates of reactions that are extremely slow under usual conditions".

Vernadsky's biogeochemical Principle II is confirmed by the most diverse empirical material. Thus, in 1956 the soil scientist V.A. Kovda*, now a Corresponding Member of the USSR Academy of Sciences, reported the results of chemical investigations on more than 1300 samples of ash of modern higher plants. On the basis of this extensive data the author came to the conclusion that (with a few exceptions) the ash content of plants increases from representatives of ancient taxons towards more recent ones. This regularity is one of the particular manifestations of biogeochemical Principle II. Generally, however, its manifestations in the biosphere are quite diverse and rather unexpected. Let us consider another example from the botanical sciences.

The Soviet botanist A.P. Khokhryakov** recently established the evolution of higher plants to have a specific tenor, residing in an intensification of changes of the organs in the course of the individual development of the organism. Thus, according to Khokhryakov, in lepidodendrons extinct (arborescent lycopods) only a part of the leaves was subject to the change. In more evolutionarily advanced plants, the ferns, the leaves are also subject to shedding, but in this case a greater part of the leaves is shed per unit time with respect to the mass of

---

* V.A. Kovda, "Mineral composition of plants and soil formation", *Soil Science*, 1, 6-38 (1956).

** A.P. Khokhryakov, *Regularities of the Evolution of Plants*, Nauka, Novosibirsk, 1975, p. 204 (in Russian).

the entire plant body than in the case of lepidodendrons. In most primitive gymnospermous
plants, the cycads, only the leaves shed, with
the exception of their stems. In conifers, the
branches and bark are shed periodically. Finally,
in the example of the angiosperms, the transition
from perennial forms (trees and shrubs) to annual
forms (herbs) is most evident. The same transition is also observed in other taxons of higher
plants: among ancient horsetails and club mosses
arborescent forms were predominant, while present-day horsetails and club mosses are herbs;
in the geological past there were many arborescent forms among ferns, while now arborescent
ferns are dying out. Such an intensification of
changes, naturally, brings about an increase in
the biogenic migration of atoms in the biosphere.
Principle II is "at work" here as well... It is
true, however, that conifers for some reason do
not want to become herbs, while mosses, on the
contrary, have never been trees.

Khokhryakov, being a botanist, examined only
plants; Perelman has given a more extensive
treatment of the problem of the purposeful
character of evolution*. He has calculated that
according to the ratio of the logarithms of annual
production to the "instantaneous biomass" of
living matter (coefficient "K") contemporary ecosystems make up the following series:
1. Taiga landscapes (0.54-0.55);
2. Landscapes of humid leaf-bearing forests:
   (a) of the moderate belt (0.59-0.62);

----

* A.I. Perelman, *Geochemistry of the Biosphere*, Nauka, Moscow, 1973, p. 168 (in Russian).

(b) of the subtropical belt (0.66);
(c) of the tropical belt (0.68);
3. Herbaceous landscapes (0.83-0.95).

It may be assumed that this is an "evolutionary series" of landscapes and that now non-existent landscapes had a value of "K" less than 0.5.

Finally, biogeochemical Principle III is also associated with the "omnipresence" or "pressure" of life. This factor ensures the endless acquisition by living matter of any territory suitable for the normal functioning of living organisms.

Several decades ago many paleontologists believed that the expansion of life over the globe proceeded very slowly. It was thought, for example, that land plants in the Carboniferous and even in the Permian period existed mainly on marshy coastal plains, and that drought-resistant vegetation formed only in the Cenozoic era. These hypotheses were recently shown to be erroneous by a detailed analysis carried out by the Soviet paleobotanist S.V. Meien. In his opinion, the presence of a developed vegatative cover on continents is proved not only by the numerous findings of plants in Paleozoic continental deposits. Facies analysis has shown that the sedimentation conditions which existed at that time did not differ principally from those existing today. Also, if land vegetation did not exist, the character of the drain from the continents would be quite different than that observed now.

Did the progressive expansion of life take place at all in the course of geological history? Vernadsky wrote: "Life penetrates everywhere where it did not exist before, but we cannot assert that these areas of the planet were always free from life, never occupied in other geological times. It appears possible that these areas free of life were formed in the most recent geological eras and we observe merely the mastering by new forms of life of those areas from which the old living matter had disappeared for some reason or other. This may be so for cave life, for example. But we may also assume that here we also see a real expansion of the area of life, there having occurred a long-term evolution of the organisms adapting to new conditions. It seems to me that otherwise it is difficult to explain with confidence the adaptation of deep-dwelling organisms living at a depth exceeding 6 km, though it cannot be regarded as proven".*

The data of modern science confirm that there actually was a "real expansion of the area of life" in geological history.

What are the functions of living matter in the biosphere? According to Vernadsky** there are nine such functions: (a) gas function; (b) oxygen function; (c) oxidation function; (d) calcium function; (e) reduction function; (f) concentration function; (g) function of destruction of organic compounds; (h) function of reducing decomposition; and (i) function of metabolism and respiration of organisms.

In the modern manual "Principles of Sedimentology"*** the following biological processes which

---

* V.I. Vernadsky, *The Chemical Structure of the Earth's Biosphere and of Its Surroundings*, Nauka, Moscow, 1965, p. 284 (in Russian).

** W. Vernadsky, "Sur les conditions de l'apparition de la vie sur la Terre", *Rev. gén. sci.*, **43**, 503-514(1932).

*** G.M. Friedman, J.E. Sanders, *Principles of Sedimentology*, Wiley, New York, 1978, p. 120.

have geological significance are distinguished: (1) metabolism of organisms, leading to the formation of skeletons from calcium carbonate; (2) subsequent destruction of these skeletons by predators and other destroyers, which leads to the formation of various forms of skeletal detritus; (3) precipitation of lime mud by the organisms; (4) its pelletization by organisms; (5) burrowing activity of the organisms and mixing of the sediments by them; (6) activity of microorganisms effecting various chemical reactions contributing to the formation of minerals.

Summarizing all the available information concerning the activity of living matter, we can single out 5 main functions of living matter in the biosphere (Table 4).

The energetic function is manifested in the assimilation of energy, mainly of solar energy. "Only life with its morphological sophistication could capture the sun's rays on the Earth for millions of years, as in the example of coal," stated the Academician V.L. Komarov at the I Congress of Soviet botanists in 1921. Indeed, only due to the "green shield" of the biosphere, to photoautotrophs, is solar energy not merely reflected from the surface of the planet, heating only the Earth's superficial layer, but instead it penetrates deep into the Earth's crust and is a source of energy for exogenous processes (we have already discussed this in Chapter One).

Not very long ago solar energy was considered to be the only energy source for all the biotic processes occurring on the Earth. It was presumed that the chemoautotrophs also use the energy that was assimilated by photoautotrophs at some

Table 4. Main Functions of Living Matter in the Biosphere

№	Function	Brief characteristics of process
1	Energetic	Absorption of solar energy in photosynthesis and of chemical energy through decomposition of energy-saturated substances; transfer of energy via the food chain of heterogeneous living matter
2	Concentration	Selective accumulation in the course of vital activity of definite kinds of matter: (a) employed for building of the organism body; (b) removed from it during metabolism
3	Destructive	(1) Mineralization of neobiogenic organic matter; (2) decomposition of nonliving inorganic matter; (3) introduction of the formed matter into the biotic cycle
4	Medium-forming	Transformation of the physico-chemical parameters of the medium (mainly due to neobiogenic matter)
5	Transportation	Transfer of matter against the force of gravity and in a horizontal direction

earlier stage. It has now been shown, however, that a living substance can also successfully utilize "primary" endogenic energy. For example, the abyssal rift concentrations of life described in Chapter Four chiefly exist at the expense of endogenic hydrogen sulphide. A living substance thus assimilates energy from both sources existing in the biosphere—cosmic and endogenic. As a result, as was concisely stated by the French botanist G. Guegamian: "The energy balance of the planet (i.e., the Earth—*A.L.*) as of a cosmic system depends on living matter".*

The supply of geological processes with energy through the activity of living matter is most clearly manifest at the stage of diagenesis. Interesting work on this problem was carried out during twenties and thirties by Professor Perfiliev.

Ingenious experiments proving the biogenic nature of diagenetic processes were more recently carried out by M.M. Yermolayev**, the author of the above-cited manual of physical geography, now a professor at Kaliningrad University.

A sample of undisturbed ground taken from the sea bottom was placed in a glass tube. Two zones were clearly observable in the sample: an upper oxidized zone and a lower reduced zone. The tube was sealed off at its upper end and turned upside down. The lower layer of the ground was thus on top. The tube was filled with water, and the water was changed every day over a period

---

* G.V. Guegamian, "On the biospherology of V.I. Vernadsky", *Journal of General Biology*, **41**, 4, 588 (1980).

** M.M. Yermolayev, "On the lithogenesis of plastic clayey marine sediments", *Izv. AN SSSR*, geol. series, 1, 121-138 (1948).

of 17 months. The result was a complete "reversal" of the ground sample: the oxidized layer at the bottom became reduced, and the formerly reduced layer became oxidized. Yermolayev explained this phenomenon by migration of the anaerobic and aerobic bacterial complexes.

To make sure that the redox process was biogenic, a second series of experiments was carried out. A sample of strongly reduced ground from the Laptev Sea was divided into two parts. One of these parts was kept in its initial state under a layer of water in a vessel; the other part was placed into another vessel, and the microflora in it were destroyed with an antiseptic. After definite intervals of time the ratio of trivalent iron to bivalent iron was measured in both vessels as an indication of the intensity of redox processes. Within eight days this ratio in both vessels increased 1.5 times. Over the next 40 days the characteristic in the vessel with the antiseptic remained unchanged, while in the control vessel it increased by as much as 8 times! This was a direct proof of the oxidation being effected by the microflora (in the vessel with the destroyed microflora the oxidation during the first eight days of the experiment proceeded under the action of enzymes).

In the course of diagenesis microorganisms carry out hundreds of various reactions. Some of the microorganisms in bottom sediments are chemoautotrophs and exist at the expense of energy-saturated inorganic compounds. In the main, however, the microbiota of bottom sediments work on biogenic fuel, namely, on detritus coming from the upper levels of the water mass.

The essence of the energetic function of living matter in the biosphere can be formulated in the words of Vernadsky: "In a limited definite region distinctly separated from the rest of the planet, in a special shell of the Earth formed by the biosphere, which is characterized by irreversible processes,—*life will increase* and not decrease in the course of time *the free energy of this shell*" (underlined by Vernadsky)*. Developing this idea, Preston Cloud, a consultant professor at the California University in Santa Barbara, defined the biosphere as "a huge metabolic device for the capture, storage and transfer of energy"**.

The second main function performed by living matter in the biosphere is that of concentration. The substance being concentrated is either employed for the growth of the soft body and skeleton of organisms, or excreted into the environment.

The concentration of matter occurs in two ways. Most commonly elements are concentrated in ionic form from true solutions. Most marine invertebrates build their skeletons in this way. The second method of concentration is sedimentation of substance from suspension colloidal solutions by filtering organisms.

The concentration of elements by living matter from true solutions was intensively investigated by the outstanding Russian mineralogist, Vernadsky's disciple and colleague, Professor Yakov

---

* V.I. Vernadsky, "On some fundamental problems of biogeochemistry", *Transactions BIOGEL*, Issue 5, p. 12 (1939).

** P. Cloud, "The Biosphere", *Scient. Amer.*, **249**, 3, 138 (1983).

Yakov Vladimirovich Samoilov. (Publishe in the Russ. ed. of "TBB".)

Vladimirovich Samoilov (1870-1925). Unlike his great teacher, Samoilov approached this problem from a mineralogical rather than geochemical point of view. At the beginning of the century little factual material existed and one sometimes had to be guided by intuition. Samoilov's intuition did not fail him. In 1910 in an article about barite deposits, Samoilov wrote: "We think it appropriate to pose the question... about the possibility that there are organisms which contain barium in their shell, and, consequently, about the possibility that this element is concentrated by virtue of the vital activity of the known organisms... ."*

At that time there were no data about the existence of barium in the shells of marine organisms. But, in the same year, the book "Investigation of Lower Organisms" by A. Shchepotiev was published, in which barite crystals found in plankters, namely, in rhizopods, were described! Samoilov's assumption was confirmed.

---

* Ya.V. Samoilov, *Bioliths*, Sci. chem-techn. Publishing House, Leningrad, 1929, p. 33 (in Russian).

It is now established that the ability to concentrate elements from rather dilute solutions is a characteristic feature of living matter. It is known that in the contemporary biosphere organisms extract large quantities of calcium carbonates, magnesium carbonates, strontium carbonates, silica, phosphates, iodine, fluorine, and other components from undersaturated solutions. Bacteria prove to be most energetic agents in this respect. The well-known microbiologist W.E. Krumbein* showed that products of the vital activity of definite species of microorganisms contain 1 200 000 times more manganese, 650 000 times more iron, 420 000 times more vanadium, and 240 000 times more silver than is found in the environment. But even bacteria do not create minerals "from nothing". The Soviet geologist A.V. Khabakov described this specific feature of living matter by the following aphorism: "Bacteria are not autocratic creators of mineral deposits, but their natural concentration specialists."

Vernadsky classified living organisms into four groups according to the degree of their concentration of chemical elements. The first group—"organisms containing some element"—include organisms which concentrate a given element to amount of 10% or more. Examples of these are siliceous organisms (diatoms, radiolarians, silisponges), calcium organisms (bacteria, algae, protozoans, mollusks, brachiopods,

---

*W.E. Krumbein, "Geomikrobiologische Prozesse bei der Anreicherung nutzbarer Minerale und sedimentärer Lagerstätten", *Erdöl und Kohle, Ergas, Petrochemie*, **31**, 3, 147-151 (1978).

echinoderms, bryozoans and corals), and iron organisms (iron bacteria).

The second group—"organisms rich in some element"—include organisms which contain a given element in quantities of about 1% or more, up to 10%. The content of these elements in the first two groups must be higher than the clarke* of the given element. The third group consists of "usual organisms", the fourth group, of "organisms low in a given element".

The prominent Norwegian scientist, one of the founders of geochemistry, Professor Wictor Moritz Goldschmidt (1888-1947) approached this problem somewhat differently. In his geochemical classification of chemical elements Goldschmidt singled out a specific group of biophilic elements, among which he included carbon, hydrogen, oxygen, nitrogen, phosphorus, sulphur, chlorine, and iodine. Along the same lines, in 1948, Academician B.B. Polynov suggested that a group of elements-organogens should be singled out and divided into two groups: (a) absolute organogens without which organisms cannot exist (hydrogen, carbon, oxygen, nitrogen, phosphorus, sulphur, potassium, magnesium); and (b) special organogens, required by many organisms but not obligatory for all. Eight years later, V.A. Kovda, in the already cited article, added six other elements to the group of absolute organogens: iodine, boron, calcium, iron, copper, and cobalt. The number of organogens increased steadily, and it has now been established that

---

* Clarke of the lithosphere—a unit of the average abundance of an element in the Earth's crust (named after the American geochemist F.W. Clarke).

if one includes those elements which are contained in small quantities. all the elements of Mendeleyev's Table enter into the composition of living matter. Some elements are concentrated by only a few organisms, but their content in these organisms can be considerable. Thus, radiolarians (a subclass of the protozoa) build their skeleton, as a rule, from amorphous silicon. But one of the families, Acantharia, prefer a less common element, strontium, for this purpose. A still rarer element in the marine medium, vanadium, is found in the blood of most primitive chordates: in ascidians, the content of vanadium pentoxide reaches 15%. In order to obtain vanadium, ascidians are now cultivated in the coastal waters of Japan: they are sessile forms and, therefore, one need not catch them. Recently, in New Zealand a shrub has been found whose dried leaves contain up to 1% nickel. These leaves are not a bad source of nickel: nowadays, even poorer ores are mined. Actually, it is only quite recently that anybody even considered including nickel in the group of organogens.

Academician A.P. Vinogradov distinguished two ways in which chemical elements are concentrated by living matter:

I. Mass increase of the content of a given element in a specific medium. For example, in volcanic regions living matter is enriched with sulphur and iron; the flora found near zinc, copper and other ore deposits is enriched with corresponding metals. The content of boron, copper, iron, manganese, barium and rubidium in calcareous sinks is determined by the salinity of water.

II. Concentration of specific elements by organisms irrespective of the medium. (Examples of a selective concentration have been given above.)

Recently research fellows of the Far Eastern Research Centre of the USSR Academy of Sciences G.N. Sayenko, M.D. Kobryakova, V.F. Makienko and I.G. Dobromyslova* discovered a new phenomenon: organisms concentrate not just one specific element from the medium, but a whole group of them, usually consisting of 4 to 7 elements.

For the biosphere as a whole it is customary to speak about the *biophilicity* of elements, i.e., the ratio of the average content of an element in living matter to the clarke of the given element in the lithosphere. Carbon is characterized by maximum biophilicity; nitrogen and hydrogen are less biophilic.

The concentration of chemical elements by living matter can manifest itself in two different forms: as morphologically shaped mineral formations** and organomineral compounds.

Mineral formations that are part of the body of living organisms are the product of secretion by special glands. As early as the 1930s Vinogradov recognized four main series of mineral composition of the skeletons of living organisms: (a) carbonate; (b) phosphate: (c) sulphate; and (d) formed by hydrates, hydroxides and silicates.

------

* *Marine Biology*, 34, 169-176 (1976).
** A.V. Lapo, "Living matter and mineral formation".—*Notes of All-union Mineralogical Soc.*, 1985, part 114, 1, 26-30 (in Russian).

In recent decades a considerable contribution to this research was made by Heinz A. Lowenstam, an outstanding scientist who was forced to leave his native Germany during the time of fascism and is now working in the United States. He is well known for his contribution to research on the biomineralization phenomenon, fossil reefs, and paleotemperatures of ancient basins using oxygen isotopic analysis data. Professor Lowenstam showed that living matter, in the course of vital activity, forms crystals of the usual shapes described in crystallography; geologists find crystals of some mineral in sedimentary mass, they consider them to have been formed abiogenically.

In living matter crystals may be encountered singly (as barite in rhizopods mentioned above), but more often they are found in the form of aggregates making up the external or internal skeleton of living organisms. Everyone knows what an internal skeleton is; an external skeleton is the housing which protects the organism from the external medium. Calcareous shells of mollusks, corneous carapaces and plastrons of turtles, crabs and various ancient fish are examples of external skeletons. Protozoans, especially plankters, commonly have external skeletons. Many algae are also found with them. The shape of the carapace can vary, and as to its composition, many years of experience (hundreds of millions) have demonstrated that amorphous silica (found in most primitive organisms, such as unicellular algae, protozoans and sponges) and calcium carbonate are most suited to the purpose. But—no accounting for tastes—some organisms "prefer" sulphates and more evolutionarily advanced animals, phosphates.

Higher plants have no skeleton, and their mineral component consists of the so-called "phytoliths"—secretion products in the form of crystals or rounded inclusions. These phytoliths are composed of inorganic (silica) or organo-mineral (calcium oxalate) matter. Some multicellular algae, in contrast to higher plants and similarly to animals, have "supports" made of calcium carbonate.

Lowenstam* compiled a table illustrating the distribution of minerals in the composition of heterogeneous living matter (Fig. 6). According to it, less differentiated organisms secrete only one mineral, though different species, orders and classes can secrete different minerals. The skeletons of more complex or differentiated organisms may be composed of two minerals, and sometimes a third mineral is also found in their bodies. Thus, the shells of mollusks from the family Patellacea are composed of aragonite and calcite, and their masticatory apparatus (radula) is encrusted with crystals of goethite (iron hydroxide). Unlike human beings, mollusks do not get their iron teeth made by the dentist: they have them from the cradle, made by nature.

Chordata and mollusks secrete the greatest number of minerals (as can be clearly seen from the Table), while some algae (diatoms, green algae

---

* H.A. Lowenstam, "Biomineralization processes and products and the evolution of biomineralization".— *27 Int. Geol. Congr.*, *Proc.*, Utrecht, VNU Science Press, 1984, 2, 79-95.

and brown algae) secrete only one mineral each.

Most mineral formations which are part of the composition of living matter are poorly soluble in seawater, and, therefore, after the organisms die, these formations accumulate in sediments (there are exceptions to this rule). The concentration of elements in organomineral compounds is of secondary importance in sedimentation, since after the organisms die such compounds rapidly decompose, and metals from the neo-biogenic substance rapidly return to the biotic cycle.

Living matter, performing the concentration function in the biosphere, may play a significant role at the stage of sedimentogenesis. The process of biofiltration accelerates the precipitation of colloidal particles by thousands of times. Many organisms are filter-feeders, including crustaceans and worms. In shallow water mussels play a particularly important role. By active filtration these mollusks accumulate dozens of centimetres of ooze a year and bury themselves in the sediments. In 1948 the hydrobiologist K.A. Voskresensky drew a noteworthy conclusion: "The involvement of a water layer of considerable thickness in benthic circulation in combination with the active removal of its suspended matter by the populated bottom requires a reconsideration of sedimentary differentiation processes. Stokes' law and its modifications which take into account only the laws of mechanics, physics and chemistry are inadequate in the dynamic field where the biomasses of filter-feeding organisms manifest themselves. Near the populated bottom of water bodies relatively simple laws are cancelled out

	MINERALS	MAJOR CATIONS	MONERA						
CARBONATES	Calcite	Ca	+	+	+			+	
	Aragonite	Ca	+		?		+		+
	Vaterite	Ca						+	
	Monohydrocalcite	Ca	+						
	Protodolomite	Ca Mg							
	Amorph hydrous carbonate	Ca							
PHOSPHATES	Francolite	Ca							
	Dohllite	Ca	+						
	$Co_3Mg_3(PO_4)_4$	Ca Mg							
	Huntite	Mg Ca							
	Brushite	Ca							
	Octacalcium phosphate	Ca							
	Calcium pyrophosphate	Ca							
	Amorph dohllite precursor	Ca							
	Amorph brushite precursor	Ca							
	Amorph whitlockite precursor	Ca							
	Amorph-Fe-Ca phosphate	Fe, Ca							
HALIDES	Fluorite	Ca							
	Amorph fluorite precursor	Ca							
OXALATES	Whewellite	Ca							?
	Weddelite	Ca							
	Glushinskite	Mg							
CITRATES	Galcium citrate	Ca							

PROTOCTISTA
FUNGAE
PLANTAE
ANIMALIA

	MINERALS	MAJOR CATIONS	MONERA	Dinoflagellata	Hoptophyta	Bacillariophyta	Phosophyta	Rhodophyta	Chlorophyta
SULPHATES	Gypsum	Ca							+
	Celestite	Sr							
	Borite	Ba							+
SILICA	Opal	Si		+		+	?		
Fe-OXIDES	Magnetite	Fe	+						?
	Goethite	Fe							
	Lepidocrocite	Fe	?						
	Ferrihydrite	Fe	+						
	Amorph "ferrihy- drites"	Fe	+						
	"Amorph ilmenite"	Fe, Ti							
Mn-OXIDES	Todorokite	Mn	+						
	Birnessite	Mn	+						
SULPHIDES	Pyrite	Fe	+						
	Hydrotroilite	Fe	+						
	Sphalerite	Zn	+						
	Wurtzite	Zn	+						
	Galena		+						
PHYLA									

Fig. 6. The diversity and distribution of biogenic mine-
an amorphous phase which upon heating to 500 °C con-

	PROTOCTISTA										FUNGAE			PLANTAE		ANIMALIA										
	Zygnematophyta	Chrysophyta	Rhizopodea	Siphonophyta	Charophyta	Heliozoata	Rodiolariata	Foraminifera	Mixomycota	Ciliophora	Basidiomycota	Deuteromycota	Mycophycophyta	Bryophyta	Trocheophyta	Porifera	Cnidaria	Platyhelminthes	Ectoprocta	Brochiopoda	Annelida	Mollusca	Arthropoda	Sipuncula	Echinodermata	Chordata
	+		+		+		+							?	+	+										
		+	+			+	+	+						+	+						+	+	+			+
									+		+	+		+	+	+					+	+ + + +	+		+ +	+ + + + +

rals in extant organisms. The term "precursor" refers to verted to the designated crystalline form.

by laws governing biohydrological phenomena".*
American scientists came to the same conclusion
after having investigated the bottom fauna of the
Florida Strait.**

It indeed became necessary to reconsider the
processes of sedimentary differentiation, as was
foreseen by Voskresensky, when sedimentation
traps, i.e., special devices used to accumulate
settling matter, began to be employed in oceanology. Already the first studies of this kind
revealed that matter settles in an ocean not "particle by particle" (as was assumed speculatively),
but mainly in the form of fecal pellets ranging
in size from dozens of micrometres to 1-4 mm. The
content of such pellets in sediments generally
exceeds 60%, while sometimes the sediments
consist entirely of pellets!***

Studies in recent years have shown that biofiltration and, correspondingly, *biosedimentation*
are carried out in the ocean mainly by multicellular animals of the planktonic and benthic
films of life. A comparatively small contribution
to biosedimentation is also made by nekton. An

---

* K.A. Voskresensky, "The belt of biofiltration or-
ganisms as a biohydrological system of the sea", *Trans.
State Oceanogr. Institute*, 1948, Issue 6 (18), p. 99 (in
Russian)

** R.N. Ginsburg, H.A. Lowenstam, "The influence
of marine bottom communities on the depositional environment of sediment", *J. Geol.*, 66, 3, 310-318 (1958).

*** P.H. Wiebe, S.H. Boyd, and C. Winget, "Particulate Matter Sinking to the Deep-Sea Floor at 2000 m in
the Tongue of the Ocean, Bahamas, with a Description
of a New Sedimentation Trap", *J. Marine Res.*, 34, 3,
341-354 (1976).

illustrative example of nekton filtrators are whales, who strain sea water for trapping krill.

By now the concentration function of living matter has been studied in sufficient detail. In Vernadsky's time, the degree of concentration of particular elements by various types of homogeneous living matter was discussed; presently information is available concerning the concentration of elements by the heterogeneous living matter of various ecosystems. E.A. Boichenko, D.Sc. (Biol.), who both studied under Vernadsky and continued his research, and her co-authors[*] succeeded in estimating the order of the concentration function of plants for the biosphere as a whole and compared these data with the world reserves of the specific raw materials (Table 5). As can be seen from these figures, the vegetational cover of our planet annually concentrates amounts of mineral matter comparable to most of the reserves of elements in the lithosphere, which have accumulated over millions of years of geological history. These data are the best illustration of the statement made by Vernadsky in 1935: "In the rapidity of concentration of solid substance from its scattered state, biogeochemical energy is probably the greatest force, in the sense of geological time, existing on our planet."[**]

---

* E.A. Boichenko, G.N. Saenko, T.M. Udelnova, "Variation in metal rations during the evolution of plants in the biosphere". In: *Recent Contribution to Geochemistry and Analytical Chemistry*, Wiley, New York, 1975, pp. 507-512.

** V.I. Vernadsky, *Works*, vol. 1, p. 535 (in Russian).

Table 5. Comparative Data on Proven Reserves of Some Chemical Elements and on Their Annual Accumulation by Photoautotrophs (after Boichenko *et al.*, 1968)

Element	Annual concentration in photosynthesis, ton	World reserves of raw materials, ton	Element	Annual concentration in photosynthesis, ton	World reserves of raw materials, ton
Carbon	10^{11}	10^{12}	Cobalt	10^5	10^6
Phosphorus	10^9	10^{10}	Nickel	10^6	10^7
Chromium	10^5	10^8	Copper	10^7	10^8
Manganese	10^7	10^8	Zinc	10^7	10^7
Iron	10^8	10^{11}	Molybdenum	10^5	10^6

The third main function of living matter in the biosphere, the destructive one, manifests itself at the stage of hypergenesis by the destruction of nonliving matter and its introduction into the biotic cycle. This function is realized in the form of three continually occurring processes (see Table 4).

In the preceding chapters we have already discussed the multiple utilization by living matter of elements introduced into the biotic cycle. Living matter, however, cannot employ the required elements in whatever form they may be found in. The organic constituent of neobiogenic matter must be decomposed into simple inorganic compounds, such as carbon dioxide gas, water, hydrogen sulphide, methane, and ammonia. As we already know, a whole army of saprotrophs is busy with decomposing the dead organics.

Another aspect of the problem is the decomposition of nonliving organic matter by the living one. Decomposition of minerals by microorganisms was established as early as the beginning of the twentieth century.*-** It has now been shown that various microflora take part in the decomposition of minerals, including algae, fungi, bacteria, and other organisms. As was already mentioned at the beginning of this chapter, in marine ecosystems an important role is played by boring organisms.

Georgi Adamovich Nadson (From: G.A. Nadson, *Selected Works*, **v.** 2, Moscow, 1967.)

The first study on boring cyanobacteria and algae was published in 1902 by the Russian scientist, who later became an academician, G.A. Nadson (1867-1940). He showed that boring algae mostly inhabit carbonate rocks and play a considerable role in returning to the biotic cycle not only calcium, but also other

---

* J. Stoklasa, "Biochemische Kreislauf des Phosphations in Boden", *Zbl. Bakteriol., Parasitenk., Infekt. und Hyg.*, Abt. 2, 1911, Bd. 29, H. 4.

** K. Bassalik, "Über Silikatzersetzung dürch Bodenbakterien", *Z. Gärungsphysiol.*, 2 (1912), 3 (1913).

vitally important elements such as magnesium
and phosphorus.*

Nadson's works did not generate interest among
biologists or geologists at the beginning of this
century. In fact, when this author requested
from a library the "Botanicheskiye Zapiski"
("Botanical Notes") of 1902 containing Nadson's
paper, the journal proved to have its pages un-
cut: nobody had bothered to read it in the course
of three quarters of a century! Nadson's works
have now been republished, and, as German
scientists have put it, "the characteristics of
microorganisms as geological agents, given by
Nadson, now begin to shine with a new light"**.

It has been shown that the role of biogenic disintegration of carbonates, carried out by other
organisms, is also significant. Recently it was
established that coral reefs (composed of calcium carbonate) are intensively grazed by some
fish (e.g., parrot fish) and sea urchins. These
animals pass the bitten-off pieces of calcium carbonate through their alimentary tract and then
excrete it as carbonate mud. It has been calculated*** that in this manner, in the region of
the Virgin Islands sea urchins deposit several
kilograms of particulate carbonates per square

* G.A. Nadson, "Les algues perforantes, leur distribution et leur role dans la nature", *CR Acad. Sci.*
(Paris), 184, 1015-1017 (1927).

** W. Schwartz, A. Müller, "Geomikrobiologie, Ent-
wicklung und Stand eines neues Forschungsgebietes",
Erdöl u. Kohle, 6, 9, 523-527 (1953).

*** J.C. Ogden, "Carbonate-sediment production by
parrot fish and sea urchins on Caribbean reefs". In: *Reefs
a. Relat. Carbon. Ecol. a. Sedimentology*, Tulsa, 1977,
pp. 281-283.

metre of the bottom surface. From this type of evidence, the Soviet lithologist I.V. Khvorova came to the conclusion that many ancient organogenic-detrital carbonate rocks originated not only from the mechanical effect of waves on sediment, but also from the crushing of shells by predatory and mud-eating animals.

While carbonates are particulated by organisms largely owing to the mechanical activity of the organisms* (second type of geological activity of living matter), in the decomposition of alumosilicates the first type of such activity—chemical—is observed. In general, the chemical decomposition of various minerals by the action of living matter occurs in the biosphere on a tremendous scale.

As early as the beginning of the twentieth century the following experiment was carried out. Fourteen species of bacteria contained in the intestines of earthworms were sown on disintegrated rock-forming minerals. The majority of the minerals had undergone biogenic decomposition, the degree of such decomposition depending on the kind of bacteria and on the composition of the minerals. Alkali elements were the first to pass into solution; next were alkaline-earth elements, as well as iron, silica and alumina. Mould fungus within a week under laboratory conditions can liberate 3% of the silicon, 11% of the aluminium, 59% of the magnesium, and 64% of the iron contained in basalt.

---

* G.E. Farrow, J. Clokie, "Molluscian grazing of sublittoral algae-bored shells and the production of carbonate mud in the Firth of Clyde, Scotland", *Trans. Roy. Soc. Edin.*, **70**, 5-9, 139-148 (1979).

Lichen on rocky ground. Chukotka. Photographed by the author.

The pioneers of life on rocks—cyanobacteria, bacteria, fungi and lichens—wage a real chemical war with rocks, using a rich arsenal of original weapons including solutions of both inorganic acids—carbonic, nitric, sulphuric (up to 10% solution capable of burning through paper!), and organic acids. Some higher plants also possess chemical weapons; for example, the roots of fir trees growing on soils, poor in nutrients, secrete strong acids which decompose the mineral compounds in abiogenic matter.

It has now been established that biogenic chemical decomposition of kaolin, serpentine, nepheline, muscovite, biotite, albite, apatite, and many other minerals takes place in the biosphere.

By decomposing minerals of one or another kind, organisms selectively extract calcium, potassium, sodium, phosphorus, silicon, as well as many microelements from them (thus introducing these elements into the biotic cycle). For example, elephant grass in the African savannas annually extracts 250 kg of silica and 80 kg of alkalies and alkali earths from one hectare of soil; jungles extract as much as 8 tons of silica from the same area! The process of introducing chemical elements in the biotic cycle occurs everywhere in the biosphere. Bacteria function even in such toxic environments (for human beings) as the oxidation zone of sulphide deposits of copper, antimony and molybdenum, and this is of importance for the formation of ores. Bacteria even oxidize gold, the metal which we consider eternal. One microbiologist remarked with sadness that the marble monument to Louis Pasteur in Paris is being destroyed by bacteria, whose activity he was so eager to prove.

Mankind has learned to use the destructive activity of microorganisms to its advantage: in some industrially advanced countries leaching of useful components from ores is carried out with the participation of bacteria.* Presently, copper, uranium, zinc and even arsenic are being extracted from ores by bacterial methods. In the United States, about 10% of the total amount of extracted copper is "delivered to the surface" by bacteria. Bacterial leaching of lead, nickel, cobalt, molybdenum, cadmium, and titanium is quite feasible. As compared to conventional methods of metallurgy, bacterial leaching is noted for a far more complete extraction of metals; therefore, the new method is especially effective

---

* D.G. Lundgren, M. Silver, "Ore leaching by bacteria", *Ann. Rev. Microbiol.*, **34**, 263-283 (1980).

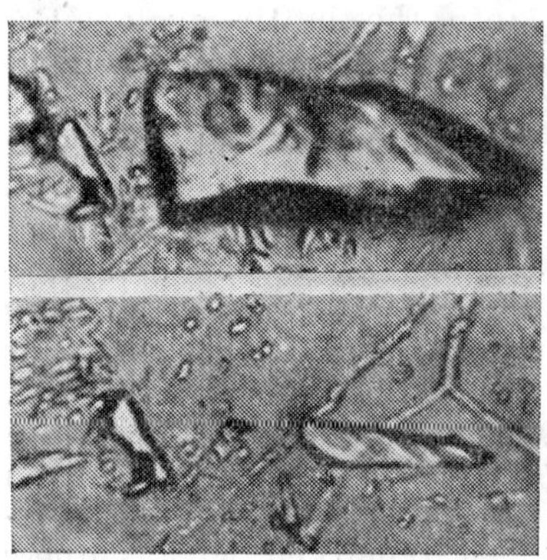

Decomposition of nepheline by micro-organisms: (a) initial particles; (b) the same particles after having been decomposed for 4 days by the microscopic fungus Penicillium. Photographed by T.V. Aristovskaya.(After T.V. Aristovskaya, *Microbiology of Soil-formation Processes*, Leningrad, 1980, Figs. 5c, 5d.)

in processing poor ores which earlier were not profitable enough to develop. Waste dumps and dressing plant tailings can also be reprocessed.

The destructive function of living matter plays an important role in the biosphere. The biosphere is not only "a factory producing macromolecules" but also a huge mill. As in a Japanese fairy tale, this mill cannot stop, but goes on milling incessantly. It has been milling for several billions of years, and it is not salt but rocks that it has been milling. The mill of life works most energetically on land, and in the near-shore area of marine ecosystems where concentrations of life are found.

The fourth basic function of living matter is the formation of a medium. The physico-chemical parameters of a medium are transformed by the processes of vital activity. While the influence of the external medium on organisms has been a traditional topic in biology since its origin, the reverse feedback—the action of the organisms on the medium (of life on "non-life")—began to appear in outline only with the discovery of photosynthesis. Vernadsky, drawing upon the investigations carried out by F. Houssay, J.S. Haldane, F. Henderson and A. Lotka, concluded that "the organism deals with the medium to which it is not only adapted, but which is adapted to it"*.

A further development of this thesis is the "Gaia hypothesis" named after the ancient Greek goddess of the Earth that gave birth to the sky, the sea, and the mountains. It was advanced by the well-known British scientist and inventor James E. Lovelock, a member of the Royal Society. As formulated by its author, the Gaia hypothesis "postulates that the physical and chemical condition of the surface of the Earth, of the atmosphere, and of the oceans has been and is actively made fit and comfortable by the presence of life itself. This is in contrast to the conventional wisdom which held that life adapted to the planetary conditions as it and they evolved their separate ways"**.

The most evident (but not the most important!) manifestation of the influence of living matter on the environment is mechanical action or the second type of geological activity of living matter. Metazoans strongly change the properties of soil by burrowing in it (for instance, by loosening the soil, earthworms increase the volume of air in it by a factor of 2.5). The roots

---

* V.I. Vernadsky, "Problems of biogeochemistry", *Transactions BIOGEL*, 1980, Issue 16, p. 22.
** J.E. Lovelock, *Gaia. A New Look at Life on Earth*, Oxford Univ. Press. Oxford a.o., 1982, p. 152.

of higher plants (particularly woody ones) also change the mechanical properties of soil: they consolidate the soil and protect it against erosion. Thus, erosion of a 20-cm surface layer of soil in prairies takes 29 thousand years, but in woods, 174 thousand years. Forest vegetation is capable of retaining soil even on slopes with a gradient of 20 to 40°. Filamentous cyanobacteria act in a similar manner: they create a kind of net which protects soil against erosion. In the mountain soils of Tajikistan there are sometimes more than 100 m of filamentous cyanobacteria in 1 g of soil! In fact, the ground underfoot does not feel like soil, and no heavy shower can wash it away.

The mechanical activity of living matter has, no doubt, a great influence on the environment; yet, as to its scale, it cannot be compared with the effect that neobiogenic matter formed by living organisms has on the environment (result of the first type of geological activity, external to organisms). For a better understanding of this influence, we shall briefly consider those two main parameters which characterize the physico-chemical conditions of the environment: the hydrogen index and the redox potential.

The hydrogen index (denoted as pH) characterizes the content of hydrogen ions in a medium and is numerically equal to the negative common logarithm of the H^+ ion concentration in the medium, expressed in gram-ions per litre; pH values vary within a range of 0 to 14. The pH of distilled water is 7. Natural water, with a pH ranging from 6.95 to 7.3, is considered to be neutral. A medium with a pH lower than this value is considered acidic, and with a pH above this value is alkaline.

The redox potential of a medium (Eh) serves as a measure of its oxidation-reduction capacity. This potential is measured in volts or in millivolts. If the redox potential values are positive,

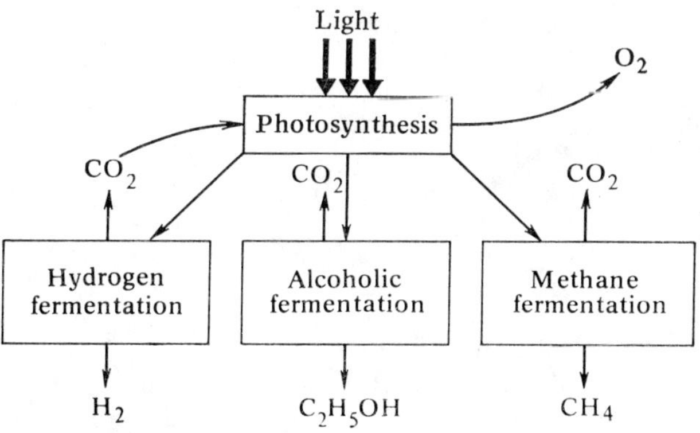

Fig. 7. Photosynthesis of living matter and microbiological decomposition of neobiogenic organic matter (after Krasnovsky, 1977)

the medium is oxidative; if they are negative, the medium is reducing. In recent marine bottom sediments, for example, Eh has been found to vary from +600 to −350 mV.

The influence of photoautotrophs on the environment is represented in a general form in Fig. 7. Photosynthesis in the biosphere proceeds by the following reaction (simplified):

$$6CO_2 + 6H_2O + 674cal \xrightarrow[\text{chlorophyll}]{\text{sunlight}} C_6H_{12}O_6 + 6O_2 \uparrow$$

In the course of their vital activity photoautotrophs continually produce oxygen. Because of this reaction, an oxidative environment exists in the surface portion of the biosphere. The intensive absorption of carbon dioxide gas by photoautotrophs also maintains a low concentration of carbon dioxide gas in the atmosphere. Not only oxygen—a strong oxidant—is evolved in photosynthesis. Organic substances also originate, which are strong reducing agents. The neobiogenic matter formed after living matter dies sinks to the bottom of water bodies and decomposes in boggy soils, creating a sharply reducing medium under the conditions of oxygen deficiency. Different types of fermentation evolve gases of various composition (see Fig. 7). The composition of the gases is also determined by the types of saprotrophs found there and by the structure of the initial products. Thus, the decomposition of organic substances under anaerobic conditions produces hydrogen, ammonia, organic acids, and the anions SO_4^{2-}, PO_4^{3-}, NO_3^-.

Products of the decomposition of steppe herbs form neutral and weakly alkaline solutions; decaying wormwoods and saxaul leaves give an alkaline reaction (pH 8-8.5), and the mass of decaying conifer needles, heather, lichens, and sphagnum gives an acidic reaction (pH 3.5-4.5). It may be appropriate to recall the words of Polynov: "Above all I consider that the statement, so frequently encountered, to the effect that this or that phenomenon (say, the formation of sediment) depends on the pH value rather than on the organisms, is wrong. I consider that the very separation of pH from organisms is wrong. Suppose that somebody was impressed by a tall tree and decided to find out why the tree had grown to such a height. In answer to his question he is informed that the height of the tree depends on the number of metres along the length of its trunk. I believe that an explanation with reference to pH does not differ at all from the explanation suggested above, since pH is also a measure, the same as a yardstick or a metre, and it cannot be the original cause; moreover, pH, as such, is quite often directly dependent on the amount of CO_2 evolved by the organisms."[*] This comment by Polynov is supported by data for all natural environments.

The atmosphere is a part of the biosphere, common to all living beings. Biogenic formation of oxygen and nitrogen, the two basic gases of the atmosphere, was demonstrated by Vernadsky himself. Today the question of the biogenic origin of other atmospheric gases is being tackled.[**] Investigations undertaken by Hutchinson have contributed much to the solution of this problem.[***] According to calculations made by geochemists, 50% of all atmospheric hydrogen is formed as a result of the activity of living matter. The formation of carbon monoxide as a result of biogenic processes has also

---

[*] B.B. Polynov, *Selected Works*, AN SSSR Publ. House, Moscow, 1956, pp. 466-467 (in Russian).

[**] Y.C.G. Walker, "How life affects the atmosphere", *Bio Science*, **34**, 8, 486-491 (1984).

[***] G.E. Hutchinson, "The biochemistry of terrestrial atmosphere". In: *The Solar System* (ed. G.P. Kuiper), v. 2, Univ. Chicago Press, Chicago, 1954, pp. 371-433.

been proven. For example, in oceanic waters (especially in algae accumulation zones) the content of carbon monoxide exceeds by hundreds of times the amount of the gas in equilibrium in the atmosphere. Land plants, on the contrary, absorb carbon monoxide. Thus, in one hour one beech tree can process 2.35 kg of this gas, which is so deadly dangerous to man.

The influence of green plants on the composition of the atmosphere has long been known, but the role of bacteria in these processes has begun to be elucidated only recently. It turns out that bacteria determine the composition of soil air*, and terrestrial atmosphere is in equilibrium with it. Bacteria are also responsible for the formation of the gases of the Earth's metabiosphere and, in particular, for the accumulations of combustible gases.

Living matter exerts a decisive influence on the composition of the natural water of the Earth— also mainly by releasing neobiogenic matter into the environment. Thus, water yields an acidic reaction which is most often associated with the biogenic substances—carbon dioxide gas and humic acids—that are dissolved in it. Photosynthesis taking place in the surface portions of water bodies causes a reduction in the partial pressure of carbon dioxide gas and an increase in pH. The algae bloom occurring in freshwater bodies, caused by the growth of Protococcaceae and cyanobacteria, increases the pH of water to 9-10 or higher. The decomposition of

---

* G.A. Zavarzin, *Bacteria and Composition of Atmosphere*, Moscow, Nauka, 1984 (in Russian).

neobiogenic organic matter occurs throughout the depth of water, and everywhere the living population of the ocean breathes, leading to opposite results: the partial pressure of carbon dioxide gas in the water increases and the water pH decreases (rotting algae can reduce the pH of seawater to 6.4).

The physico-chemical conditions existing in the bottom sediments of reservoirs are determined mainly by the presence of organic substance: in the presence of organic substance the conditions are reducing; in its absence, they are oxidative. A reducing environment is created during the stagnant conditions created by the decomposition of dead organic matter by sulphate-reducing bacteria with the formation of hydrogen sulphide. This process occurs everywhere, provided there are accumulations of organic neobiogenic substance, humidity and sulphate-ion (SO_4^{2-}). If hydrogen sulphide is not removed, autointoxication of the medium takes place (recall the zones of the Black Sea and the Cariaco Depression contaminated with hydrogen sulphide). In this case the medium-forming ability of living matter is particularly obvious: the layer of sulphate-reducing bacteria, located just above the bottom, with a thickness of up to 5 cm, poisons the sea with hydrogen sulphide to a depth of over one kilometre, limiting the habitat of zooplankton and large sea animals to the upper 200 or 300 metres.

Of all the representatives of the Earth's organic world, microorganisms are the most important regarding their role in the formation of media. Many of them are capable of actively changing the environment in accordance with their vital requirements. For example, in an excessively acidic medium such microorganisms secrete neutral products instead of acidic ones, and in an alkaline medium they intensively produce acids. According to I.L. Rabotnova, the evolution of microorganisms proceeded by way of developing an ability to change the external medium, while the perfection of more highly organized organisms depended on the isolation of their internal sphere from the environment.

Sulphate-reducing bacteria and thiobacteria play an important role in the biosphere: sulphate-reducing bacteria convert sulphate-ion into hydrogen sulphide; thiobacteria perform the reverse reaction, i.e., they oxidize hydrogen sulphide to sulphuric acid. It is hardly necessary to prove the medium-forming role of these reactions.

Almost dramatic situation was created by thiobacteria during the Kiev metro construction. Before tunneling began they led a miserable existence in Paleogene sands. At those depths, the bacteria suffered from oxygen deficiency. During tunneling, compressed air was pumped to the faces and the bacteria livened up. The hydrogen index (pH) of the medium reached values of less than 1 (to put it in other words, subterranean water turned into a strong solution of sulphuric acid). Within a month or two, massive reinforced concrete bolts were half destroyed. The situation became critical, and subway engineers could only shake their heads: nothing like it had ever happened before. It was microbiologists, however, who came to the rescue. They found the guilty ones and recommended that the method of tunneling should be changed. The subway engineers had to stop pumping compressed air into the tunnel.

The case of the Kiev subway is not the only example when microbiologists have come to the aid of construction engineers. It is well known how much trouble is caused by landslides in construction engineering. The ground scientist V.V. Radina* has proved their bacteriogenic origin. When an investigation of the grounds of the Nizhne-Obskaya hydroelectric power plant project was undertaken she established that soil acquires a plastic state (becomes plasticized, as construction engineers say) because of the slimy substances (and, as later became apparent, gases and surface active substances) produced by bacteria. The degree of soil liquefaction depends on the availability of food for bacteria (such as potassium, phosphorus, and dead organic matter). Evidently, biological control of landslides is not far off.

In aqueous ecosystems the medium-forming role of living matter is, perhaps, manifested more clearly and in a manifold way. "The heterogeneous living matter of the ocean, the life of the sea, taken as a whole, may be regarded as a special mechanism which completely changes the chemistry of the sea," wrote Vernadsky.** Indeed, organisms that absorb carbonates and

---

* V.V. Radina, "The role of microorganisms in the formation of the properties of grounds and of their stressed state", *Gidrotechnicheskoje stroitel'stvo*, 9, 22-24 (1973).

** W. Vernadsky. *La géochimie*, Alcan, Paris, 1924, p. 295.

silica from seawater not only change its mineral composition, but also change the acidity of the medium by increasing the relative content of alkalies. Rookeries also exert a considerable influence on the aqueous medium. Near the rocks where they are located 50 m wide coastal strips are intensively enriched with the feces of birds. During the nesting period the content of phosphates and nitrates in seawater may increase by a factor of over 100, and the area of sea locations enriched with these elements sometimes exceeds 200 km². Poorly populated rocky shores have many inshore water areas stretching for dozens of kilometres that are under the influence of colonial sea birds.

Recently, it was established that living matter changes not only the chemical, but also the physical parameters of the medium, its thermal, electrical and mechanical characteristics. For instance, it is believed that Indian summers are caused by the activity of living matter, or, more precisely, by the autumn peak in the activity of saprotrophs. The explanation is rather simple: the accumulation of a lot of decomposing organic matter during this period results in the liberation of heat through decomposition. It turns out that Indian summers are caused by fungi...

Recently, an interesting manifestation of the medium-forming activity of living matter was found first in the Black Sea and later in the White Sea. It was called the "bioelectric effect". This effect consists in that living substance (phytoplankton) creates an electric field with a negative charge, and accumulations of neobiogenic matter (dead plankton) create positive fields.*

In recent years the medium-forming activity of living matter is being revealed to an ever-increasing extent and in the most diverse manifestations. One of the more general conclusions has been formulated recently by Yu.V. Davydov, Yu.P. Kazansky and V.N. Kataeva: "The vegetable world actively affects the composition of gases in the atmosphere and, accordingly, the ionic composition of oceanic water, but animals exert almost no influence on the atmosphere, although they do change the cationic composition of seawater."

Evidently, still much remains unknown about the influence of living matter on the medium, and what is known requires comprehensive evaluation in order to form general conclusions. This is why we have discussed the medium-forming role of living matter in such detail and with the use of diverse examples. The development of a general theory about the medium-forming role of life still lies ahead.

Finally, the fifth main function of living matter in the biosphere is that of transportation. Even in Newton's time it was known that the flow of matter on our planet is determined by the gravitational force of the Earth. Nonliving matter on the Earth moves by itself only downwards. Rivers, glaciers, avalanches, and taluses move only in this direction.

---

* R.M. Demenitskaya, A.M. Gorodnitsky, "Measurement of electric fields in the ocean", *Transactions of the Institute of Geology of the Arctic*, **181**, 88 (1979).

Rookery on the coast of the Bering Sea in Chukotka.
Photo taken by the author.

Living matter is the only factor (in addition to surface tension) which effects the reverse movement of matter, upwards, from the ocean to the continents. "Terrestrial organisms feed on marine food on such a large scale," Vernadsky wrote, "that this may compensate for—or at any rate return to the land—a commensurable portion of those chemical elements that rivers take from the land to the sea in solution. Since the Mesozoic era mainly birds have fulfilled this function."* Shoals of sea fish going up rivers for spawning also contribute. And a considerable portion of matter is transferred from fresh-water bodies to land by countless hordes of winged insects. As regards horizontal shifts, here only tornados and hurricanes can compete with accumulations of homogeneous living matter in the mass of the substance transferred and in the distances over which it is transported. There are no other competitors.

These are the five main functions of living matter in the biosphere. Vernadsky wrote: "Living matter embraces and reconstructs all the chemical processes of the biosphere... Living matter is the most powerful geological force, growing with time"** (from this statement we borrowed the title for this chapter). To pay homage to the great founder of the theory of the biosphere, Perelman suggested that the following generalization should be called "Vernadsky's Law": "The

---

* V.I. Vernadsky, *Works*, v. 4, Book 2, p. 93 (in Russian).
** V.I. Vernadsky, *The Chemical Structure of the Earth's Biosphere and of Its Surroundings*, Nauka, Moscow, 1965, p. 127 (in Russian).

Krill—routine diet of whales. Tens of times natural size. (From: A. Lory, *The Living Ocean*, Leningrad, 1976, p. 41.)

Benthic film of life of the antarctic shelf at a depth of 91 m. Numerous starfish are visible. (From: B.C. Heezen, C.D. Hollister, *The Face of the Deep*, N.Y. a.o., 1971, p. 62.)

migration of chemical elements in the biosphere is accomplished either with the direct participation of living matter (biogenic migration) or it proceeds in a medium where the specific geochemical features (O_2, CO_2, H_2S, etc.) are conditioned by living matter, by both that part inhabiting the given system at present and that part that has been acting on the Earth throughout geological history."*

---

* A.I. Perelman, *Geochemistry*, Vysshaya Shkola, Moscow, 1979, p. 215 (in Russian).

4. Three Factors: Bio-, Eco- and Tapho-

The final quantity and quality of natural products depend not only on the conditions of formation but also to a considerable extent on the conditions of preservation.

Johannes Walther, 1895

The formation of paleobiogenic matter in the Earth's crust is controlled by the following three factors:

First, the productivity of living matter which serves as initial material in the formation of biogenic matter, i.e., the biological factor (bio-factor);

Second, conditions that are favourable for concentration of neobiogenic matter, i.e., the ecological factor (eco-factor);

Third, circumstances ensuring the transition of biogenic substance into the fossil state, i.e., the taphonomic factor (tapho-factor).

In this chapter we shall consider how the above factors work in the contemporary biosphere.

It has been established that the distribution of living matter in the biosphere is extremely non-uniform.

To characterize the distribution of living matter in the biosphere Vernadsky introduced the concept of areas where there is a maximum concentration of life, "which is perpetually varying, but occupies the same locations in the

Earth's envelopes corresponding to the biosphere"*. Vernadsky has characterized two forms of life concentrations: films of life which cover tremendous areas (e.g., the planktonic film of life which covers the entire upper part of the water body of the ocean), and local concentrations of life in more localized areas (e.g., concentrations of standing water bodies). The degree of life concentrations is usually measured by a few metres or dozens of metres; it is rare for the degree of life concentrations to extend to one or two hundred metres. Thus, in relation to the biosphere as a whole, it is measured in negligible magnitudes. The rest of the biosphere is a zone of rarefaction of life.

Developing Vernadsky's idea further, Perelman** noted that the entire biosphere is distinctly divided along the vertical into two zones: an upper zone where photosynthesis occurs, and a lower zone where photosynthetic reactions cannot proceed. He suggested that the upper zone be called the "phytosphere" and the lower zone, the "redusphere." Vassoyevich,*** however, has criticized these designations and suggests instead the terms "photobiosphere" and "melabiosphere" (from the Greek root 'μελαζ', dark). But the term "melabiosphere" is not quite appropriate either, since it differs in only one let-

* W. Vernadsky, *La biosphere*, Alcan, Paris, 1929, p. 198.

** A.I. Perelman, *Geochemistry of landscape*, Vysshaya Shkola, Moscow, 1975, p. 34 (in Russian).

*** N.B. Vassoyevich, "Various interpretations of the concept of the biosphere". In: *Investigations of the Organic Matter of Recent and Fossil Sediments*, Nauka, Moscow, 1976, pp. 381-399 (in Russian).

ter from other terms which have been introduced by Vassoyevich, e.g., "metabiosphere" and "megabiosphere".

In scientific terminology the Greek root 'μελαζ' is transliterated more often as "melan" than "mela"; for example, there are such terms as "melanium", "melanite", "melanines," "melanoresinite". Accordingly, we shall use the term "melanobiosphere".

The border between the photobiosphere and the melanobiosphere almost coincides with the surface reached by daylight: light penetrates the soil to a depth of several millimetres. In an aqueous medium the position of the border is determined by the transparency of water. The depth of the photosynthesis zone varies from several centimetres, in torrential rivers carrying significant quantities of mud, to a hundred metres or more (180 m at most), in parts of the ocean remote from land. Thus, the thickness of the photobiosphere varies from several centimetres to a hundred metres (measured upwards from the daylight surface on land and downwards from the surface of the sea in the ocean: the photosynthesis zone).

The thickness of the melanobiosphere is one to two orders of magnitude greater: in oceans it encompasses the entire mass of water lying below the zone of the photobiosphere and the populated bottom; on continents it is the layer of the biosphere, extending from the daylight surface to the lower boundary of active bacterial life.

The photobiosphere and the melanobiosphere may be subdivided vertically into smaller zones (or horizons). Thus, the Soviet researcher

Yu.P. Byallovich introduced the concept of a biogeocoenotic horizon, and defined it as follows:

"The biogeocoenotic horizon is a vertically isolated and structural part of the biogeocoenosis that is further indivisible vertically. From top to bottom this horizon is uniform in its biogeocoenotic components, in their interconnections, and in the transformations of matter and energy occurring in it, and in these same ways it differs from the neighbouring biogeocoenotic horizons, functioning as a roof and bed for them.* Biogeocoenotic horizons, for the sake of brevity, are called biogeohorizons. In ecosystems of all ranks it is possible to observe not only these elementary biogeohorizons, but also strata of higher ranks, which may be called ecohorizons.** The photobiosphere and the melanobiosphere are ecohorizons of the highest—global—rank. The films of life distinguished by Vernadsky may be regarded as specific examples of ecohorizons.

According to the landscape principle, all ecosystems of the Earth's biosphere may be classified into three main groups: marine ecosystems, land ecosystems, and ecosystems of inland water bodies.

Let us consider the distribution of living matter and the method of accumulation of biogenic substance in these main types of ecosystems of the biosphere.

---

* Yu.P. Byallovich, "Biogeocoenotic horizons", *Trans. MOIP*, 3, 44-45 (1960).

** A.V. Lapo, "The Earth's biosphere, its boundaries and ecohorizons". In: *Sedikakhites on Different Stages of Lithogenesis*, Moscow, Nauka, 1982, pp. 43-49 (in Russian).

Yu.Yu. Marti aphoristically expressed the main problem in marine ecosystems as follows: "Biogenic salts in the depths and the presence of light at the surface". The World Ocean consists of water body (oceanologists call it the pelagic zone) and the bottom (the benthic zone). In oceanology, the pelagic zone within the limits of the photobiosphere is termed the euphotic zone; the lower part of the pelagic zone is termed the aphotic zone. In essence, these are three self-contained ecohorizons of the ocean (looking downwards): an euphotic zone, an aphotic zone, and a benthic zone, each of them characterized by its specific living matter and environmental conditions. In some half-closed basins with limited circulation of water (such as the Black Sea), another unique weakly-populated ecohorizon is found—a zone contaminated with hydrogen sulphide, where only a few species of anaerobic bacteria exist.

Vernadsky* distinguished two films of life (planktonic and benthic) in the ocean and three types of local life concentrations (littoral, sargasso, and reef). Both films of life are confined to the interfaces: planktonic to the gaseous/liquid and benthic to the liquid/solid one (Fig. 8).

Vernadsky's planktonic film of life basically corresponds to the euphotic zone of the ocean. In the composition of living matter it drastically differs from land ecosystems: organisms passively suspended in water and incapable of withstanding currents dominate here (these organ-

---

* W.J. Vernadsky, "Ozeanographie und Geochemie", *Mineralog. u. Petrograph. Mitteil.*, **44**, 2/3, 168-192 (1933),

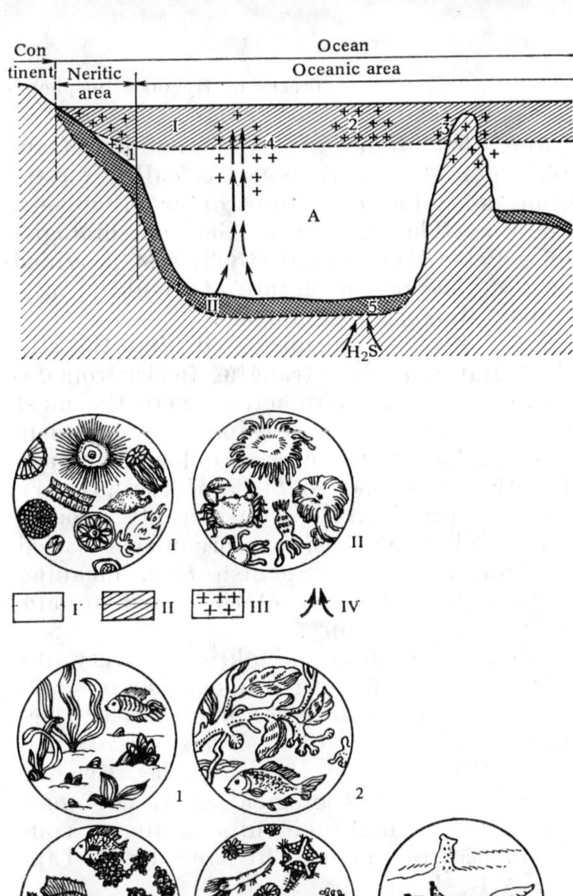

Fig. 8. Ecohorizons, concentrations and rarefactions of life in the World Ocean:

I—planktonic film of life; *II*—benthic film of life; *III*—local concentrations of life: *1*—near-shore; *2*—sargasso; *3*—reef; *4*—upwelling; *5*—abyssal rift; *IV*—upwelling of abyssal water; *A*—rarefaction of life

isms are called plankton). A community of autotrophic planktonic organisms is called phytoplankton, and that of heterotrophic organisms, zooplankton. The renowned German biologist Johannes Peter Müller (1801-1858) first provided evidence of the specific nature of plankton as a community of marine organisms.

Until recently it was considered that the single-celled diatomic algae (ranging in size from dozens to hundreds of micrometres) were the most important contributers to the primary products of the ocean, but studies carried out not long ago revealed that from 30 to 80% of the primary products are provided by considerably smaller (0.4-1 μm) photosynthesizing organisms called picoplankton (from the Spanish *pico*, meaning small quantity). Cyanobacteria predominate among the picoplankton*.

The composition of zooplankton is very diverse. Its most significant group consists of small Crustaceans (Copepoda and Euphasicea); accumulations of these Crustaceans are called "krill". Krill is the basic diet of whales. Regarding biospheres of the geological past, the composition of their planktonic film of life is considered in detail in an excellent paper by H. Tappan and A.R. Loeblich**.

------

* R. Iturriaga, B.G. Mitchell, "Chroococcoid cyanobacteria: a significant component in the food web dynamics of the open ocean", *Mar. Ecol. Progr. Ser.*, 28, 3, 291-297 (1986).
** H. Tappan, A.R. Loeblich, Jr., "Geobiological implications of fossil phytoplankton evolution and time-space distribution", *Geol. Soc. Am., Spec. Paper*, 127, 247-340 (1970).

The population density in the planktonic film is such that nine tenths of the living organisms, be they plants or animals, are devoured before the term of their natural death: Copepoda devour diatoms and, in their turn, are devoured by larger Crustaceans, etc. The number of living organisms

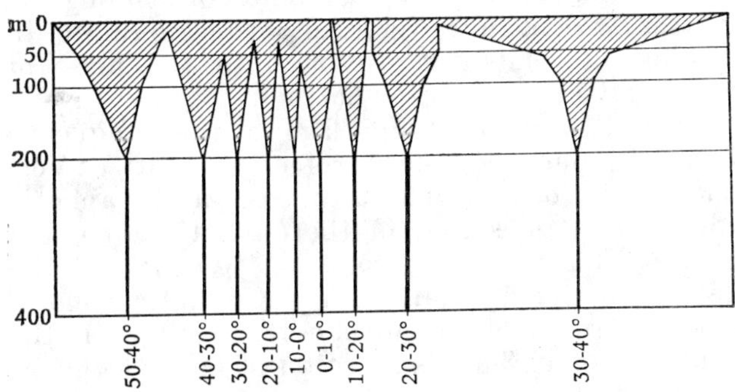

Fig. 9. Distribution of plankton biomass along the depth depending on geographic latitude (after Lohmann)

in the planktonic film rapidly decreases with depth (Fig. 9). According to the data obtained by an expedition that took place in the 1930s, the population of living organisms in 1 litre of sea-water was as follows: in the surface layer, 10 147 individuals; at a depth of 50 m, 9443; at the depth of 100 m, 2749. The thickness of the plank-tonic film as a peculiar concentration of life was estimated by Vernadsky to be 50 to 60 m.

The euphotic zone is the kitchen-garden of the ocean. Here is where the major part of the au-totrophic living matter of the ocean is synthesized (we shall discuss the exceptions on a later page).

It feeds almost the whole ocean (which is not a simple matter!), and the energy it accumulates is the energy source for most of the geochemical processes occurring in the ocean. The geological role of plankton is tremendous: it supplies raw materials for future rocks. The planktonic film of life produces enormous amounts of neobiogenic matter which, however, cannot accumulate in it, but descends by gravity into the mass of water until it reaches the bottom.

Under the planktonic film a thick aqueous aphotic zone of "life rarefaction" (after Vernadsky) is located. The thickness of the aphotic zone is 40 times that of the euphotic zone (the average depth of the ocean is 3800 m) and the density of living matter in the aphotic zone is several orders of magnitude lower than in the euphotic zone. This is a region of eternal gloom. There is no indigenous autotrophic living matter in the aphotic zone. Heterotrophic organisms feed on detritus, i.e., on nonliving organic matter, or they are predators. The detritus chiefly consists of pellets, which are reutilized many times by living organisms during its descent through the oceanic zones. The nutritional value of the detritus steadily diminishes.

The aphotic zone is thus a transient zone. Biogenic matter in the solid state also does not accumulate there, though the content of mineral feeding elements in dissolved state is higher there than in the euphotic zone.

Vernadsky's benthic film of life corresponds to the concept of the benthic zone as understood by oceanographers. Out of the 160 000 existing species of sea animals 157 000 live here. As we shall see later, the concentration of living matter in the benthic film within the shelf may be quite considerable. In Vernadsky's time, the benthic film had been studied only within the shelf, and owing to this he mistakenly extrapolated the shelf data to the benthic film as a whole, regarding it as a receptacle even richer in life than the planktonic film*. It has now been established, however, that in the deepest regions of the ocean the biomass of benthos does not reach even 1 g per m^2 of the bottom.

Recently, scientists from Columbia University (USA) carried out an interesting experiment in the east-equatorial region of the Pacific**. A camera placed at a depth of 4873 m automatically photographed the ocean floor every 4 hours over 202 days. During this period, only 35 animals crawled or walked within the camera's field of view. In other words, an animal passed by, on the average, only once in six days!

There is a close correlation between the distribution of the biomasses of the planktonic and benthic films of life; and, as a rule, areas with a high biomass of plankton correspond to areas with an increased content of living matter in the benthic zone. In honour of the well-known Soviet oceanologist who discovered this dependence, it is called "the Zenkevich correspondence principle".

---

* W.J. Vernadsky, "Ozeanographie und Geochemie", *Mineralog. u. Petrograph. Mitteil.*, 44, 2/3, 168-192 (1933).
** A.Z. Paul, E.M. Thorndike, L.G. Sullivan, B.C. Heezen, R.D. Gerard, "Observation on the deep-sea floor from 202 days of time-lapse photography", *Nature*, 272, 5656, 812-814 (1978).

While formation of the planktonic (surface) film is dependent on the penetration of sunlight into the upper layers of the ocean, the accumulation of life in the benthic film of life is determined by the presence of... a bottom or floor. Naturally, the bottom or floor as such does not feed the organisms; however, it retains all that was not eaten earlier (and leftovers are said to be the tastiest). Moreover, solid substrate provides a hiding place.

All that lives in the benthic zone (except predators) feeds on detritus. Mud-eaters indiscriminately devour mud and assimilate the detritus contained in it. The most active mud-eaters in the benthic film are worms, holothurians, sea urchins, and starfish. In addition to them, other representatives of the benthos bury themselves in the bottom sediments (thus changing the sediment texture) such as the Cephalopoda (e.g. cuttlefish) and bivalved mollusks, Ophiuroidea, Malacostraca (Isopoda, Amphipoda, crabs) and even some fish (plaice). As a result of this activity the surface layer of bottom sediments is continually "shovelled up" to quite a considerable depth*.

The Soviet scientists A.S. Alekseev and D.P. Naidin** recently showed how diverse the effects of the burrowing benthic fauna can be (Fig. 10). Under the action of organisms textures

---

* K.K. Turekian, J.K. Cochran, D.J. De Master, "Bioturbation in deep-sea deposits", *Oceanus*, **21**, 1, 34-41 (1978).

** A.S. Alekseev, D.P. Naidin, "Disturbances of sedimentary bedding by littoral invertebrates", *Lithol. a. Miner. Resour.*, **4**, 435-444 (1973).

are often formed which resemble shrinkage
cracks, traces of small erosions and roiling.
Sometimes such textures "manifest themselves"
only in the process of diagenesis. The main action produced by organisms on the sediment is
mechanical intermixing which increases sediment

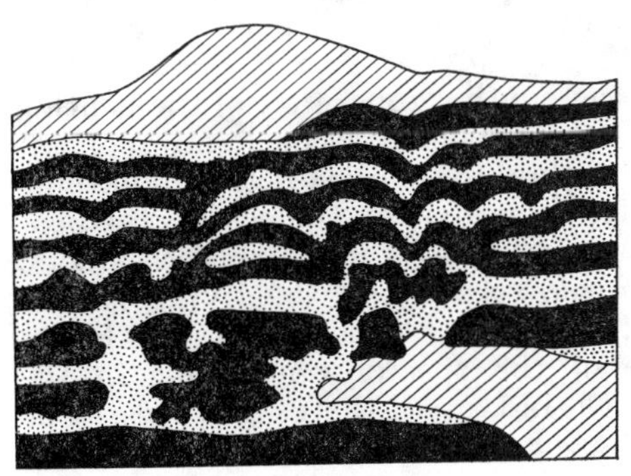

Fig. 10. Disturbances in the bedding of bottom sediments, caused by lugworm. Sediments of different composition are indicated by hatched and filled-in areas
(after Alekseev and Naidin, 1973)

homogeneity. But there are animals which act in
an opposite direction: they sort out sediments*
and make, for example, sand "still more sandy".

Most diagenetic reactions are carried out by
bacteria. This "biological reactor" in the diagenesis of bottom sediments works on detritus. As
a result of biogenic decomposition the detritus

---

* J.D. Howard, "The sedimentological significance
of trace fossils". In: *The Study of Trace Fossils* (ed.
R.W. Frey), Berlin a.o., Springer, 1975, pp. 131-146.

slowly disappears from the muds, whereas the bottom water is markedly enriched with the decomposition products, first of all with carbon dioxide gas, hydrogen sulphide, hydrogen, and ammonia; the pH of the bottom water drops, free oxygen disappears from the mud solution, and the formerly oxidizing medium becomes reducing, accompanied by an Eh drop to a negative value.

The role of the benthic zone, i.e., of the benthic film of life, in the biosphere is no less important than that of the planktonic film. If the planktonic film is the kitchen-garden of the ocean, the benthic zone is a storehouse for its finished products. After having been created by the living matter of the ocean, all that escapes from the biotic cycle because of the specific conditions in the benthic zone is immured there for ages. The planktonic film of life supplies raw materials for sediments, while the benthic film is the main oceanic ecohorizon where their accumulation takes place. The benthic film is the main, but not the only zone of accumulation, as has been shown by recent investigations.

J.P. Zaitsev*, Corresponding Member of the Academy of Sciences of the Ukrainian SSR, discovered an interesting phenomenon—"an anti-rain of cadavers". It turned out that not only the bodies of large organisms float up after their death (as was earlier believed), but also those of various small marine organisms. They finally sink, but when passing through the surface layer,

---

* J.P. Zaitsev, *Life of Sea Surface*, Naukova Dumka, Kiev, 1974, p. 112 (in Russian).

there is time for substantially enriching it with dissolved organic matter.

Another source of nonliving organic matter in the near-surface layer is organic matter absorbed by gas bubbles rising from the ocean depths. The nonliving organic matter, transported in gas bubbles to the near-surface layer, exceeds the formation of living matter in the process of photosynthesis by as much as 10 times. As a result, a lot of organic matter is accumulated at the surface of the sea*, mainly in colloidal form. During storms this matter is churned into a snow-white foam—that very foam, out of which, according to ancient mythology and as depicted by Sandro Botticelli, Venus, the goddess of love and beauty, was born.

The population of the near-surface layer of the water mass is quite distinct. The five-centimetre layer of water intercepts 40% of the solar radiation. The ultraviolet region of the spectrum is mainly absorbed. It is paradoxical that photosynthesis is suppressed here. The base of the trophic pyramid consists of saprotrophic microorganisms which process nonliving organic matter, which is found in excess. The number of bacteria in the near-surface layer is hundreds and thousands of times greater than in the lower horizons of the water mass. The second level of the trophic pyramid consists of the minutest heterotrophs: protozoans, larvae of all kinds of mollusks, worms, crustaceans, fish, and other animals. There are quite a lot of young fish and

---

* J.T. Hardy, "The sea surface microlayer: biology, chemistry and antropogenic enrichment", *Prog. Oceanogr.*, **11**, 4, 307-328 (1982).

gametes and zygotes of organisms—fish eggs—
in the near-surface layer, all keeping to the
very surface of the water. Finally, subsequent
levels of the trophic pyramid consist of larger
invertebrates, fish, and sea birds.

Zaitsev called the near-surface layer of the
ocean "the incubator of the pelagic zone". Future
generations of sea inhabitants are concentrated
there. At the same time, it is the surface of the sea
that is most susceptible to contamination with
petroleum and petroleum products, which cause
innumerable quantities of tender young fish to
perish. As Zaitsev put it, "the region of maximum negative effect on the living coincides with
the region of greatest population sensitivity".
The future of the ocean is in danger...

In addition to life films, concentrations and
rarefactions of life are found in the ocean. Deserts
on land have been known to mankind for ages; in
the ocean they were discovered rather recently.
A vast water desert was found in the Pacific
Ocean in the region of the Hawaian Islands,
where the concentration of living matter was
calculated to be $3 \times 10^{-6}\%$. In other words,
in order to collect a one-litre jar of marine organisms, one would have to filter 30 million litres
of oceanic water.

Vernadsky classified the local concentrations
of life in the ocean into three types: (a) near-shore;
(b) sargasso; and (c) reef (see Fig. 8).

Near-shore concentrations correspond to neritic
regions of the ocean. As a matter of fact, they
originate there, where both films of life, the planktonic and the benthic, meet and combine those
good things of life which they carry—sunlight

A mussel bank. (Publ. in the Russ. ed. of "TBB".)

and solid substrate. Moreover, the near-shore concentrations of life are characterized by an abundant influx of mineral and organic substances from the continent and are subjected to still another good thing: intensive stirring of the water mass (this enables repeated use of mineral elements). As a result of all these positive factors, in near-shore concentrations the biomass of plankton is hundreds of times, and that of the benthic fauna, many thousands of times, greater than in bathypelagic regions. Correspondingly, the degree of processing of sedimentary material proves to be high. In the near-shore concentrations of life the excrements of marine organisms often turn out to be the main component of the sediment.

A distinctive feature of the near-shore concentrations of life is the predominance of metazoans

rather than protozoans. In this case a comparative
monotony of life is characteristic: from one to 12
species of organisms may constitute up to 95%
of the biocoenoses. An example of such homogeneous accumulations are mussel banks. In all
seas, except tropical ones, mussels make up a
thick littoral border. Their biomass sometimes
reaches dozens of kilograms per square metre of
the ground.

A high concentration of organisms with skeletons of calcium carbonate leads to the appearance
of coquina accumulations. Based on data from
the Azov Sea, A.A. Aksenov demonstrated
that formation of large coquina accumulations
takes place in the case of a high productivity of
the benthos, shallow sea or shallow regions of the
sea, a predominance of coquina in the composition of detrital deposits, etc.

Other aspects of the activity of near-shore concentrations of life are illustrated by the previously mentioned investigation of mussel banks in
the White Sea, carried out by K.A. Voskresensky
in the 1940s and directly inspired by Vernadsky's
ideas. Voskresensky's research was both remarkable and, if not the only one of its kind, one of
the few at that time, and therefore of particular
value. In laboratory experiments and field observations he proved that the activity of mussel
banks controls the colloidal composition of
coastal water, sedimentation within the shore
limits, and—even more difficult to believe at
once—no less than the circulation of water within
the littoral zone!

All these functions (in the preceding chapter
they were discussed as the concentration, medium-

forming and transportation functions) are accomplished through filtering of inshore water by mussels. Biogenic circulation is set up due to the fact that water, free from colloidal particles, becomes lighter and ascends (Fig. 11). Later on it was also established that many organisms from

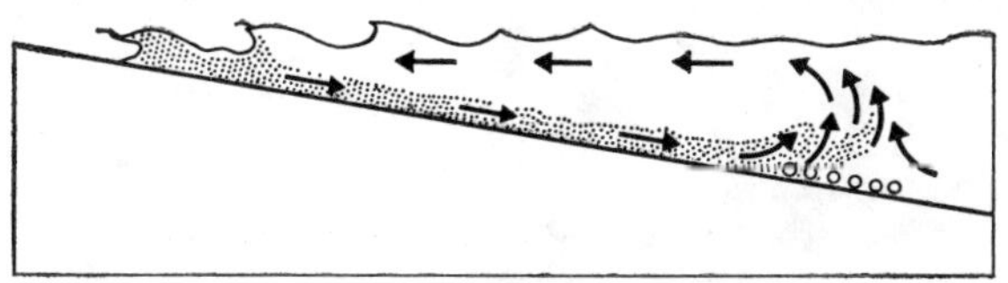

Fig. 11. Scheme of biogenic circulation of water in a near-shore concentration of life (after Voskresensky, 1948)

the near-shore concentration of life secrete mucous substances into the bottom sediments. Bivalved mollusks, crustaceans, echinoderms, and Hemichordata are among such organisms. These mucous substances, as well as mollusk byssuses (sticky, easily solidifying filaments with the aid of which mollusks attach themselves to a substrate), homes of polychaetes, and other formations add to the mechanical strength of bottom sediments. In this way, conditions are created for the preservation of sediment grains in an apparently foreign hydrodynamic medium.

A local life concentration of another type is represented by sargasso concentrations; these are sea areas, overcrowded with multicellular algae, Sargassum or Phyllophora, which are not attached to the sea bottom. This type of concentration is characterized by a very high biomass and an extremely low productivity of living matter.

Christopher Columbus first described this wonder of nature, this "grass" floating in the open sea where the depth reaches 4 to 6 km. "At dawn we

Fig. 12. Brown alga Sargassum natans. (From: K. Sterne, *Evolution of the World*, Moscow, 1909, v. 1, p. 332.)

came across so much grass that the sea seemed to be covered with it as with ice. The grass was coming from the west", Columbus wrote in his diary on September 21, 1492. The following day he wrote: "For part of the day there was no grass, then it became quite dense."

The brown alga Sargassum owes its name to the Portuguese word "sargaço", a cluster of grapes. These algae are yellowish-brown plants with strongly sectioned "leaves". Their characteristic feature is the presence of spherical air sacs or bladders which resemble grapes. A tangled mass of the algae with its animal inhabitants is the sargasso concentration of life, distinguished by Vernadsky (see Fig. 12).

A classical example of a local concentration of life of this kind is the ecosystem of the Sargasso Sea located southeast of North America. Its biomass amounts to four to eleven million tons, i.e., to about 1% of the entire biomass of the autotrophic living matter of the World Ocean. The low annual productivity of this sea can be explained by its specific hydrological conditions: its boundaries are defined by an elliptical stream, and vertical intermixing of the water is poor.

Another similar local concentration of life was found in the northwestern part of the Black Sea by one of the founders of Russian hydrobiology, Academician S.A. Zernov (1871-1945). There, in an area of about 11 000 km^2 in shallow water, a concentration of the red alga of the genus Phyllophora, not attached to the bottom, is located. The biomass of this concentration of life (5.5 million tons) is comparable to that found in the Sargasso Sea. Presently, in "Zernov's Phyllophora field" (so called in honour of its discoverer) Phyllophora is being collected to be used in the production of agaroid.

Reef concentrations of life are the third and last type of local concentrations of life known in Vernadsky's time (we shall consider them in the next chapter). In our times two other characteristic local concentrations were established: upwelling and abyssal rift ones.

While in sargasso concentrations the productivity of living matter is limited by the weak intermixing of water, in upwelling regions, where

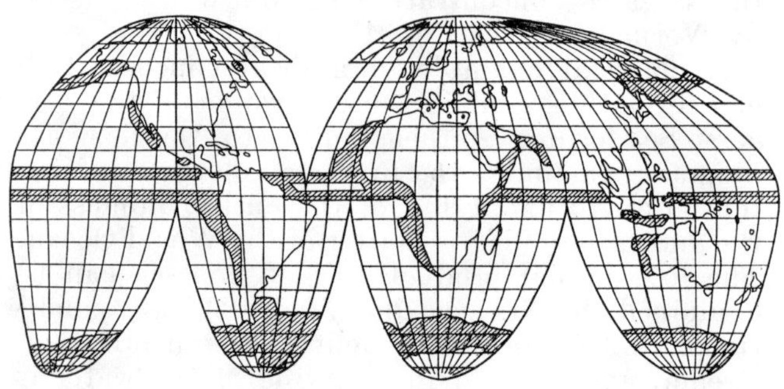

Fig. 13. Upwelling **concentrations** of life in the World Ocean (after Lafond, 1966)

water enriched with phosphorus and nitrogen rises from a deeper to a shallower depth, the productivity is tremendous. This tendency is especially obvious in tropical and subtropical **regions** (Fig. 13), and explains why all the largest upwellings on a planetary scale, namely, the Peruvian, Canary, Bengali, Somali, and Californian ones, are in exactly these regions. The most productive system in the World Ocean is located in the zone of the Peruvian upwelling. Its area, occupying only 0.02% of the total water area of the ocean, yields up to 15-20% of the world catch of fish.

Finally, the last of the concentrations of life in the ocean known to date are the abyssal rift concentrations (not to be confused with reef ones!). These life concentrations (undoubtedly the most remarkable ones!) were discovered on February 15, 1977, when the American deepwater vessel "Alvin" reached the bottom of the Pacific Ocean at a depth of 2540 m, at a distance of 280 km to the northeast of the Galapagos Islands.

"The typical basalt landscape had quite a dismal appearance: monotonous fields of brown "pillows"* were cut up by numerous fissures; in an area of several square metres it was not always possible to find a living creature", wrote a participant of this expedition, Professor J.M. Edmond. "But here we found ourselves in an oasis. Reefs of mussels and whole fields of giant bivalve mollusks, crabs, actiniae, and large pink fish seemed to bathe in the twinkling water... We had encountered a field of hot springs. Inside a circle approximately 100 m in diameter, warm water flowed out of every fissure, every opening in the sea floor".

The word "oasis" was immediately caught up by the world's press. Numerous photographs of them appeared in many illustrated journals. But initially it was absolutely unclear whence such a flourishing of life appeared in an abyssal zone, in the kingdom of eternal darkness. All the handbooks on ecology, including the very latest ones, constantly repeat the same idea: "Ecosystems cannot exist without plants because they will have no sources of organic matter, and this is the same as the absence of food". So what did these strange giants feed on *in the complete ab-*

---

* What is meant is pillow lava.

sence of plants (where could they appear from at a depth of 2.5 km?)? One can bask, even in the warmest water, only when a dependable source of food is present!

As Shakespeare's Hamlet once remarked: "There is a lot in the world, dear Horatio, which our men of wisdom have not even dreamed of". Indeed, who could imagine that in rift concentrations, not photoautotrophs, as everywhere on the Earth, but chemoautotrophic microorganisms would be the basis of life? Investigations revealed, however, that this is exactly the case.

The hydrothermal springs at the ocean bottom carry endogenic hydrogen sulphide that is utilized by most chemoautotrophic eubacteria and archaebacteria* (some microorganisms utilize hydrogen, ammonia, NO_2, Fe^{2+}, Mn^{2+}). The next trophic link—macrofauna—feeds on chemoautotrophic microorganisms (archaebacteria and eubacteria), and, in this way, these abyssal communities (the only ones of their kind!) are receivers of *endogenic* (not solar) energy. This is the first and most important distinguishing feature of abyssal rift concentrations of life. (Biogenic oxygen also participates in the reactions carried out by microorganisms; in this respect, abyssal communities are not quite autonomous** and retain a relation to communities based on photosynthesis.)

------

* H.W. Jannasch, "The chemosynthetic support of life and the microbial diversity at deep-sea hydrothermal vents", *Proc. Roy. Soc.*, London, 225, 1240, 277-297 (1985).

** E. Boyle, "Ecosystems of deep-sea vents (a letter)", *Science*, 230, 4725, 498 (1985).

The second feature is the widespread propagation of symbiotrophic organisms*. Chemoautotrophic bacteria frequently (but not always!) function directly in the body of multicellular organisms and even form small crystals of virgin sulphur there. Thionic bacteria are concentrated in a special organ in rifties (*Pogonophora* species), and their number there reaches 3700 million cells per gramme of weight.

The third distinguishing feature of rift concentrations of life is the wonderful peculiarity of their organic world (Fig. 13). Already 16 new families of segmented worms, pogonophors, gastropods, and crustaceans, not to mention new genera of various types, have been described in abyssal rift concentrations**. Many inhabitants of the abyssal concentrations have not yet gotten into the manipulators of the deep-sea research vessels and are thus far known only from photographs.

The most typical inhabitants of the rift concentrations of life are the rifties—representatives of the newly discovered genus of pogonophors—whose name is explained by their inhabiting the vicinity of rifts. Rifties are worm-like symbiotrophic animals up to 1.5 m long and with a diameter of 3.5-4 cm that dwell in flexible cylindrical tubes of protein and chitin.

Other typical inhabitants of the abyssal rift

---

* C.M. Cavanaugh, "Symbiosis of chemoautotrophic bacteria and marine invertebrates from hydrothermal vents and reducing sediments", *Bull. Biol. Soc. Wash.*, 6, 373-386 (1985).
** J.F. Grassle, "Hydrothermal vent animal: distribution and biology", *Science*, 229, 4715, 713-717 (1985),

concentrations are tube worms, which, like the rifties, live in tubes (made of lime instead of chitin). One of the newly discovered representatives of the tube worms has been named the "Pompeian worm" because of its close settlement near hydrothermal springs discharging smoke (they are called "white" and "black" smokers).

Blind crabs and fish in the rift concentrations of life graze on the "groves" of rifties and tube worms, like livestock on floodplains. Giant (up to 30 cm) bivalve mollusks settle along the fissures from which the hydrothermal springs escape. Their flesh, like that of rifties, is incrustated with thionic bacteria.

The gigantism of the inhabitants is another feature of the rift concentrations of life. In "The Zoology of Invertebrates" published in 1975, two years before the rift concentrations of life were discovered, a species that reached 0.5 m in length, with a body diameter of 6 mm, was considered to be a giant among the tube worms. On the other hand, the rifties, as mentioned above, are larger by more than three times in length and six or seven times in diameter. It is interesting that the "mania of gigantism" in the rift concentrations has even affected the bacteria, which here reach 0.11 mm—a size previously unheard of for bacteria!

The abyssal rift concentrations of life have very restricted dimensions—dozens of metres in cross section around the active vents of hydrothermal springs—but the density of life in them is from three to five orders of magnitude (!) higher than is usual in abyssal zones. This fact alone demonstrates that the rift concentrations of life are independent of a direct influx of solar energy while depending entirely on the existence of hydrothermal springs whose life is apparently only a few dozens of years. Scientists of the French expedition "Biocyarise", who in 1984 revisited the oases of abyssal life they had discovered earlier, registered serious changes in the structure of the communities that had occurred in only two years*. Where the hydrothermal activity had terminated during this period, the communities of organisms had also fallen apart. Only accumulations of giant mollusk shells sometimes remained as indications of the recent flourishing of abyssal life.

All the rift life oases known at present are located in the eastern part of the Pacific Ocean at depths of 1500-3000 m; their major part is located on the axis of the midocean East-Pacific upheavals**, namely, at 21° N.Lat., 10-13° N.Lat., at the equator (the Galapagos rift), and at Easter Island (27° S.Lat.). The northmost concentration of life is beyond the limits of the East-Pacific upheaval, on the Juan-de-Fuca ridge. Within the confines of each of these sections, there are generally several isolated ephemeral oases dozens of metres in diameter spaced several hundreds of metres apart. The overall length of the meridianal belt of rift concentrations of life in the Pacific Ocean is about eight thousand kilometres.

---

* L. Laubier, D. Desbruyères, "Les oasis du fond des océans", *La recherche*, **15**, 161, 1507-1517 (1984).
M. Roux, "L'impact écologique de l'hydrothermalisme dans les océans actuels et anciens", *Bull. Soc. Geol. France*, 7 Sér., **26, 1, 25-31 (1984).

In March, 1984, scientists from the Scripps Institute of Oceanography made another sensational discovery*, namely, a "rift" concentration of life was found *outside of a rift zone*, in the Bay of Mexico, not far from the Florida coast, at a depth of 3266 m. Its discoverers did not register any specific features distinguishing it from the previously known, "truly rift" concentrations of life. Here also hydrogen sulphide was the source of nutrition for the chemoautotrophic microorganisms, but the hydrogen sulphide escaped not from a rift, but from the shelf zone. On this basis, the authors arrived at the far-reaching conclusion that such communities can exist not only in rift zones and that they do not require elevated temperatures. All they need are reduced inorganic compounds as food. We shall wait for new discoveries.

The abyssal rift concentrations of life appeared in the biosphere at least 350 million years ago— this is precisely the age of the presently known most ancient find of their fossil remains which was made on the territory of Ireland**. However, B.S. Sokolov described fossil remains found in vend deposits (670-590 million years old) of the tubular organism *Sabelliditide*, which the French scientists, the Termiers (a husband and wife team)***, presently presume to be predecessors of

---

* *Oceanus*, **27**, 3, 32-33 (1984).
** D.A. Banks, "A fossil hydrothermal worm assemblage from the Tynagh lead-zinc deposit in Ireland", *Nature*, **313**, 5998, 128-131 (1985).
*** H. Termier, G. Termier, "Formes panchroniques ou fossiles vivants?", *Bull. Soc. Zool. France*, **108**, 4, 534-546 (1983),

the rifties. It is quite possible that rift concentrations of life are among the most ancient ecosystems existing on our planet. Not requiring sunlight, they could have appeared on the Earth even before the first photoautotrophs*.

The discovery of the abyssal rift concentrations of life is truly considered to be one of the major biological discoveries of the seventies. We can agree with the American scientist J.F. Grassle, who said that after the discovery of the abyssal rift concentrations, "our image of life in tho deep sea has been altered, and more surprises are likely in the near future". Even more can be said — our previous notion of the *biosphere as a whole* has also changed radically. We can now no longer speak of the biosphere as of a system, in which the course of life is sustained exclusively by the primary products of photoautotrophs.

The abyssal concentrations of life play a special role in the biosphere. Nature, following the principle "there is safety in numbers", likes to create spare variants. The abyssal concentrations of life are a spare variant of development of the biosphere, its "spark plug". And if, at some time or other, life based on photosynthesis terminates in the biosphere—its "big flame" extinguishes— then autonomous abyssal life will still remain in the inconceivable depths of the ocean as the "spark plug" that can ignite the flame of new life on the Earth.

---

* J.A. Barros, S.E. Hoffman, "Submarine hydrothermal vents and associated environments as sites for the origin and evolution of life", *Orig. Life*, 15, 4, 327-345 (1985).

The existence of abyssal concentrations of life also extends the possibilities of searching for life on other planets. If previously a definite minimum of solar energy delivered to the planet's surface was considered to be an essential condition for the existence of a biosphere, then after the discovery of abyssal concentrations of life this condition stopped being obligatory. We can now presume that on cold celestial bodies, at considerable distances from the Sun, life exists based exclusively on chemosynthesis.

But this is within the sphere of hypotheses. Let us return to our planet, which to our fortune is well situated relative to the Sun.

In the early sixties, at the Institute of Oceanology of the USSR Academy of Sciences on the base of a large corpus of empirical data, a map of the bottom sediments of the World Ocean was compiled. It was established that the accumulation of neobiogenic matter in oceanic sediments is controlled by three types of zonation: climatic, vertical, and circumcontinental. Climatic zoning is of primary importance. In different climatic zones organisms assimilate different components from seawater: in cold parts of moderate zones mainly silica is mobilized; in arid parts, only carbonates; and in equatorial and humid parts, carbonates and silica*.

Vertical zonation of accumulation of neobiogenic matter is determined by the so-called "level of carbonate compensation"—the critical depth, below which, because of the high pressure

---

* A.P. Lisitsyn, "Biogenic sedimentation in the oceans and zonation", *Lithol. a.Miner. Resour.*, **12**, **1**, 1-17 (1977).

and low temperature of seawater, the carbonate skeletons of calcium organisms dissolve. This phenomenon, discovered in the 1970s by the well-known British oceanologist J. Murray (1841-1914), explains the absence of carbonate sediments at depths exceeding 4.0 to 5.5 km. It has been established that the carbonate compensation level in the oceans has changed in the course of geological history. In the present time, it is at its maximum depth; however, in the Mesozoic era it was 1.0 to 1.5 m higher than now.

Circumcontinental zonation (from the Latin word "circum", around) is determined by the changing composition of sediments as one moves away from continents towards the oceanic area of the ocean. The density of life in this direction decreases, and we should expect a decrease in the content of neobiogenic matter in the sediments as well. However, this is not the case. As one moves farther from the continents, the content of biogenic matter in the sediments increases. Why? The explanation is simple. It is not the absolute quantity of biogenic matter that is less in proximity with the continent, but its percentage in the sediments decreases because of its strong dilution with a terrigenous admixture coming from the continent. On the periphery of the ocean 92% of terrigenous material is deposited! Terrigenous sedimentation is more abundant than the biogenic sedimentation, but in central parts of the ocean, remote from the land, the situation changes. Having brought together a considerable amount of factual material, the Soviet oceanologist and Corresponding Member of the USSR Academy of Sciences,

A.P. Lisitsyn came to the following conclusion: "The biogenic process in the pelagic zone of the ocean, on the whole, is scores of times more powerful than the terrigenous one, and the processes of preparation, transportation, and deposition of sedimentary material by the bios are dominant here"*.

Those are some of the natural phenomena in the distribution of living matter and the accumulation of neobiogenic matter in the ecosystems of the contemporary World Ocean. The ecosystems of land differ considerably from the marine ones, though there are some similarities. As in the ocean, there are two films of life on land: the upper film is located in the photobiosphere; and the lower film is in the melanobiosphere. Here the similarity ends.

The upper film of life on land is terrestrial; it exists, as we already know, from the surface of the soil to the upper boundary of the biosphere. These are the landscapes we are accustomed to, and there is no need to describe them.

Located below is a soil film of life. This is a specific world, where the concentration of life is higher than in the terrestrial film. For example, in one gram of forest soil there are, on average, 400 million bacteria, 2 million microscopic fungi, 100 thousand microscopic algae, and 10 thousand protozoans.

In contrast to the ocean, both films of life on land are in direct contact: they are not sepa-

---

* A.P. Lisitsyn, "Terrigenous sedimentation, climatic zonation, and interaction of terrigenous and biogenous material in the ocean", *Lithol. a. Miner. Resour.*, **12**, 6, 617-632 (1977).

Table 6. Hydrobiochemical Zonation of the Subterranean Part of the Biosphere of Land (after L.E. Kramarenko, 1975)

Zones	Eh	Types of microorganisms	K*	Neobiogenic matter—products of vital activity of bacteria
Aerobic	From +800 to +100 mV	Thiobacteria, nitrifying, methane-oxidizing, hydrogen-oxidizing bacteria	Up to ∞	SO_4^{2-}, NO_3^-, NO_2^-, CO_2, oxide forms of metals
Mixed	From +100 to +200 mV	Thiobacteria, nitrifying, hydrogen-oxidizing, denitrifying, sulphate-reducing, methane-producing, hydrogen-producing bacteria	About 1	SO_4^{2-}, NO_3^-, NO_2^-, CO_2, oxide forms of metals; H_2S, N_2, H_2, CH_4, reduced forms of metals
Anaerobic	From −200 to −400 mV and lower	Sulphate-reducing, denitrifying, methane-producing, hydrogen-producing bacteria	Down to 0	H_2S, N_2, H_2, CH_4, reduced forms of metals

* K is the ratio of occurrence of aerobic to anaerobic bacteria.

15—01293

rated from each other vertically by several kilometres of rarefaction of life. Here there are no problems limiting the productivity of the ocean ("biogenic salts at the depth"), and autotrophic organisms obtain the elements they need from the soil. After death their remains—neobiogenic organic matter—also enter the soil.

Further down below the thin layer of soil (its thickness is usually equal to several decimetres and seldom reaches 1-1.5 metres) an area of life rarefaction is located. This is a world almost unexplored by science. With the rare exception of caves, here everywhere—from the lower boundary of soil to the lower limit of the biosphere—mainly bacterial, i.e., microscopic life, is possible. These subterranean prisoners search out moisture for their habitat. They live in subterranean water and where the water is in contact with rocks. From the studies of microorganisms that dwell in subterranean water, the Soviet microbiologist L.E. Kramarenko has distinguished "zones of hydrogeochemical zonation of the Earth's crust"* (Table 6). In essence, these zones are specific ecohorizons of the subsoil part of the melanobiosphere in its continental portion.

Giving these circumstances it is possible to distinguish on land (Fig. 14) the following five ecohorizons of the biosphere (going downwards): (1) terrestrial film of life; (2) soil film of life; (3) aerobic subterranean ecohorizon (corresponding to the aerobic zone, after Kramarenko); (4) aerobic-anaerobic subterranean ecohorizon

---

* L.E. Kramarenko, "Microorganisms of subterranean water and their geochemical importance", *Transactions of the All-Union Geological Institute*, **241**, 156-165 (1975).

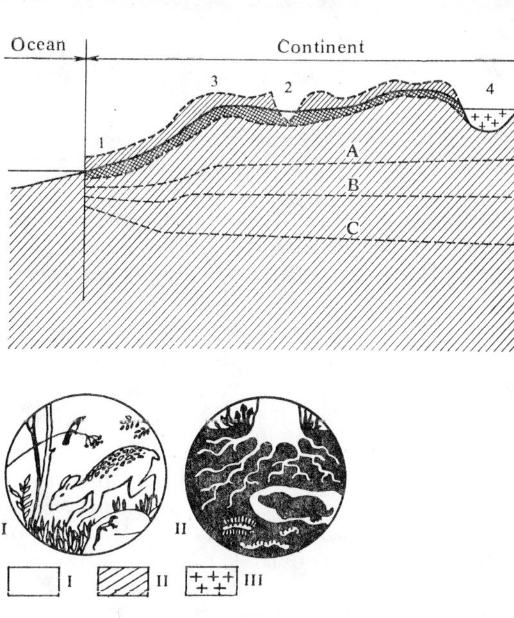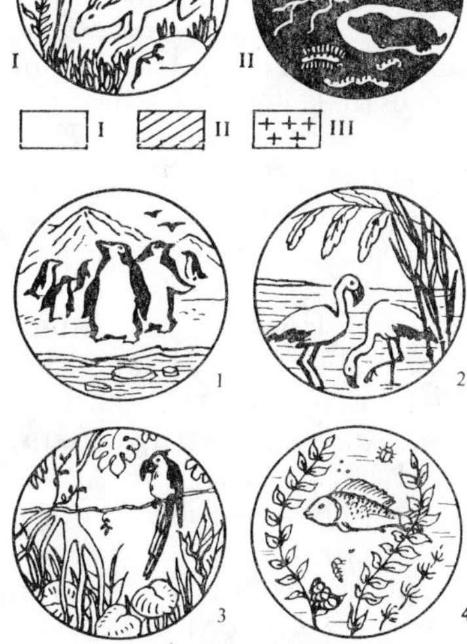

Fig. 14. Ecohorizons, concentrations and rarefactions of life on the continent:

I—terrestrial film of life; *II*—soil film of life; *III*—local concentrations of life: *1*—coastal; *2*—flood-plain; *3*—tropical and subtropical forests of humid areas; *4* – concentrations of stagnant water bodies; *A-C*—rarefactions of life: *A*—aerobic subterranean ecohorizon; *B*—aerobic-anaerobic subterranean ecohorizon; *C*—anaerobic subterranean ecohorizon (the mixed zone, after Kramarenko); (5) anaerobic subterranean ecohorizon (the anaerobic zone, after Kramarenko).

Living matter is distributed nonuniformly not only in the vertical section of the biosphere, but also laterally. On land, Vernadsky distinguished (a) coastal and (b) flood-plain local concentrations of life. Taking into account present-day data on the determination of the biomass of various ecosystems, it is possible to distinguish a third type of concentration—tropical and subtropical forests of humid areas.

According to Vernadsky, coastal concentrations of life include inshore territories of continents and islands. The high concentration of living matter is due here to the favourable circumstances created by contact between the two fundamental habitats of living organisms—the sea and land. Two neighbouring communities of the sea and shore (littoral) directly adjoin each other and are in close interaction.

But are seashore concentrations of life found everywhere on the Earth? Let us look at the physical map of the world. An appreciable part of the coastal territories of America, Africa, Asia, and Australia is occupied by deserts. The Arctic and Antarctic coasts, as regards the absolute figures on the density of living matter, also cannot be considered concentrations of life. Hence, the climatic factor also has a great influence on the concentration of life. But if we compare the density of life in the centre of the Antarctic continent or Greenland, and on their coasts, we shall see that for the given climatic conditions the coast is indeed a concentration of life. While in favourable climates such as that in the Mediterranean, the seashores are in absolute (not just comparative) terms a graphic example of concentrations of life.

The second, flood-plain, type of concentration of life on continents was characterized by Vernadsky in his "Essays on Geochemistry" as the "accumulation of life in the basins of great rivers", including not only fertile river valleys but their deltas as well. According to present-day data, these ecosystems are characterized by the highest productivity on land: though their area is negligible (less than 1%), they produce 10% of all living matter. An increase in production by more than an order of magnitude compared with the average standard of land ecosystems is explained by an abundant supply of flood plains and, particularly, deltas with mineral nutrients. As examples of flood-plain concentrations of life Vernadsky cited the Amazon, the Orinoco, the Zambezi, the Ob, and the Irtish. Contemporary biomass estimates necessitate making amendments to Vernadsky's conceptions: ecosystems possess a more considerable phytomass only within the limits of the subtropical and tropical belt; therefore, the valleys of our great rivers the Ob and the Irtish cannot be cited as examples of local concentrations of living matter.

Finally, tropical and subtropical forests of humid areas are the third type of concentrations of living matter on continents. Their phytomass reaches a record level of 650 t/ha (in the taiga of the Soviet Union the respective figures are 200 to 250 t/ha). D.V. Panfilov states that tropical forests resemble a gigantic green cascade

Tropical forest. Malaysia. (From: P.W. Richards, *Tropical Rain Forest*, Moscow, 1961, Photo 16.)

frozen in its downfall. Not only the flora, but also the fauna of tropical forests is abundant and diverse. Mammals, birds, reptiles, amphibias and, especially, insects are represented by a large number of species. Insects, mainly termites, very rapidly destroy the dead parts of plants (the fallen leaves, branches, fallen or still standing trunks of dead trees). Thick branches of trees are almost completely destroyed by insects after a period of 3 to 5 years; dry leaves and small branches lying on the ground disappear within a few months. As a result, in humid

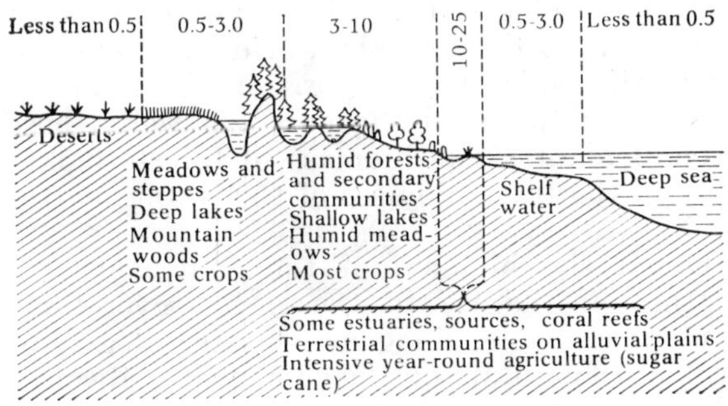

Fig. 15. Productivity of various ecosystems of the Earth's biosphere (in grams of dry matter per m² per day) (after Villee and Dethier, 1971)

tropical forests possessing a colossal biomass, neobiogenic organic matter practically does not accumulate.

Figure 15 shows how great differences in the productivity of the ecosystems of the Earth can be. Both the total quantity of living matter and its annual production are distributed over the area of the continents in an extremely nonuniform manner; for example, the reserves of biomass in the richest and in the poorest belts on land differ almost by a factor of 100. The distribution of the absolute masses of living matter and of annual production is determined here by global climatic factors: by temperature, by the quantity of precipitation, and by the fertility of soils.

A distinctive feature of the living matter of land is its composition: higher plants are characterized by absolute predominance in the biomass and productivity. The remaining eight subkingdoms of the organic world are found in a drastically subordinate position. But among higher plants there are "leaders" as well: these are woody plants. The biomass of forests makes up 84% of the total biomass of the living matter of land.

Although the biomass of the continents exceeds that of the World Ocean by several orders of magnitude, biogenic matter does not generally accumulate on the continents. Regarding this, Vernadsky wrote: "Here we have a rather perfect dynamic equilibrium which results in the tremendous geochemical work of the living matter of land leaving, after scores of millions of years of its existence, negligible traces in the solids constituting the Earth's crust"*.

This phenomenon can be explained by inorganic biogenic matter almost not being formed on land. Higher plants prefer their carcass to be built from lignine rather than from calcium carbonate or silica, which is preferred by marine organisms. As a result, after the plants die away, their remains are completely decomposed under normal conditions.

---

* W. Vernadsky, *La biosphère*, Alcan, Paris, 1929, p. 192.

Finally, let us examine the last type of eco-system of the Earth—continental water bodies. The main mass of the surface water of land is concentrated in pools, lakes and swamps, rather than in rivers. On continents, Vernadsky singled out a characteristic type of concentration of life: "concentrations of stagnant water bodies". The main water bodies here are lakes.

In the concentrations of shallow stagnant water bodies, synthesis of the living matter of auto-trophs occurs in the entire mass of the water. The activity of mud-eating animals in the bottom sediments of lakes is quite considerable. The most active mud-eaters in lakes are worms and larvae of dipterans (in particular, mosquito larvae, so familiar to aquarists). Under favourable conditions worms build up several millimetres of excrement a year.

Concentrations of stagnant water bodies are of great importance in sedimentation. Thus, in the littoral part of many lakes, coquina is often accumulated, but this is not the only product of accumulation in lakes. The Soviet limnologist, Professor L.L. Rossolimo (1894-1977) suggested that the following types of lakes should be distinguished by the type of sediments: (a) lakes which are accumulators of drift; (b) lakes which are concentrators of dissolved mineral substances; (c) lakes which are accumulators of organic matter.

In lakes which are concentrators of dissolved mineral substances the accumulation of matter can proceed under the influence of abiogenic processes (evaporation) and biogenic processes (concentration of elements by living organisms).

Further elaborating his classification, Rossolimo distinguished iron-accumulating, calcium-accumulating, and silicon-accumulating lakes.

Lakes which are accumulators of organic matter are most typically shallow lakes (having a depth of 2 to 10 m), not vast in area, with either small-drainage or no-drainage at all, protected from the wind, and located in the forest zone of moderate climates.

We have discussed the distribution of living matter and the potentiality of sedimentation in various ecosystems of the Earth's biosphere. But was it always like this? Did films and local concentrations of life exist in the geological past as well, and were they the same as now? Can one justify the extrapolation of the situation observed today to the geological past?

Vernadsky wrote: "There can be no doubt that beginning with the most ancient Paleozoic era there are indications as to the existence in nature of the same concentrations and rarefactions of living matter as those observed today. It is easy to verify that already in the Cambrian the same types of marine biocoenoses existed as we have today. In all geological periods the same picture is observed, though the morphological composition of these concentrations and rarefactions changes sharply."* The data obtained by modern science confirm Vernadsky's understanding. According to Academician A.V. Sidorenko, the sedimentogenesis of the Precambrian and of the Phanerozoic eras is essentially similar as a single

---

* V.I. Vernadsky, *Living matter*, Nauka, Moscow, 1978, pp. 299-300 (in Russian).

whole, found at different stages of continuous evolutionary development. Evidently, since the appearance of the ozone shield on the Earth, the distribution of living matter and conditions of sedimentation in the biosphere did not fundamentally change and, if there were changes, they were mainly fluctuating in character. This does not exclude the possibility that during some specific periods other, presently nonexisting facies, may also have existed on the Earth. "Never in the Earth's history will there again appear facies of archaeocyathean limestone (Cambrian), stromatoporous limestone (Silurian and Devonian), graptolitic shale (Silurian), fusuline and Schwagerina limestone (Carboniferous, Permian), nummulitic limestone (Paleogene), etc., because the organisms characteristic of these facies have become extinct", was written by Academician L.S. Berg, a younger contemporary of Vernadsky*.

All the sedimentary rocks of the Earth (of the past 3.4 billion years of its development) have formed in the biosphere. This thesis renders in the most concise form the geological aspect of Vernadsky's theory. Living matter takes an active part in the formation of sedimentary rocks, and all sedimentary rocks comprise a certain (even if very small) amount of paleobiogenic matter. The ratio of the abiogenic and paleobiogenic matter in rocks may vary: the low-ash varieties of coal are composed almost completely of paleobiogenic organic matter; limestones con-

---

* L.S. Berg, *Selected Works*, Moscow, Izd. AN SSSR, 1958, v. 2, p. 336 (in Russian).

tain some paleobiogenic inorganic matter; and sandstones may contain very little paleobiogenic material. Paleobiogenic matter in sedimentary rocks is of diverse origin: vegetable detritus, various remains of organisms (miospores, large-size fragments of plants, microscopic remains of plankton, spicules of sponges, shark teeth, shells, bones of vertebrates, etc.), amber, coprolites, and such microbiogenic minerals as sulphides, carbonates, hydroxides of iron, and others.

Thus, we have considered the accumulation conditions of biogenic matter in the contemporary biosphere. On the basis of this material we now return to the question of the three factors of formation of paleobiogenic matter in sedimentary rocks—the biological, ecological, and taphonomic factors.

The general connection between biological productivity and the quantity of neobiogenic matter accumulating in an ecosystem is not questioned. The biological productivity of ecosystems depends, in turn, on a number of factors: climate (mainly, ambient temperature and amount of precipitation), availability of mineral nutrients, intensity of solar radiation, and degree of mineralization of natural water.

The influence of temperature on the quantity of living matter varies: in oceanic ecosystems there is no direct relationship, while on continents a direct relationship does exist. In terrestrial ecosystems the average yearly temperature determines not only the quantity of the biomass, but also the type of predominant vegetation. Thus, forests grow only in those regions, where the mean monthly temperature exceeds $+10\ ^{\circ}C$

at least four months of the year. In the middle latitudes, usually only a few species of plants prevail (e.g. coniferous forests or spear-grass steppes in the Soviet Union), but the fauna is extremely diverse. In tropical forests, the opposite is observed: a tremendous diversity of plants and relatively few, though specialized animal species, participating in the life of the former are found.

Aridity of the climate influences both terrestrial and oceanic ecosystems to the same degree. Ecosystems of the humid belt are considerably "saturated with life". The introduction of abiogenic matter from the internal strata of the Earth's crust is also beneficial to biological productivity. We have already mentioned specific rift concentrations of life in the ocean. Generally high productivity of phytoplankton is observed everywhere in the region of the Pacific volcanic belt; for the land vegetation in areas of recent volcanicity, gigantism is characteristic. The introduction of endogenic matter probably not only increases the productivity of matter in the biosphere, but also contributes to the formation of species. This, at least, was the opinion of Vernadsky's colleague, Professor B.L. Lichkov (1888-1966).

Is it always true that an increase in biological productivity—the bio-factor—causes an increase in the quantity of biogenic matter in the sediments? In some cases such a relationship is quite obvious; for example, in the ocean, at depths above the level of carbonate compensation, the accumulation of carbonate ooze is directly dependent on the productivity of phytoplankton. In lakes, the situation is quite the reverse: it has been established that lakes with a low level of biological productivity produce muds with a high content of neobiogenic organic matter. Evidently, other factors exist in addition to the biofactor, which control the accumulation of biogenic matter in sediments.

Scientists were confronted by these factors for the first time in the middle of the last century, when "a telegraphic rope" (the word "cable" had not yet come into use) was laid across the Atlantic. This was the beginning of specific investigations of the oceans, the birth of a new science—oceanology. Sediments from oceanic depths were studied for the first time and their composition proved to be unexpected.

"Why have no fish bones, teeth, scales, shells, starfish, corals, or other parts of animals, not liable to rapid decay, been found?" wrote a scientific reviewer of that time. The correct explanation was found: "When these inhabitants of the near surface water die, their corpses become the spoils for animals with a lower organization, which, in turn, in the same way, become the spoils for even more primitive organisms. Long before the remains of animals dwelling on the surface of the sea reach the bottom and become assimilated with its mass, they, possibly, pass, through various levels and finish this descent in microscopic animals that inhabit the deepest parts of the sea."

Let us try to imagine for a moment that the living matter existing on the Earth is exclusively autotrophic. In this case, the accumulation of neobiogenic matter would be controlled only by its productivity (it is another matter that life would have been exhausted after several hundred or thousand years). In reality, however, heterotrophic living matter also exists on the Earth. In most cases, saprotrophs, with the potent assistance of abiogenic factors, honorably accomplish their difficult task of decomposing neobiogenic matter into the following simple components suitable for re-use by living matter: carbon dioxide gas, water, hydrogen sulphide, ammonia, and others.

Sometimes, however, complete decomposition of neobiogenic matter does not take place. The activity of saprotrophs may be suppressed by the aridity of the climate (in a desert), or by excessive humidity (in a swamp), by low temperatures (in tundra), or, by the toxicity of the medium. In the water of sphagnum bogs, for example, there are phenols which render it inhospitable to most organisms. It was for a specific purpose, however, that in the Middle Ages sailors, when setting out on long voyages, provided themselves with just such water. This water now also renders an invaluable service to archaeologists: it conserves for ages such wooden relics as piles, pavement plankings, boats, oars and small articles.

The completeness of neobiogenic matter decomposition is also materially dependent on the physical depth of the area in which the destruction processes take place. Thus, in lakes and in shallow parts of the ocean, where the planktonic film is separated from the benthic film by only a few metres of water, the quantity of detritus decomposed during precipitation will be, naturally, much smaller than in deep sea basins.

At the XXIII International Geographic Congress in Moscow in 1976, the Soviet scientist Panfilov suggested that three main types of ecosystems should be distinguished*: transit, autonomous, and accumulative. Transit ecosystems are characterized by a constant supply and removal of mineral nutrients used by plants; autonomous

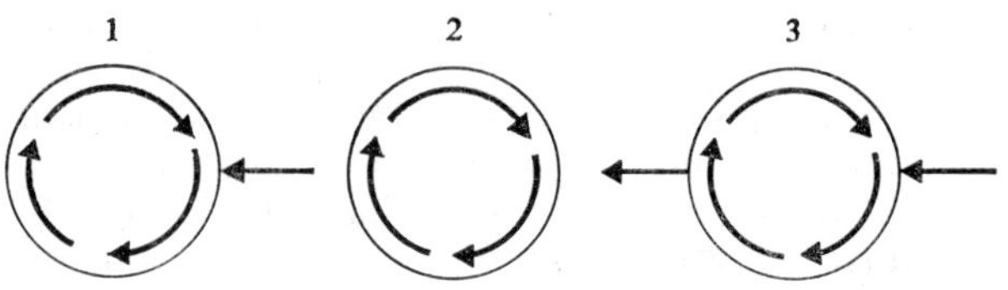

Fig. 16. Types of ecosystems (after D.V. Panfilov, 1976):

1—accumulative type; *2*—autonomous; *3*—transit; the flow of nutrient substances is indicated by arrows

ecosystems, by a weak supply and removal; and accumulative ecosystems, by a considerable supply but weak removal of matter (Fig. 16). Panfilov mentioned oceanic abyssal zones, mangroves, swamps as examples of accumulative systems. Nothing other than neobiogenic matter accumulates there, both organic (in mangroves and swamps) and inorganic (in oceanic abyssal zones).

It has recently been suggested that the factor ensuring the concentration of neobiogenic matter

---

* D.V. Panfilov, "Natural-history classification of natural ecosystems". In: *International Geography-76*, Section 4, Moscow, 1976, pp. 91-96.

Vladimir Ottonovich Tau-
son. (Published in the
Russ. ed. of "TBB".)

Johannes Walther. (Pub-
lished in the Russ. ed. of
"TBB".)

in ecosystems should be called the eco-factor*.
The well-known Soviet microbiologist V.O. Tauson (1894-1946) was the first to emphasize the
importance of this factor in the accumulation
of caustobioliths.

The eco-factor is also responsible for conditions which preclude the supply of considerable
amounts of terrigenous material to the ecosystem, material which dilutes neobiogenic matter.
Such conditions include the levelled-out relief of
the surrounding territory and weak oscillatory

---

* A.V. Lapo, "Living matter of the biosphere and formation of sedimentary rocks and ores", *Izv. AN SSSR*,
geolog. series, 11, 121-130 (1977).

motions of the Earth's crust. Those areas of the biosphere, in which formation of biogenic or chemogenic sediments takes place, not disturbed by the supply of terrigenous material, are called concentration basins. According to Academician D.V. Nalivkin (1889-1982), examples of such basins are those in which phosphate, manganese, ferruginous, and other sediments accumulate. Peat land is also a concentration basin*. (It should be noted that some people, still thinking in the old-fashioned way, consider that for the accumulation of peat downwarping of the peat land bed is required. This assumption is based entirely on a misunderstanding, on the incorrect extrapolation of the laws of mechanics to a biological object, namely, to the peat accumulation ecosystem.)

All the above arguments are pertinent to sedimentogenesis, to the stage of the accumulation of sediments, occurring in the biosphere. On the geological time scale, conservation of neobiogenic matter in ecosystems is an altogether temporary phenomenon, something like leaving one's luggage in an automatic luggage locker. Normally life retrieves its luggage, or rather, neobiogenic matter. Extraordinary circumstances are required to keep the locker locked and the luggage immured in it. Under the conditions of the biosphere such an extraordinary circumstance is the process of burial. Only when isolated from the processes of active decomposition can neobiogenic matter be preserved over millions of years of

---

* D.V. Nalivkin, "An important reserve of mineral resources", *Priroda*, 2, 14-15 (1959).

geological history. Only by having ceased to be a sediment can it become a rock.

Johannes Walther (1860-1937), the German geologist who was quoted in the epigraph to this chapter, laconically formulated the following thesis: "We call deposits all the accumulations of matter that are forming. Only those that have remained preserved become rocks."

The transition of biogenic matter into the fossil state, its transformation from neobiogenic to paleobiogenic matter, which occurs at the stage of diagenesis, may be called the tapho-factor of the formation of sedimentary rocks (from the Greek "taphos", tomb).

The burial of neobiogenic matter on land commonly occurs as a subsidence basin of its accumulation. But there can be sudden burials too. Within the memory of mankind catastrophic burials of whole cities have taken place. A well-known case is that of Pompeii, which was buried under a layer of volcanic ash up to 4 metres thick. And another, not so commonly known example: on May 31, 1970 when the city of Yungay, in the mountains of Peru, was flooded with a ten-metre (!) layer of mud in the space of a few seconds.

Similar sudden burials have occurred in the geological past as well. For example, findings of "fossil forests", i.e., accumulations of mineralized trunks of trees, buried at the site of their growth, are not unusual. If the tree had not rotted before it was covered by sediments it indicates that the process of burial was very rapid. In oceans, burial of low-stability biogenic matter may also occur as a result of very intensive sedimentation and resulting portions of the sediment become isolated from the aggressive action of seawater and from the activity of the benthic fauna.

The general situation on land is not favourable for biogenic sedimentation. I.A. Yefremov (1907-1972), both a paleontologist and writer, founder of the science studying the regularities of the burial of organic remains in the Earth's crust (taphonomy), suggested that situations favouring the burial of biogenic matter should be called ultrafacies*. Yefremov noted that all that remains from a continent is a hiatus in the geological chronicle, surrounded by a belt of ultrafacies.

In this respect the ocean, or, more precisely, its benthic film of life, is a complete antithesis to the continent. It has already been mentioned that the benthic film of life is of extreme importance in the formation of sedimentary rocks, since conditions exist for the preservation of biogenic matter for a long geological time. "As the remains of life and roiled parts of inert matter gradually descend, the lower layers of marine mud become lifeless, and chemical bodies formed by life have no time to pass into gaseous states or to enter into new living matter. The living layer of mud never exceeds a few metres, though it grows continually from the surface. It always dies down from below"**. It is there that the final chords of the grand symphony of life sound, and

---

* I.A. Yefremov, "Taphonomy and geological chronicle", *Trans. of Paleontol. Inst. of the USSR Acad. Sci.*, 24, 1-178 (1950).
** W. Vernadsky, *La biosphère*, Alcan, Paris, 1929, pp. 177-178.

neobiogenic matter, departing from the biosphere, is transformed in the course of geological time into paleobiogenic matter.

The quantity of biogenic matter that passes into the fossil state is negligible in relation to the annual production of living matter. In the case of carbon, for example, it amounts to 0.05% for the biosphere as a whole, and to 0.4% for

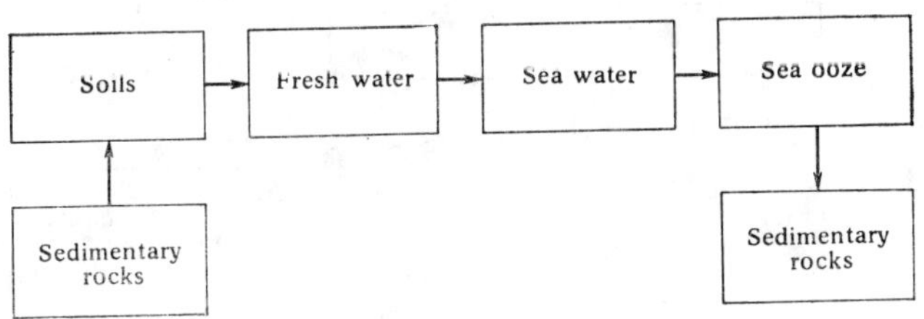

Fig. 17. The formation of sedimentary rocks (after Vernadsky, 1926)

the World Ocean (0.7% for the underwater outskirts and 0.1% for the oceanic region). Such negligible fractions of matter, which escape from the biotic cycle by entering the fossil state, are the constituents of the biogenic matter of the metabiosphere.

Vernadsky diagrammed the formation of sedimentary rocks* as shown in Fig. 17. From this diagram it follows that during the 1920s and 1930s Vernadsky thought of the formation of sedimentary rocks as being an exclusively under-

---

* W. Vernadsky, "Sur l'analyse des sols au point de vue géochimique", *Acte IV conf. int. pedol.*, t. II, Rome, 1926, p. 573.

water process. In the 1940s, however, L.S. Berg and B.L. Lichkov* (Fig. 18) substantiated their opinion that sedimentary rocks can also be formed on the surface of continents, in the course of soil formation processes. Vernadsky supported this idea: at any rate it was he who presented a paper by Lichkov treating this topic to the *Izvestiya*

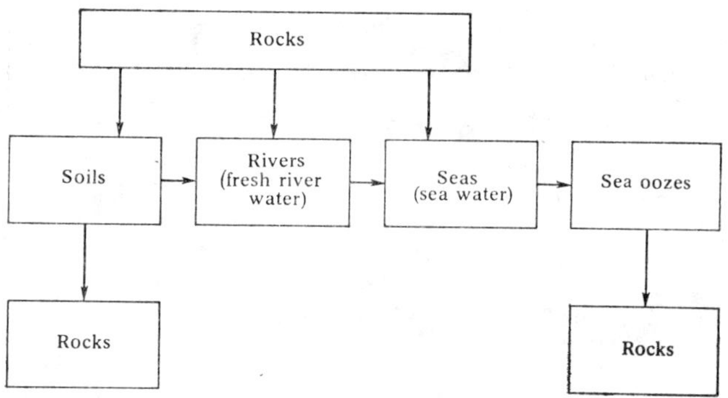

Fig. 18. The formation of sedimentary rocks (after Lichkov, 1946)

AN SSSR and mentioned Lichkov's work with favour in his book "The Chemical Structure of the Biosphere and Its Surroundings" (1965, p. 128). The accumulation of sediments and their diagenetic transformations occur in dynamic systems of a specific kind, which Vernadsky called bio-inert natural bodies.

----

* B.L. Lichkov, "Changes in the relief and evolution of the soil and mud formations of land and sea in the Earth's history (theory of sedimentation)", *Izv. of the Tajik Branch of the USSR Acad. Sci.*, 11, 3-28 (1946).

In 1938, Vernadsky* introduced this concept to distinguish not only living and inert bodies in the biosphere, but also systems in which their interaction is realized. As examples of bio-inert natural bodies Vernadsky cited soils, forests, crust of weathering, ooze, surface water, oceans, and biosphere as a whole. "Organized bio-inert bodies account for a considerable portion of the biosphere in terms of its weight and volume", wrote Vernadsky. "Their remains, after the death of the organisms of which they are composed, make up biogenic rocks which take up a tremendous part of the stratisphere".** Whether sedimentary rocks are formed as a result of the diagenetic transformation of the bottom sediments of water bodies or of soils, in either case their formation proceeds in bio-inert natural bodies (or, in bio-inert systems, after Perelman***). What role does living matter play and what processes occur in the bio-inert systems? Let us consider Fig. 19.

A distinctive feature of bio-inert systems is the presence of living matter in them. If living organisms composing the system die, it can no longer be considered to be bio-inert. In all bio-inert systems the content of living matter (in relation to the total mass) is small, but it is this living matter that plays the leading role in the functioning of the system.

---

* V.I. Vernadsky, "Problems of biogeochemistry", pt. 2. *Trans. Conn. Acad. Arts a. Sci.*, **35**, 483-517 (1944).
** V.I. Vernadsky, *The Chemical Structure of the Biosphere and Its Surroundings*, Nauka, Moscow, 1965, p. 128 (in Russian).
*** A.I. Perelman, *Bio-inert systems*, Nauka, Moscow, 1977, p. 160 (in Russian).

Since there is living matter in the system, there must also be products of its vital activity, and dead organic matter, i.e., neobiogenic matter. In bio-inert systems, abiogenic matter must necessarily be present as well. It may be additionally incorporated there as a terrigenous admixture, as products of volcanism, or as extraterrestrial material (terrestrial and extraterrestrial

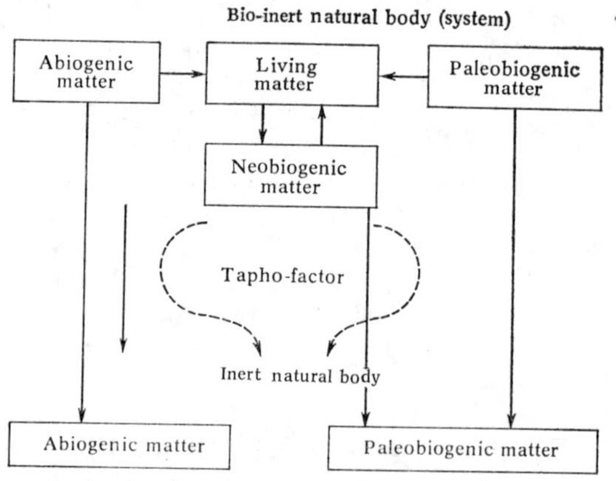

Fig. 19. Formation of sedimentary rocks in bio-inert systems with subsequent burial

matter are combined in the diagram). Paleobiogenic matter such as limestones and phosphorites may also (though not necessarily) be present.

In the course of the processes of vital activity living matter continually consumes and introduces new portions of abiogenic matter into the biotic cycle (it should be remembered that this is one of the basic functions of living matter in

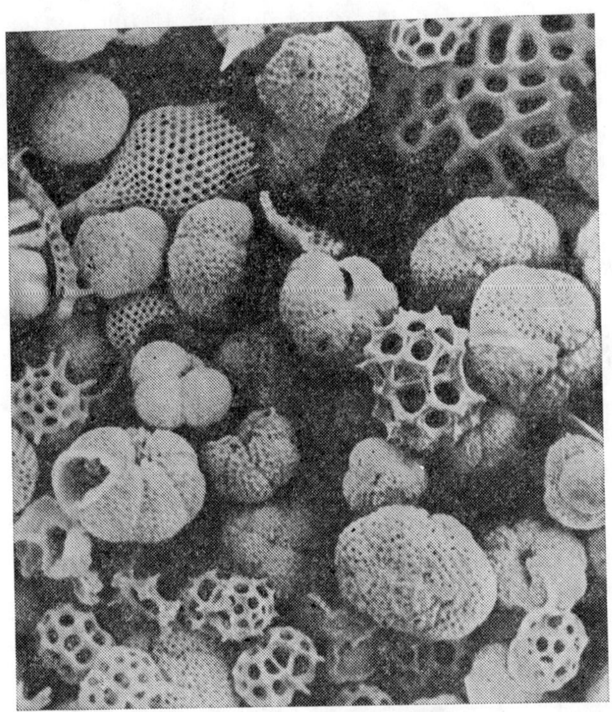

Abyssal oceanic ooze consisting of remains of foraminifers and radiolarians. Scanning electron micrograph. 170-fold magnification. The Pacific Ocean, depth of 2850 m. (From: B.C. Heezen, C.D. Hollister, *The Face of the Deep*, N.Y. a.o., 1971, p. 280.)

the biosphere). Mostly abiogenic matter of terrestrial origin is assimilated, but, evidently, a part of abiogenic matter of extraterrestrial origin is also used.

In addition to abiogenic matter, living matter consumes neobiogenic matter. Living matter also utilizes paleobiogenic matter (e.g., shells of borers require biogenic limestones for their making). Higher plants assimilate phosphorus-containing minerals, and some species of bacteria, organic matter of coals and petroleums. Thiobacteria oxidize biogenic sulphides created by their predecessors, i.e., by sulphate-reducing bacteria, etc.

Thus, just as forty rivers flow into Lake Baikal and only one river flows out of it, so living matter introduces into its cycle all types of nonliving matter and produces only one type—neobiogenic matter.

Bio-inert systems create sedimentary rocks. After burial, life in them comes to a standstill, the bio-inert natural body is converted into the inert one. As a result, from the four types of matter, comprising bio-inert systems, two types of nonliving matter of inert systems are formed: abiogenic and biogenic.

The sedimentary envelopes of the Earth, in the most simplified form, are stratigraphically superposed traces of the bygone biospheres of our planet. Taken together, they make up the meta-biosphere of the Earth—envelope many kilometres in length—whose character is to a considerable extent determined by the activity of four thin films of life: the planktonic, benthic, terrestrial and soil films.

5. The Metabiosphere

The unity of the Earth's stratisphere resulting from the developement of the bygone biospheres of the planet has become apparent.

B.S. Sokolov, 1975

At the end of Sredny Prospect in Leningrad the area between the 19th and 20th Lines is occupied by a magnificent edifice clad in grey stone. It is called the Palace of Geology. At one time the Geological Committee, practically the sole geological establishment of pre-revolutionary Russia, was located there. Now three leading establishments of the Ministry of Geology of the USSR are accommodated in this building: the A.P. Karpinsky All-Union Geological Research Institute, the All-Union Geological Library, and the F.N. Chernyshev Central Museum of Geological Prospecting. The building houses a grand hall and a wide staircase reaching up to the top. In the hall there are creations of nature and not of human hands: a block of coal from the Donets Coal Basin petrified trunks of extinct trees, a masterpiece of the Mesozoic Era—an ammonite. These are all traces of bygone biospheres.

In January 1959 in the Palace of Geology, the Fifth Session of the All-Union Paleontological Society was opened. It seemed as if there was nothing special about it (such sessions are held every year, but the topic of that session was unusual: "The importance of the biosphere in geological processes."

This representative forum (more than 500 scientists participated in it) was the first scientific conference at which the role of living matter in the formation of the Earth's crust was considered in so many aspects and so comprehensively. Its initiator, the well-known Soviet paleontologist and later Lenin prize winner, B.P. Markovsky (1895-1966), delivered a programmatic report entitled, "Life as a Geological Factor"*. Numerous special communications were about investigations on the biogenic origin of carbonate rocks, combustible minerals, iron and manganese ores, phosphorites, bauxites, etc.

The Fifth Session of the All-Union Paleontological Society summarized the results of investigations carried out during the decades that had passed since publication of the first works by Vernadsky about the geological role of life. But the importance of this session lay not only in this: at the same time it opened up a new stage in the development of Soviet geology. Such sessions were also conducted later, but this was the first one.

Vernadsky's ideas have justly won general recognition. The brilliant pleiad of scientists who meritoriously developed his ideas includes many contemporaries (also younger contemporaries) of Vernadsky.

---

* *"The Importance of the Biosphere in Geological Processes. Problems of Interconnection of Paleontology and Tectonics"*, Moscow, Gostoptekhizdat, 1962, p. 248 (in Russian).

Owing to the efforts of these investigators, out-standing advances have been made in studying the role of life in the formation of the Earth's crust. The last chapter of our narrative is devoted to this question. The present can be said to be the clue to the understanding of the past. We shall use this clue to gain a better understanding of the way in which sedimentary rocks were formed in the geological past.

According to present-day classifications, sedimentary rocks are subdivided into the following groups: (1) detrital; (2) shales; (3) allites; (4) iron-bearing; (5) manganese; (6) phosphatic; (7) carbonate; (8) siliceous; (9) salines; and (10) caustobioliths.* Among the sedimentary rocks, carbonate and siliceous rocks, as well as caustobioliths, are characterized by the highest concentrations of paleobiogenic matter. We shall begin our treatment of the rocks forming the Earth's sedimentary crust with carbonate ones.

Different authors estimate the content of carbonate rocks in the sedimentary layer of the Earth's crust to be within the range of 10 to 18 per cent. Vernadsky attributed particular importance to the role of life in the formation of carbonate rocks and even distinguished, as has already been mentioned, a specific "calcium function" of the living matter of the biosphere. The mechanism of formation of calcium carbonate by living organisms has been considered recently by the well-known West German scientist E. De-

---

* N.V. Logvinenko, *Petrography of Sedimentary Rocks*, Vysshaya Shkola, Moscow, 1974, p. 400 (in Russian).

gens*, and the specific role of algae and bacteria in this process has been examined by W.E. Krumbein**.

Not so long ago the ratio of the chemogenic (abiogenic) and biogenic sedimentation of carbonates in marine ecosystems was a subject of heated discussion. Some lithologists held that the role of chemogenic carbonate accumulation was essential in marine water bodies of the Black Sea type, which have restricted communication with the World Ocean. However, recent investigations of the Black Sea have proved that the carbonate accumulation there was of biogenic origin. Also, on the Bahama Bank, carbonate sedimentation was for a long time considered chemogenic; but detailed investigation have revealed that finely dispersed carbonate material is composed of the remains of microscopic algae, bacteria, and fragments of shells***.

In the contemporary living matter of marine ecosystems, carbonates play an important role. At great depths the distribution of carbonates on the ocean floor is limited by the level of carbonate compensation.

Lisitsyn**** classifies neobiogenic carbonate

---

* E.T. Degens, "Why do organisms calcify?", *Chem. Geol.*, **25**, 3, 257-269 (1979).

** W.E. Krumbein, "Calcification of bacteria and algae". In: *"Biogeochemical Cycling of Mineral-forming Elements"* (ed. P.A. Trudinger, D.J. Swaine), Amsterdam a.o., Elsevier, 1979, pp. 47-68.

*** R.D. Stieglitz, "Scanning electron microscopy of fine fraction of recent carbonate sediments from Bimini, Bahamas", *J. Sediment. Petrol.*, **42**, 1, 211-226 (1972).

**** A.P. Lisitsyn, *Processes of Ocean Sedimentation*, Tokyo, 1983.

sediments of marine ecosystems into two types: planktogenic and benthogenic. Both life films of the ocean thus create their own types of carbonate sediments.

The planktogenic type, in turn, is subdivided into three classes: foraminiferal, coccolithic, and pteropodal. At least half of the area of recent carbonate accumulation in the open sea is composed of foraminiferal ooze.

Foraminifers belong to the subkingdom of protozoans. Their contemporary representatives are microscopic in size. Among extinct forms there existed rather large organisms. These include nummulites, giants among one-celled animals, which reached 10 to 16 cm in diameter. Their Latin name means "stone coins"; indeed, nummulites resemble petrified small coins. An Azerbaijanian legend recounts that this is the money of a rich man who refused to give alms to a pauper. Nummulites were first classed with organic remains only in the eighteenth century, whereas nummulitic limestones had been used much earlier—the Egyptian pyramids are built of them.

Other foraminifers are rather diverse but less important sources of carbonate sediment. There are approximately a thousand species now existing; only 30 of them are planktonic; the rest are inhabitants of the benthic film of life. The body of foraminifers is rather diverse in shape: it can be spherical, tubular, dendritic, etc. The body is covered on the outside with a thin calcareous test through which tiny openings run. Recent foraminiferal oozes are composed of the tests of these organisms, mostly, of their fragments. Foraminifers appeared in the Cambrian period and acquired an important role in calcareous sedimentation since the Carboniferous era.

Recent coccolithic oozes are considerably less abundant than foraminiferal ones. They are composed not of the remains of animals, but of the remains of the microscopic yellow-green algae Coccolithophorida (this is a good example of how biogenic matter is formed in the photobiosphere and accumulated in the melanobiosphere, in the benthic film of life). The skeletons of coccolithophoridae consist of calcareous plates which contain crystals of calcium carbonate. After their death coccolithophoridae disintegrate into a fine carbonate powder.

Finally, pteropodal oozes are the least abundant among the recent carbonate planktogenic sediments. The initial material for their formation was furnished by the remains of tests of small (0.3 to 10 mm) gastropod mollusks called pteropods.

These are the main types of recent carbonate planktogenic oozes. It has been calculated that they cover about 128 million km^2 of the floor of the World Ocean, or about 36% of its area. Their average thickness is about 400 m, and the accumulation rate is approximately 1 cm in 1000 years. There are sufficient grounds to believe that for the biospheres of the geological past the planktogenic carbonate accumulation rate was not smaller. It has been calculated that coccoliths alone, under stable favourable living conditions, could have produced, for example, over the Cretaceous period a 7-km thick layer of ooze.

The second type of recent biogenic carbonate sediment is formed by the benthic film of life.

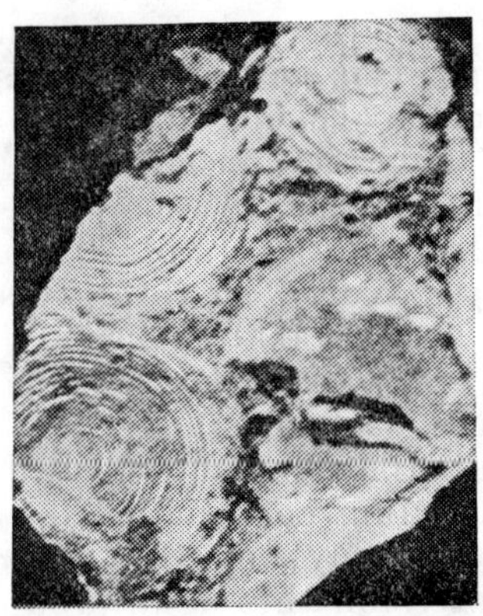

Nummulitic limestone from the Pyramid of Cheops. 1.5-fold magnification. (Published in the Russ. ed. of "TBB".)

These sediments are called benthogenic, and Lisitsyn subdivides them into several classes.

The first class—coquinoid deposits—is encountered mainly on shelves and on summits of seamounts. Among the shelves, areas most favourable for the accumulation of coquina are those adjacent to the coast with a flat relief and without a developed river drainage. These include the colossal coquina fields at the eastern and northern edges of the Caspian Sea, in the northwest corner of the Black Sea, on Bahama Cay, off the coast of Florida. Included among these is also the Sea of Azov, which is even called "molluskan". In the near-shore zone, coquina undergoes intensive crushing, and the sediments are often represented by shell sands. In the past geological epochs, shell deposits were also composed of molluskan remains, though during certain periods, brachiopods also acquired great importance.

Another class of benthogenic carbonate deposits is coral-algal. These deposits are formed in reef concentrations of life.

The reef concentrations are one of the most highly productive ecosystems of the biosphere. Reefs grow at a rate of 10 and sometimes up to 25 cm per year. The total area of all the reefs in the world is 600 thousand km^2.

The Great Barrier Reef alone, stretching along the east coast of Australia, exceeds in volume all the buildings made by man. Reefs consist of calcium carbonate. Nowadays this will not surprise anybody, but just try to imagine the impression this news produced during the last century on a planter, who lived on a coral island and had been importing lime from England for years! This story was told by a traveller of that time.

Corals are the best known contemporary reef-builders. Therefore all reefs are sometimes called coral reefs, though it is not quite correct. In addition to corals, reefs are created by the activity of the following living beings: green and red algae, mollusks, echinoderms, and other organisms; the palm being borne by green algae of the genus Halimeda and by red algae Lithotamnion. As mentioned in Chapter Two, the tissues of corals themselves are literally packed with the photosynthesizing symbiotic algae zooxanthellae. Cyanobacteria also play an important role in the creation of the autotrophic living matter of coral reefs.

The high productivity of the ecosystem of coral reefs can to a considerable extent be explained by the porosity of the reef structure itself: reef-forming organisms can "pass through" tremendous

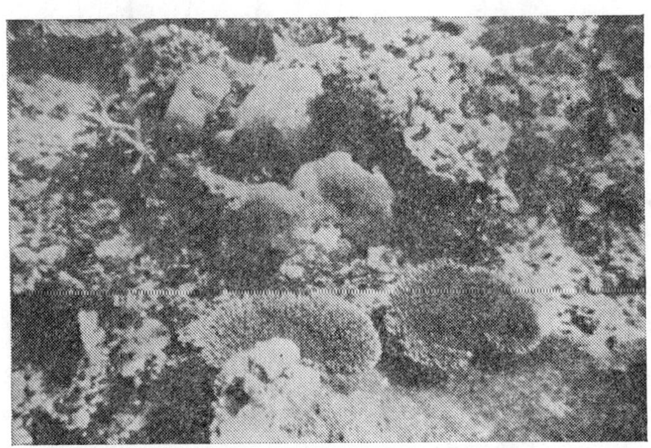

Part of the underwater portion of the Great Barrier Reef.
Australia. (From: W.G.H. Maxwell, *Atlas of the Great
Barrier Reef*, 1968.)

volumes of water, filtering out nutritious materials. Credit for the discovery of this most interesting phenomenon must be given to the Soviet
biologist Yu.I. Sorokin. Because of the biofiltration of tremendous amounts of water, a low
concentration of biogenic elements does not limit
the development of coral reefs. This ecosystem
successfully solves the eternal problem of oceanic
life—"biogenic salts in the depth". Sorokin*
believes that the concentration of dissolved organic matter in the ocean is controlled on the global
scale by the filtering activity of coral reefs. Ac-

---

* Yu.I. Sorokin, "Ecosystems of coral reefs", *Bull.
AN SSSR*, 11, 29-35 (1978).

cording to his estimations, the entire volume of
ocean water is filtered through the reefs over a
period of 40 thousand years.

Recent reefs are limited to areas where the
water maintains an average annual temperature
of at least 18 °C. Reef builders are also hard to
please in some other respects too: the seawater
must have a definite salinity (from 2.7 to 4.0%);
it must not be turbid; and it must be rich in oxygen. Finally, corals require light, and therefore
they live at a depth not over 40 to 50 m. The thickness of coral reefs sometimes reaches 1200 to
1400 m. How could it happen that the remains of
organisms in shallow water extend to such a depth?

Charles Darwin was the first to give a correct
answer to this question. In his classic work "The
Structure and Distribution of Coral Reefs"* he
showed that the formation of coral reefs occurs
during the continuous subsidence of the sea floor.
Corals (and other organisms) compensate for this
subsidence by their growth, and the depth of
the sea remains approximately the same. This
fact enables one to use reefs for reconstructing
the tectonic conditions of the geological past.

Fossil reefs are noted for their widespread occurrence. According to Nalivkin, in the Cenozoic and Mesozoic eras, reef limestones accounted
for the major portion of all limestones. In Leningrad, one can see reef limestones not only at
the Museum of Geological Prospecting but also in
the decoration of the underground hall of the
subway station "Ploshchad' Vosstaniya". Look-

---

* Ch.   Darwin, *The Structure and Distribution of
Coral Reefs*, Smith, Elder a. Co., London, 1874.

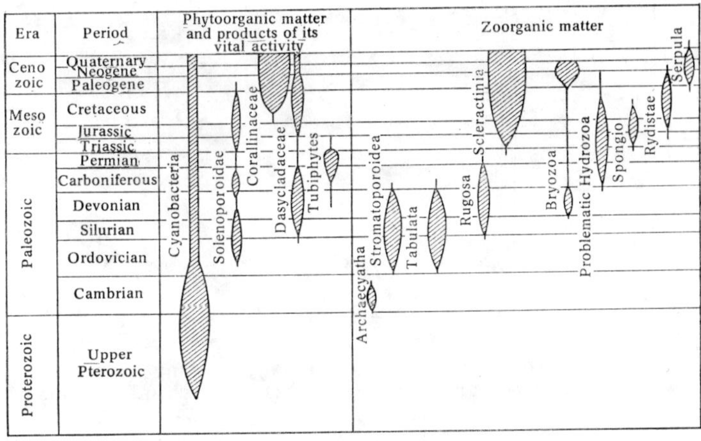

Fig. 20. The evolution of the main builders of carbonate biogenic structures (after Osadchaya and Krasnov, 1977)

ing carefully at these limestones, one can discern organic remains, relics of feather stars, or crinoids. Complexes of reef-builders have undergone considerable changes over geological history. D.V. Osadchaya and E.V. Krasnov* distinguish several stages in the development of reef-building complexes (Fig. 20).

In addition to coquinoid and coral-algal, there exist three more classes of recent benthogenic carbonate sediments which are not so widespread: (a) foraminiferal (as you remember, foraminifers

---

* D.V. Osadchaya, E.V. Krasnov, "Evolution of reef-building organisms", *Trans. of the Institute of Geology and Geophysics*, Siberian Division of the USSR Academy of Sciences, 1977, Issue 302, pp. 113-125 (in Russian).

Algal reef of Carboniferous age on the Amga river in
Yakutia. Photographed by V.D. Nalivkin. (From:
D.V. Nalivkin. *Essays on the Geology of the USSR*. Le-
ningrad, 1980, p. 51.)

can be not only planktonic, but benthic as well);
(b) bryozoan; and (c) sediments composed of
the remains of echinoderms, ostracods, serpulids,
and barnacles. All these types of carbonate
sediments are predominant on the shelf, on the
upper part of the oceanic slope, and on underwater
uplifts.

Recent benthogenic carbonate sediments of
marine ecosystems are formed by two concentrations of life—near shore concentration and reef
concentration. In the remaining water area of
the ocean, calcareous sediments are formed by
the planktonic film of life. In the geological past
the scheme of carbonate accumulation was, evidently, the same (see Fig. 24), though the species
of carbonate-depositing organisms and the position of the carbonate compensation level were
different.

Modern carbonate accumulation proceeds not only in marine ecosystems, but also in lakes, though the character of the processes occurring there is substantially different. In the opinion of S.I. Kuznetsov*, a prominent Soviet microbiologist and Corresponding Member of the USSR Academy of Sciences, the precipitation of carbonates in lakes takes place both by evaporation of oversaturated solutions (as observed, for instance, in Lake Sevan in Armenia) and owing to the geochemical activity of bacteria. In lakes, bacteria do not function as direct concentrators of calcium carbonate, they merely create conditions favourable for its precipitation (the medium-forming function of living matter is thus manifested). The resulting microcrystalline calcite, in combination with the debris of charophytes, crustaceans and thin-valved mollusks, produces the so-called "lacustrine chalk" or "lacustrine marl". In the near-shore part of the lakes, coquina is aggraded in some places.

Thus, in the contemporary biosphere there takes place the accumulation of carbonate sediments which then undergo further diagenetic transformations. Neobiogenic carbonate sediments are characterized by the presence of minerals unstable under biospheric conditions (Academician V.F. Chukhrov called such minerals "geological ephemerae"): aragonite, vaterite, and calcite monohydrate are later transformed into calcite. Formerly loose sediments undergo cementation, conditioned to a considerable extent by the activity of

---

* S.I. Kuznetsov, *The Microflora of Lakes and Its Geochemical Activity*, Austin, Univ. of Texas Press, 1970.

sulphate-reducing bacteria*. Sometimes, dolomitization of these sediments takes place. Neobiogenic matter is thus converted into paleobiogenic matter, i.e., into sedimentary carbonate rocks.

According to their mineral composition, carbonate rocks are classified as calcite rocks ($CaCO_3$ is predominant), dolomite rocks ($CaMg(CO_3)_2$ prevails), or rocks having a mixed composition.

Calcite rocks include mainly diverse types of limestones and one more rock with which we are most directly concerned between the ages of seven to seventeen—chalk. As investigations on carbonate rocks yield more extensive data, an ever greater portion of these rocks proves to be biogenic. This was already noticed by one of the founders of Soviet lithology, Professor M.S. Shvetsov (1885-1975). He wrote: "It has become a thing of the quite recent but already almost legendary past, that even a prominent geologist, having glanced in the field at a dolomite bed, would pin a label of sandstone on it in his publications, which would stick for decades, or, examining limestones consisting of algae, would declare them to be of a specific, tectonic 'conchoidal' texture." These words date back to the early thirties, but the process of "biolithization" of limestones (and of rocks in general) has not been completed and continues even today.

Nicolaus Steno (1638-1687) first recognized that many limestones derived from the skeletal remains of organisms. The first microscopic in-

* J.C. Deelman, "Two mechanisms of microbial carbonate precipitation", *Naturwissenschaften*, **62**, **10**, **484-485** (1975).

vestigations of limestones were carried out in the 1870s by the well-known British naturalist Henry Clifton Sorby (1826-1908), President of three Scientific Societies of Great Britain: Microscopic, Mineralogical, and Geological.

No small contribution to the "biolithization" of limestones was made by the excellent "Atlases of Rock-forming Organisms" published in the thirties by the French scientist Lucien Cayeux (1864-1944) and the Russian scientist, a student

Lucien Cayeux. (From: L. Cayeux, *Sedimentary Rocks of France*, Darien, 1970.)

of Ya.V. Samoilov, V.P. Maslov (1891-1968). By now, foraminiferal, pelecidopodal, brachiopodal, bryozoan, crinoidal*, and many other types of limestones have been separated and have been found to be composed of various skeletal remains of organisms (Fig. 21). Precambrian limestones of various regions, which earlier were all lumped together under the classification of chemogenic, are now being gradually re-classified as biogenic.

---

* One of the finest examples of crinoidal limestones forms the polished slabs in the staircase leading to the Enquiry Office at Paddington Station, London. In these polished slabs sections of crinoids are abundant.

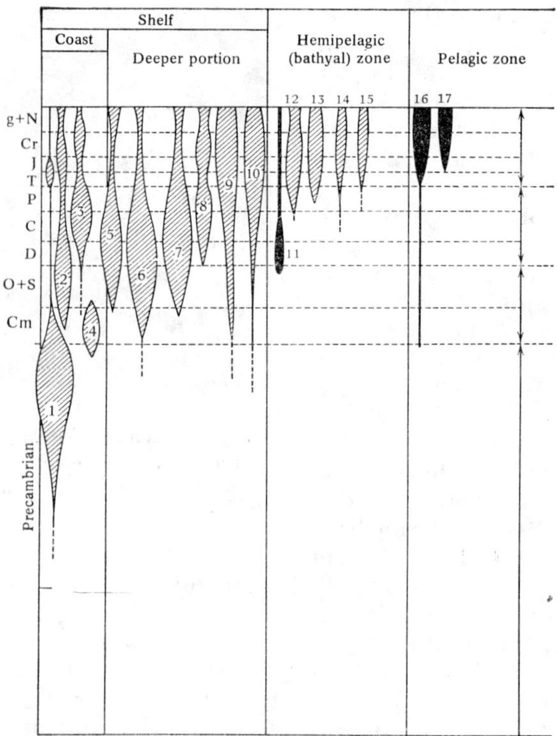

Fig. 21. Evolution of biogenic carbonate accumulation (after Strakhov, 1949):

1—calcareous algae; 2—corals; 3—benthic foraminifers; 4—archaeocyata; 5—bryozoans; 6—brachiopods; 7—crinoids; 8—sea urchins; 9—pelecypods; 10—gastropods; 11—pteropods; 12—abyssal brachiopods; 13—crinoids; 14—abyssal bivalved mollusks 15—abyssal sea urchins; 16—coccolithophorids; 17—planktonic foraminifers. Hatched—benthos; filled-in—plankton

Biogenic limestones are composed not only of the skeletal remains of organisms and calcified thallomes of algae. Coprolite limestones, which are rocks whose initial material consists of the excrement of mud-eaters that processed lime mud, are also biogenic. Limestones of this type are aggregates of fine pellets—coprolites (discernible only under the microscope) in combination with microgranular calcite. They have been known to exist since at least the Ordovician and often make up whole strata that are from 0.5 to 3 m thick, and sometimes even up to 6 m (found in the Moscow Syneclise, Kuznetsk Basin, and South-West of England). Detrital limestones are also biogenic. Both the constructive and destructive life-processes are dramatically manifested in them: comminution and redeposition of the calcareous substrate occur as a result of the activity of living organisms (as was mentioned in Chapter Three*-**.

Formerly, limestones were considered to be abyssal formations, although this conclusion was purely speculative. Detailed ecological analysis has demonstrated that many biogenic limestones are extremely shallow-water marine or freshwater deposits. Thus, Shvetsov (1922) found stigmariae (rhizomes of arborescent lycopods, provided with thin root appendages) in the Lower Carboniferous limestones of the Near-Moscow Basin. Vegetable remains of such a kind could

---

* J. Schneider, "Biological and inorganic factors in the destruction of limestone coasts", *Contr. Sedimentology*, 6, 112 (1976).

** S.V. Maksimova, *Essays on Applied Palaeoecology*, Moscow, Nauka, 1984 (in Russian).

Bryozoan limestone of the Carboniferous age. 7-fold magnification. The Kuznetsk Coal Basin. Photographed by
S.V. Maksimova. (From: S.V. Maksimova, *Lithology
and Formation Conditions of Bituminous Limestone Mass
of the Lower Carboniferous in th Kuznetsk Coal Basins,*
AN SSSR Publ., Moscow, 1961, Table XVI.)

not have been transported; one can only suppose
that the basin had been extremely shallow and
that it was periodically infested with arborescent lycopsids (their carbonified remains make
up the coal beds of the Near-Moscow Basin).
The evolution of carbonate accumulation conditions in geological history was considered by
J.L. Wilson in his circumstantial monograph*.

Chalk is a peculiar calcite rock. A zone of deposits containing chalk extends throughout the
whole of Europe: from England to the banks of

____

* J.L.   Wilson, *Carbonate   Facies   in   Geological
History*, Berlin a.o., Springer, 1975.

Chalk cliffs on the south coast of Great Britain between Eastbourne and Seaford. In the background is Beachy Head. (From: *Nat. Geogr.*, 1945, v. 87, 4, p. 425.)

the Emba. The ancient name of Great Britain, "Albion" (from the Latin "albus", white) supposedly refers to the chalk cliffs of Dover.

Early investigations on chalk were carried out in the last century by the famous German naturalist Christian Gottfried Ehrenberg (1795-1876). He assumed that chalk originated from foraminifers and particles of abiogenic origin. It has now been established that chalk is a fossil analogue of coccolithic ooze. Ninety to ninety eight per cent of its fine dispersed portion is composed of coccoliths. There are from 10^{10} to 10^{11} coccoliths in one cubic centimetre of chalk! In addi-

Recent coccolith ooze in the Black Sea. Scanning electron micrograph. 8000-fold magnification. Photographed
by S.I. Shumenko. (From: *Priroda*, 1978, 6, p. 121,
(article by S.I. Shumenko.)

tion to coccoliths, exoskeletons of sea urchins,
rostra of belemnites, and shells of mollusks are
found in chalk.

For a long time it was not clear why chalk is
not laminated. This problem was solved using
the method of impregnating chalk with lubricat-
ing oil*, elaborated by the Soviet lithologist
G.I. Bushinsky (1903-1980). By this treatment,
traces of mud-eaters filled with their excrement
become apparent. It is clear that coccolithic
ooze, from which chalk formed, has been intensively processed by mud-eaters and repeatedly

---

* G.I. Bushinsky, S.I. Shumenko, "Chalk and its
origin", *Lithology a. Miner. Resour.*, 2, 37-54 (1979).

passed through their own alimentary tract, which results in the absence of lamination in chalk. The bioturbation of mud-eaters in the English Chalk rocks has recently been considered by W.J. Kennedy*.

Chalk is characteristic only for Upper Cretaceous deposits, this being associated with the coccolithophorids that thrived in the seas of that time and with conditions favourable for the accumulation of calcareous sediments.

Chalk composed of remains of coccoliths. Scanning electron micrograph. 4300-fold magnification. (Published in the Russ. ed. of "TBB".)

Dolomites are a specific type of carbonate rocks. They are named after their discoverer, the French mineralogist D. Dolomieu (1750-1801).

In appearance dolomite rocks are very similar, to limestone, but, in contrast to it, they do not foam in reaction with cold dilute hydrochloric acid. Well-preserved remains of organisms are also rarely encountered in these rocks. This, evidently, is an indication of increased salinity of the basin in which they had formed deposits. Dolomite rocks are encountered mainly in Pre-

---

* W.J. Kennedy, "Trace fossils in the chalk environment". In: *Trace Fossils* (ed. T.P. Crimes, J.C. Harper), Liverpool, Seel House Press, 1970, pp. 263-282.

Cambrian dolomite composed of the remains of Cyanobacteria of the genus Collenia. Siberian Platform. Photographed by I.K. Korolyuk. (From: *Trans. Geol. Inst. AN SSSR*, 1956, Issue 4, paper by I.K. Korolyuk.)

cambrian and Paleozoic deposits; they are considerably less common in the Mesozoic and, particularly, in the Cenozoic.

As soon as it comes to do omites, a dolorous note can be detected in geological papers and manuals. "The problem of the formation of dolomite rocks is known to be one of the most difficult in theoretical lithology", writes Academician N.M. Strakhov (1900-1978), the founder of theoretical lithology and geochemistry of sedimentary rocks in the Soviet Union. "Not many rocks are known, about which so many contradictory opinions have been voiced and suggestions put forward on the question of their origin, and whose origin, nevertheless, still remains as dubious and obscure as that of dolomites", testifies Shvetsov.

The complexity of the problem lies in that dolomite cannot be found in the composition of contemporary living matter (see Fig. 6). True, quite recently it has been found in an urolith in a Dalmatian dog*. Recent dolomite sedi-

---

* C.E. Mansfield, "An urolith of biogenic dolomite —another clue in the dolomite mystery", *Geochim. cosmochim. acta*, 44, 6, 829-839 (1980).

ments were not discovered for a long time. It was only in the thirties and forties that such sediments were found in salt lakes and lagoons in the Soviet Union (Balkhash), on the south coast of the Persian Gulf, on the Bahama Shoals, in southern Florida, and in Australia (Coorong Lagoon)*. It was established that in the recent geological epoch dolomite accumulates in aqueous ecosystems characterized by high salinity, a high pH of the water, and abundant vegetation.

As has been shown by Strakhov, dolomite formation in this case is conditioned by the medium-forming activity of autotrophic living substance: in the course of photosynthesis plants extract from water the carbon dioxide dissolved in it; this leads to an increase in the pH and contributes to the precipitation of dolomite. American scientists came to the same conclusion, based on the study of Precambrian dolomites found in California**. The connection between an increased content of organic matter and dolomite formation can be directly well traced on fossil material: dolomite rocks often smell of hydrogen sulphide, and if the rock consists of alternating calcite and dolomite intercalations, then dolomite is found concentrated in the dark bands, and calcite, in the light ones.

------

* C.C. von der Borch, D. Lock, "Geological significance of coorong dolomite", *Sedimentology*, **26**, 6, 813-824 (1979).
** L. Wright, E.G. Williams, P. Cloud, "Algal and cryptalgal structure and platform environments of the late pre-Phanerozoic Noonday Dolomite, eastern California", *Geol. Soc. Amer. Bull.*, **89**, 3, 321-333 (1978).

Thus, in many cases there exists a marked positive correlation between the content of biogenic organic matter and the content of dolomite found in rock. This correlation can be explained by two interrelated factors. In the first place, magnesium, as we know, is contained in chlorophyll (its content there reaches 2%), and an increased productivity of photoautotrophic living matter may result in a rather high percentage of magnesium in bottom sediments. On the other hand, ammonia, originating in the decomposition of neobiogenic organic matter, produces an alkaline medium which, in turn, favours the formation of magnesium hydroxides and carbonates. The latter combine with carbonate sediment to form dolomite.

A variety of evidence exists proving that dolomite forms as a result of the vital activity of organisms. Thus, already by the end of the last century the Russian scientist Professor A.A. Verigo (1837-1905) reported on interesting experiments elucidating the influence of bacteria on the formation of dolomites. According to his data, ooze, placed in a test tube and infected with the bacteria Proteus vulgaris, substantially changed after a period of one and a half years. Yellowish-white beads appeared in the ooze, which, upon analysis, proved to be dolomite; in control test tubes formation of dolomite was not observed.

In the 1950s similar experiments in aquaria were conducted by the French researcher C. Lalou. He came to the conclusion that bacteriogenic carbonates (including dolomite) can be obtained from any sediment, provided that the quantity of organic matter is sufficient, the temperature is high enough, and the bacterial processes proceed in shallow water under conditions of intensive illumination. All these factors are characteristic of tropical lagoons.

By now the wide-spread occurrence of dolomites composed of the remains of cyanobacteria has been established in deposits of various ages: Permian (the Donets Basin, the Urals Territory, North America); Cambro-Silurian (the Siberian Platform); and Late Cambrian (north of Siberia, the Kara-Tau Range). Most characteristic of them are dolomites produced by various species of Collenia, though other forms of cyanobacteria are also encountered. Reef and other biogenic structures are often composed of such protosedimentary dolomites. Recently, another example of dolomite formation with the participation of biogenic matter—formation inside the shells of dead gastropods*—has been demonstrated. In this case the carbonates (including protodolomite) are formed by the action of microorganisms which process organic matter (the body of the dead mollusk and the matter which gets inside its shells together with terrigenous material).

The mystery of dolomite is beginning to be solved.

Thus, biogenic carbonate rocks are formed as a result of the activity of both the planktonic and (to a lesser extent) the benthic film of life in the ecosystems of the World Ocean and of

---

* L.E. Sterenberg, L.S. Fomina, A.B. Sheko, "One of the ways of formation of carbonate minerals", *Doklady AN SSSR*, **229**, 6, 1430-1432 (1976).

inland water bodies. The intensity of carbonate accumulation in the geological past was to a considerable extent determined by paleogeographic factors and by the content of carbon dioxide gas in the atmosphere evolved by volcanic processes. A.B. Ronov, Corresponding Member of the USSR Academy of Sciences, formulates the main law of carbonate accumulation as the following: "The quantity of carbonate sediments deposited during the epochs following the Precambrian is directly proportional to the intensity of volcanic activity and to the area of inland seas"*.

Referring to the tables illustrating the character and localization of the processes performed by living matter, and the main functions of living matter in the biosphere (see Tables 3-4), it can be seen that the function of living matter in the formation of calcite rocks is most manifest in that of concentration that occurs inside the organism (construction of the skeleton). Dolomite rocks, however, are formed under the action of both the concentration and medium-forming functions of living matter, occurring not inside but outside the organism.

The origin of siliceous rocks is similar in many respects to that of carbonate rocks. Siliceous rocks are those consisting mainly of silicon minerals such as opal, chalcedony, or quartz. Clastic quartz rocks (sandstones and siltstones) do not belong to this group.

---

* A.B. Ronov, "Volcanism, carbonate accumulation, life (regularities of the global geochemistry of carbon)", *Geochemistry*, 8, 1268 (1976).

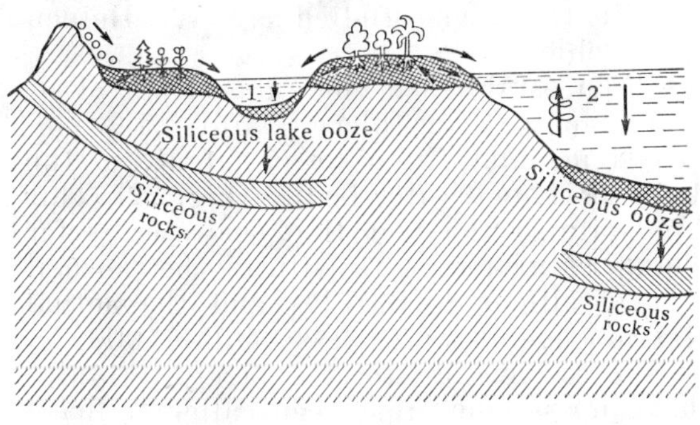

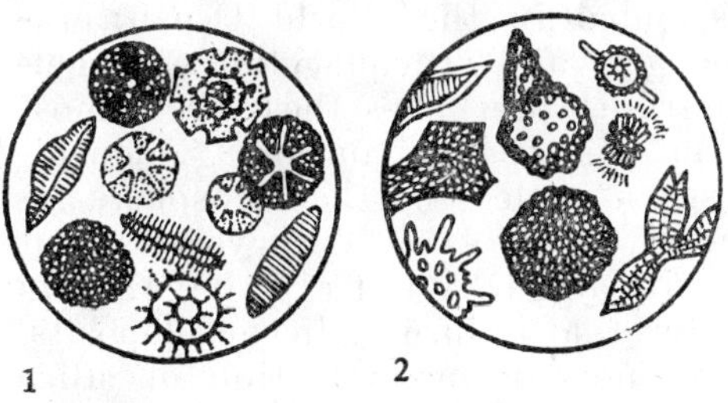

Fig. 22. Diagram of formation of siliceous rocks:

1—fresh-water siliceous plankton; *2*—marine siliceous plankton

"The entire history of silicon in the ocean is completely dependent on life processes", wrote Vernadsky*. Scientific advances during the last half century have confirmed this. The mechanism of silicon concentration by living mat-

---

* W. Vernadsky, "La matière vivante et la chimie de la mer", *Rev. gén. des. sci*, **35**, 1, 5-13; 2, 46-54 (1924).

ter has recently been studied by W. Heinen and J.H. Oehler*.

It has been established that deposition of siliceous sediments takes place mainly in marine ecosystems and, to a lesser extent, in the ecosystems of inland water bodies (Fig. 22). This is so in spite of the fact that seawater is far from being saturated with silica: the normal solubility of silicon is 0.012% and the actual concentration is 30 times less—only 0.0004%.

Organisms responsible for the precipitation of silica have for a long time been called "siliceous". These are diatoms (containing 90% of all the silica suspended in the World Ocean), radiolarians, sponges, and silicoflagellatae (flagellate algae); in fresh-water lakes these are almost exclusively diatoms. Some authors** consider that the silica cycle in the biosphere is regulated exclusively by the eucaryotes. But W. E. Krumbein and D. Werner*** have shown that cyanobacteria also form siliceous deposits. No signs of chemogenic precipitation of silica

* W. Heinen, J.H. Oehler, "Evolutionary aspects of biological involvement in the cycling of silica". In: "*Biogeochemical Cycling of Mineral-forming Elements*" (ed. P.A. Trudinger, D.J. Swain), Elsevier, Amsterdam a.o., 1979, pp. 431-443.

** A.N. Knoll and S.W. Awramik, "Ancient microbial ecosystems". In: *Microbial Geochemistry* (ed. W.E. Krumbein), Oxford a.o., Blackwell Sci. Publ., 1983, pp. 287-315.

*** W.E. Krumbein and D. Werner, "The microbial silica cycle". In: *Microbial Geochemistry* (ed. W.E. Krumbein), Oxford a.o., Blackwell Sci. Publ., 1983, pp. 125-157, *op. cit.*, pp. 125-157.

Modern marine diatoms. Scanning electron micrograph. 2000-fold magnification. (Published in the Russ. ed. of "TBB".)

have been detected in modern aqueous ecosystems*.

Among siliceous rocks, predominantly composed of the skeletal remains of organisms, four types are distinguished: diatomites, silicoflagellites, radiolarites, and spongolites. The first three types of siliceous rocks are planktonogenic; spongolites are benthogenic formations.

Silicon accumulation in the ocean occurs mostly in areas where there is mass proliferation of diatoms (the greatest concentrations of them are observed in upwelling zones). In the contemporary biosphere, however, siliceous sediments are not accumulated in all the areas where diatoms are extensively developed. The hydrodynamic factor and supply of terrigenous and carbonate biogenic material also play an important role: pure siliceous sediments, naturally, do not accumulate in those locations where the role of these sedimentation components is significant.

---

* H.E. Harper, Jr., A. H. Knoll, "Silica, diatoms, and Cenozoic radiolarian evolution", *Geology*, 3, 4, 175-177 (1975).

Diatomites are light (white or yellowish) finely porous rocks, the main bulk of which is composed of the microscopic tests of diatoms*. The number of unbroken tests of diatoms in 1 cm³ reaches several million. Diatomites exhibit uncommon properties for rocks: they are very soft (one can write on a board with a piece of diatomite), porous (their porosity reaches 70-90%), and finally, they are light-weight: the volume weight of a lump does not exceed 1, and in some cases is equal to as little as 0.5-0.7 and even 0.25-0.3 g/cm³. (There is an interesting story about Fersman. Apparently even when he was on vacation, he collected stones all the same. The porter at the railway station could not help wondering: "What a heavy suitcase! You have not stuffed it with stones, have you, sir?" Had Fersman collected diatomites, the porter would have had no grounds for grumbling.)

To understand the unusual properties of diatomites, one should consider the initial material they are composed of—diatoms.

The word "diatom" stems from the Greek "diatomos", meaning cut in two. Tests of diatoms, indeed, consist of two parts, one part entering the other. If we compare the tests of diatoms with things customary to us, then, perhaps, they most closely resemble a perforated split case for a toothbrush, the difference being in that diatoms are porous over the entire surface of their body and have a more diverse

---

* T.E. Ross, "Diatomite: origin, occurrences, and uses", *Rocks a. Minerals*, **57**, 4, 145-147 (1982).

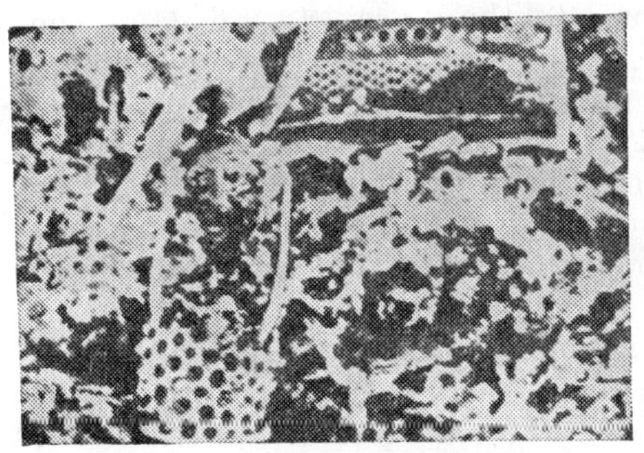

Marine diatomite. Scanning electron micrograph. 750-fold magnification. (Published in the Russ. ed. of "TBB".)

shape: they can be disk-shaped, fusiform, prismatic, etc. It is, therefore, not surprising that rocks consisting of these tests are lighter than water and avidly absorb moisture (apply the test rock to your tongue, and, if the rock is diatomite, it will stick to it).

Diatoms proliferate at a tremendous rate of reproduction. Under favourable conditions the number of cells may double every 4 hours. The layer of biogenic silica accumulating in the World Ocean owing to diatoms alone may reach from 7.5 to 30 cm in one thousand years.

Marine diatomites have been known since the Late Cretaceous period and occur as strata with a thickness of dozens and even hundreds of metres. The thickest beddings of diatomites, reaching 1600 m, are found in the United States, in California (Lompoc Field of Miocenic age).

Lake diatomites are younger (fresh-water diatoms appeared only in the Eocene epoch) and are less widespread; they are found in the Caucasus, in the Far East, in the Carpathians, in the north of Western Europe.

The regularities of silicon accumulation in small lakes have been studied in detail by L.L. Rossolimo. It was established that these accumulations occur mostly in moderate and high latitudes. In some cases (but far from always) they occur in volcanic areas: volcanism is an additional source of mineral food for diatoms. If volcanic material is not introduced, an extensive development of persilicic crystalline rocks subject to intensive weathering is a prerequisite for silicon accumulation in lakes. Specific morphological features of the lakes in which silica is accumulated have also been established as follows: shallow water (predominantly with a depth of 3-4 m) ensuring sufficient aeration of the entire mass of water, and a small water area of the lake or its subdivision into autonomous parts (this precludes the motion of water at a considerable speed and hinders the accumulation of oozy sediment). A smooth relief of the surroundings and the presence of mossy cover favour silicon accumulation. A. A. Arutyunyan has noted that diatomites of small lakes are characterized by high purity, whereas in large lakes they are of usually low purity, and the preservation of the tests of diatoms is poor. As regards silicon accumulation in large lakes, it obeys marine rather than lake "laws".

If diatomites are the most widespread among biogenic siliceous rocks, then silicoflagellites, which have been recently described for the first time, are the most rare. They are composed of the skeletons of other representatives of phytoplankton—siliceous flagellate algae or silicoflagellatae. Usually skeletons of these algae can also de encountered in small quantities in diatomites, but in Neogenic formations in South-East Europe silicoflagellites make up individual strata.

Radiolarites, like the preceding types of siliceous rocks, are composed of plankton remains, but, in contrast to diatoms and silicoflagellatao, they are composed of zooplankton rather than phytoplankton. Accordingly, they occur below the euphotic zone, encompassing a portion of the aphotic zone. The major part of the radiolarian biomass is, nevertheless, confined to the upper 250 metres of the ocean water (radiolarians are exclusively marine animals). The name "radiolarian" stems from the Latin "radius", meaning ray. The microscopic skeleton of radiolarians is an intricate spherical openwork structure, with long spicules extending in all directions from the sphere with strict regularity. One might think that radiolarians were created by nature specially to illustrate the laws of symmetry and perfection.

In one book radiolarians were described as the "most elegant and beautiful formations which exist in the animal world". And though this author is inclined to share the opinion of the ancient Greeks, who maintained that the beautiful human body is the most perfect creation of nature, the elegance of radiolarians is, indeed, worthy of our admiration (Fig. 23).

Radiolarians occurred in the Cambrian peri-

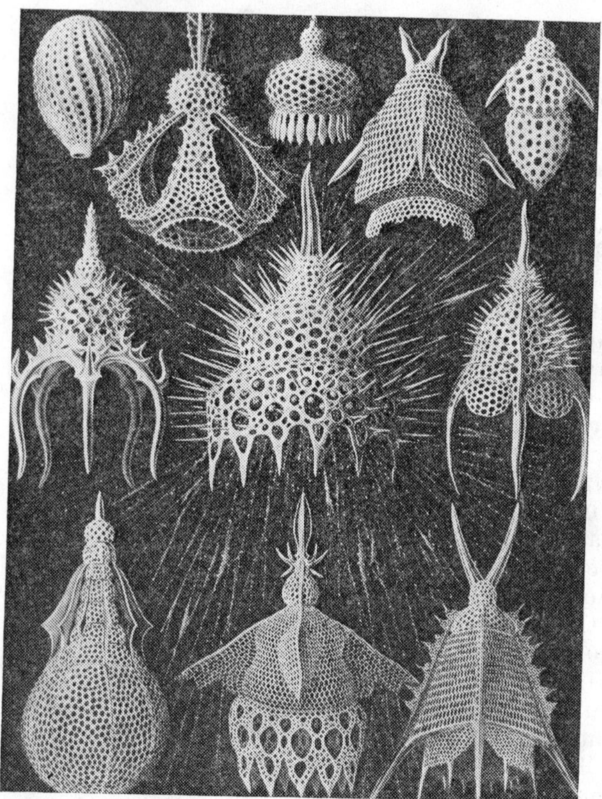

Fig. 23. Radiolarians (sheets from E. Haeckel's album "The Beauty of Forms in Nature")

od. They belong to the number of those rare organisms which were first discovered in the fossil state and only later found in the present-day biosphere.

Radiolarites are less widespread in the meta-biosphere than diatomites, but the thickness of their strata reaches 38 m (Paleogene of Barbados). The distribution of radiolarites in the sedimentary shell of the Earth has recently been studied by H.R. Grunau* and M. Steinberg**. Radiolarian clays, i.e., rocks in which radiolarian skeletons are liberally diluted with terrigenous material, are considerably more widespread (as compared with "normal" radiolarites).

Regarding spongolites, some time ago they were considered as quite rare, but now beddings of marine spongolites, with a thickness of up to 10-15 m, have been discovered in the Cretaceous and Paleogene deposits of the Ukraine, in the Paleogene of the Caucasus, in the Cretaceous deposits of Central Europe, in the Paleozoic of the Urals Territory and the North-East of the Soviet Union, and in other regions. Freshwater spongolites have also been found; their thickness in the Eocene of Kazakhstan reaches 6-10 m.

Spongolites are rather diverse in appearance. They are homogeneous fine-grained rocks, greyish-green and black in colour, consisting of spicules of bottom-dwelling animals—the so-called "siliceous" sponges. Spicules are structural elements of the skeleton of sponges. When the sponges are alive, these structural elements are bound together into a skeleton by

---

* H.R. Grunau, "Radiolarian cherts and associated rocks in space and time", *Ecl. Geol. Helvetica*, 58, 157-208 (1965).

** M. Steinberg, "Biosiliceous sedimentation radiolarite periods and silica budget fluctuations", *Oceanologica acta*, suppl., No. spec., pp. 149-154 (1981).

organic matrix; after the death of the sponges their skeletons disintegrate into separate spicules. The length of the spicules may reach 2 to 3 mm, their cross-section is as little as a few hundredths of a millimetre, and their shape may be quite diverse ranging from simple (needle-like) to bent and star-like. Spicules resemble the letters "C" or "S", all kinds of fish-hooks, tridents, yokes, etc.

Recent spongolites have been found in the Barents Sea, where "glass wool" from the spicules of siliceous sponges makes up a layer as thick as 30 to 60 cm. Since spicules account for only a few percent of the total volume of the body of siliceous sponges, considerable accumulations of these organisms are required for the formation of spongolites. Recent spongolites are found at depths of 250 to 500 m; at greater depths the population density of sponges is, evidently, insufficient for the accumulation of pure varieties of spongolites.

It's beyond dispute that all of the four types of rocks discussed above are composed of biogenic silica (opal). The origin of some other siliceous rocks: (tripolis, gaizes, jaspers) is, however, a subject of discussion. Organic remains in them are rather rare, and many lithologists consider these rocks to be chemogenic. There is one opinion, however, that gaizes and tripolis have formed from diatomites, and spongolites and jaspers, from radiolarites, which lost their initial structure in the course of diagenetic and katagenetic processes*.

____

* S.I. Shumenko, "Nanopetrography of tripolis and gaizes in connection with the question of their genesis", *Doklady AN SSSR*, **240**, 2, 427-430 (1978).

As early as at the end of the last century, Academician F.N. Chernyshev, after whom the Museum of Geological Prospecting in Leningrad is named, found remains of a rich fauna of radiolarians in jaspers from the South Urals. "Our jaspers are, without a doubt, abyssal slime", wrote Chernyshev in 1889, "and the silica of radiolarian skeletons furnished the fundamental material for the accumulations of quartz, scattered throughout the rock mass". In the first decades of the twentieth century, Ya.V. Samoilov* suggested the predominantly biogenic origin of siliceous rocks.

Siliceous sediments are formed in the biosphere as a result of the concentration function of living matter. Both in the recent geological epoch and in the geological past (beginning with the Cambrian Period), the accumulation of biogenic silica has proceeded mainly in marine ecosystems. If initially it was effected by the benthic film of life (siliceous sponges) and by zooplankton (radiolarians), beginning with the end of the Mesozoic era, the main role in silicon accumulation has been taken over by phytoplankton (diatoms).

Silicon accumulation in lakes began only in the Eocene epoch with the appearance of fresh-water forms of diatoms and sponges, and it is less significant.

A specific factor controlling the biogenic ac-

---

* Ya.V. Samoilov, E.V. Rozhkova, "Deposits of silica of organic origin", *Trans. of the Institute of Applied Mineralogy*, 1925, Issue 18, pp. 1-76 (in Russian).

cumulation of silicon is a rich supply of silica to the ecosystem. This can be effected in different ways: in marine and fresh-water ecosystems, by the supply of volcanic products or dissolved products from the weathering of acidic rocks; in marine ecosystems, in addition to the above sources, by the upward movement of abyssal water, which is enriched with silicon and phosphorus.

Geological evidence (starting from the Paleozoic era) and recent data have established that the supply of volcanic products intensifies the vital activity of all groups of siliceous organisms. These organisms, however, are not omnivorous, and the type of volcanic products determines the predominant development of this or that species. As has been shown by I.V. Khvorova, the formation of substantially radiolarian deposits in geosynclinal strata is localized in areas where the main effusive volcanism develops, while the accumulation of diatomites is associated with the appearance of large amounts of a fine suspension of acid volcanic glass in the mass of water.

When an undertaking is hopeless, people sometimes say they are "going on a wild-goose chase". A task, perhaps still more difficult than wild-goose chasing, is that of tracing currents which existed millions of years ago in the sea. Siliceous rocks provide us with a clue here: guided by these rocks, one can successfully reveal ancient upwelling concentrations of life. Thus, recently the Ukrainian scientist Yu.N. Sen'kovsky, based on investigations of siliceous rocks, outlined an upwelling in the sea which existed in the Cretaceous Period on the territory of the Carpathians, and N.A. Brewster of the United States outlined an upwelling in the Neogene sea of the Antarctic.

We shall conclude our story about siliceous rocks with a recently published statement by Vernadsky: "Though in the history of silicon the role of organisms is not as dramatic as in the history of calcium, even here the history of the given chemical element cannot be understood by us without it (i.e. the role of siliceous organisms.—*A.L.*)*.

Caustobioliths are a third group of sedimentary rocks, characterized by considerable concentrations of biogenic matter. About one hundred years ago mankind was forced to become interested in caustobioliths. "Now, when Russia will shortly be pierced by railways in various directions, when even in Moscow one has sometimes to pay 45 roubles in banknotes for a tolerable sazhen of birch firewood, now public attention is of necessity directed to finding new combustible material, which is expected to be obtained either in coal, or in peat." These lines date back to 1857, and today mankind annually burns a quantity of caustobioliths equal to that accumulated by bygone biospheres over a million years. It is an ill wind that blows nobody good, and humanity has again, of necessity, turned its attention to renewable sources of energy, to living matter, and more specifically, to the green mass of plants, from which, by

---

* V.I. Vernadsky, *Living Matter*, Nauka, Moscow, 1978, p. 60 (in Russian).

processing with anaerobic bacteria, combustible gas is produced*.

The term "caustobioliths" is composed of three Greek words: "kaustos" (burning), "bios" (life), and "lithos" (stone). Peats, sapropels, coal, oil shales and petroleum—recent sediments and rocks, composed mainly of biogenic organic matter, are caustobioliths.

"Organic matter, penetrating all the substances of the Earth's crust accessible for study, is all of biogenic origin... Through the agency of slow geological processes these organic substances, the remains of the bodies and metabolism of organisms enter the stratisphere from the biosphere, into the metamorphic envelope"**, wrote Vernadsky.

The most intensive accumulation of organic matter in the present-day biosphere occurs in swamps and in some lakes. The accumulation of neobiogenic organic matter in oceans is a separate question.

It is not always easy to define everyday concepts. For instance, it is difficult to define what a swamp is. One definition reads as follows: "A swamp can be characterized as a lake, but with bound water, or as land, but containing 90% water and only 10% dry matter." Indeed, one part of dry peat is capable of retaining from 15 to 25 parts of water! Vast areas of the Soviet Union are characterized by optimal conditions

---

* J.G. Zeikus, "Chemical and fuel production by anaerobic bacteria", *Ann. Rev. Microbiol.*, **34**, 423-464 (1980).

** **V.I. Vernadsky**, *Works*, v. 4, Bk. 2, p. 93 (in Russian).

for peat accumulation, e.g., adjacent to the Baltic Sea, Byelorussia, the northern part of the Ukraine, the north of the European part of the USSR, West Siberia, and the Far East. Sixty percent of the world's resources of peat are in the Soviet Union.

Climatic conditions are a "triggering mechanism" for the formation of swamps. As the peat lands develop, the role of climatic factors diminishes. The main factor becomes the accumulation of peat itself, which changes all the environmental conditions. The swamp gradually turns into an ecosystem, developing to a considerable extent in accordance with its own internal laws and relatively independent of the environment.

In addition to the landscape-climatic prerequisites for peat accumulation there also exist ecological ones: these are factors limiting the development of consumers of autotrophic living matter (this has already been discussed in the preceding chapter), e.g., deficiency of nitrogen. Thus, for intensive mineralization of neobiogenic organic matter by saprotrophs, the carbon/nitrogen content ratio must be within the range of 20 to 25. In swamps this ratio is higher and, therefore, the decomposition of biogenic organic matter proceeds at a slower rate.

Emphasizing the specific conditions for caustobiolith formation, the well-known Soviet geologist K.G. Voinovsky-Krieger (1894-1979) wrote: "The accumulation of vegetable mass, evidently, obeys other regularities than those for the accumulation of sand and silt. In this case, in addition to the geomorphological factor, a biological factor participates, and perhaps even plays the main role".

Thus, the accumulation of the neobiogenic organic matter of peats is controlled by the ecological factor. The transformation of peats into paleobiogenic matter is determined by another factor—the geological one (tapho-factor). Seaside and littoral-lake peat bogs in the zones of subsidence of the Earth's crust have maximum chances of passing into the fossil state.

Another type of ecosystem in which the accumulation of neobiogenic organic matter takes place is inland water bodies. It is of interest to consider the relationship between the depth of the water body and the percentage of organic matter subject to burial. Thus, in the lakes of Lithuania with an average depth of 3 m, 2/3 of the annual production of phytoplankton is buried; with a depth of 3 to 10 m, 1/3; and in those deeper than 10 m, only 1/10.

In contrast to peat bogs, in inland water bodies it is not the remains of higher plants, but of sapropel (from the Greek "sapros" + "pēlos", meaning "rotten from phytoplankton slime"): an accumulation of debris and zooplankton, bottom-dwelling and freely floating organisms, and excrements of animals. A large contribution to the study of recent sapropels has been made by N.V. Cordet.

Finally, biogenic organic matter in the present-day biosphere accumulates also in marine ecosystems, mainly in shallow lagoons. The basic factor which controls the accumulation of neobiogenic matter in the World Ocean is circumcontinental zonation. According to data reported by the Soviet geochemist E.A. Roman-kevich,* V.I. Vernadsky prize winner of 1978, in the peripheral areas of the ocean, comprising shelves, continental slopes and near-continent abyssal troughs, 87% of the entire organic matter of the ocean is accumulated; in the marginal portion of the ocean bed, 10%; and in central areas, about 3%.

This is how the accumulation of organic matter occurs in the present-day biosphere. (The formation of caustobioliths is diagrammatically presented in Fig. 24.) The accumulation of biogenic organic matter in the geological past proceeded in a similar manner. "The formation of coals is associated with bogs, with large accumulations of plants, characteristic of countries with moist climates, in the outfalls and deltas of large rivers, in the plains of their basins, on the coasts of continents and islands, and in tidal flats. All these are large concentrations of life, where the mass of organic matter, found in a state of slow decomposition, is tremendous. Possibly, these are the largest concentrations of life on land that we know of",** wrote Vernadsky.

Coals have existed since the Devonian, i.e., since the time when plants spread from the sea to the littoral areas of continents. Black and, at first sight, unprepossessing, coals (in thin sections), when viewed under a microscope, fascinate one by the range of orange-red hues they display. They are composed mainly of coalified

---

* E.A. Romankevich, *Geochemistry of Organic Matter in the Ocean*, Berlin a.o., Springer-Verlag, 1984.
** W. Vernadsky, *La géochimie*, Alcan, Paris, 1924, p. 253.

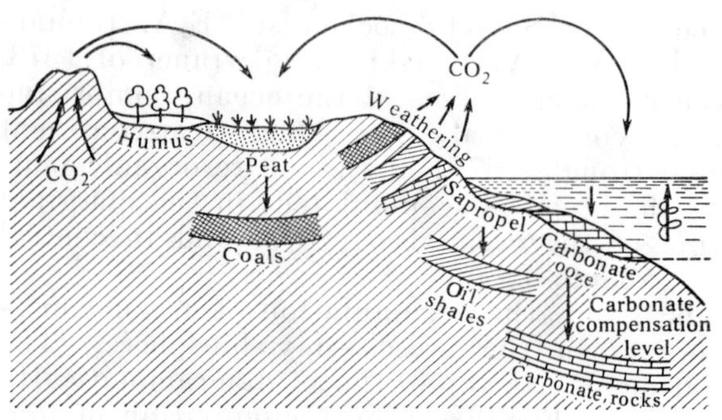

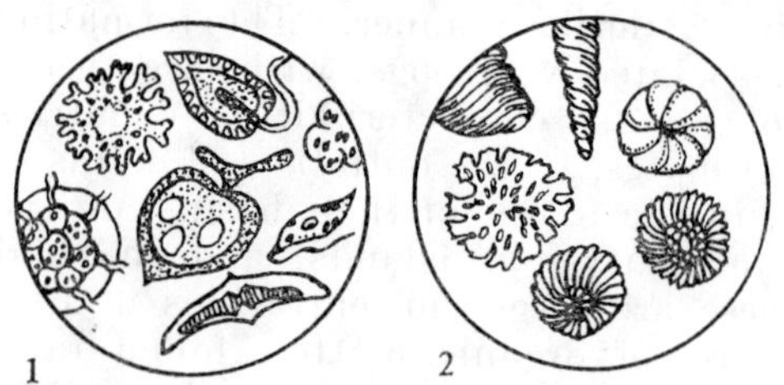

Fig. 24. Formation of caustobioliths and carbonate rocks:

1—sapropel-forming organisms; *2*—carbonate organisms

vegetable tissues, which are called phyterals (the suffix is the same as in the word "mineral", and the Greek root "phyto-" means "a plant"). In recent years methods for their analysis have been elaborated. With these methods the initial organ of a plant, its taxonomy, and the process of its conversion into coal are determined*.

---

* A.V. Lapo, "Phyterals of Jurassic coals of Tuva", *The Palaeobotanist*, **25**, 205-216 (1978).

Mesozoic coal composed
of compressed leaves of
Czekanowskia. The Lena
Coal Basin. Photographed
by the author. Somewhat
diminished. (Published in
the Russ. ed. of "TBB".)

From these data one can get an idea about the
vegetation which served as the initial material
for the formation of coal.

The composition of coal was subject to substantial changes during the course of geological
history.*   In Carboniferous coals there are
many spores; in Late Carboniferous coals massive trunks of woody plants appear for the first
time (earlier, woody plants were predominantly
tubular like present-day bamboo, or had a loose
central portion like reed); in the Mesozoic era
the coals are pressed from leaves or from resin
needles; for the Paleogene and Neogene periods
lignites are characteristic, which are remains of
conifers with a macroscopically distinguishable

---

* Yu.A. Zhemchuzhnikov, "Development of coal
accumulation in geological history", *Izv. AN SSSR*, geol.
series, 3, 57-82, (1955).

Lignite—a trunk of Sequoioxylon, buried at the site of its growth in a coal bed of Neogene age. Hungary. (From: *A Magyar Allami Földtani Intézet... az 1977 évröl* (1979), p. 48.)

structure of wood, etc. From the composition of phyterals it is possible to determine approximately the age of coals.

Biogenic matter formed by heterotrophs is rather seldom encountered in coals. These are mainly fungi, most widespread in Paleogene and Neogene coals. Remains of bacteria, anthropods, and vertebrates have also been found. The most surprising findings were made in two brown coal fields of Central Europe: Geiseltal (Paleogene) in the German Democratic Republic and Turow (Neogene) in Poland. There, remnants of a surprisingly rich and diverse fauna of vertebrates were found (recall the above-cited statement by Vernadsky about the "largest concentrations of life"): fishes, amphibians, reptiles (crocodiles, lizards, snakes), birds, and, finally, mammals (tapirs, horses, marsupial rats, bats, prosimians). In the coal from one of the small coal fields of Italy, M. Teichmüller, the prominent West German specialist in coal petrography,* found the remains of a young individual of a "near-man"—an anthropoid ape belonging to a genus allied to ours. The baby had drowned in a swamp.

While coals correspond to ancient peats, combustible shales were formed from sapropels which sometimes accumulate in lacustrine, and more often, in marine ecosystems. Strakhov, who studied this problem in detail, distinguishes the following types of oil shales: (a) pelagic planktonogenic oil shales; (b) pelagic benthogenic oil shales; (c) oil shales of flood and pre-estuarine types; (d) oil shales of reef type (the latter are rarely encountered). It is easy to see that these types of oil shales are formed by various concentrations of life, by the planktonic and benthic films of life, by the rear-shore and reef concentrations of life.

In all cases the biogenic material of oil shales was intensively processed by benthic organisms and, therefore, it is difficult to identify organic remains in oil shales. Nevertheless, the Soviet paleobotanist M.D. Zalessky (1877-1946) has carried out classical investigations of the initial vegetable material of some Paleozoic and Mesozoic oil shales. The French specialist in coal petrography Boris Alpern came

---

* M. Teichmüller, "Die Oreopitecus—fuhrende Kohle von Bacinello bei Grosseto (Toskana, Italien)", *Geol. Jahrb.* **80**, 69-80 (1963).

to the conclusion that the predominant constituets of the organic matter of Paleozoic oil shales are the remains of the fresh-water alga Botrycoccus braunii, while for Mesozoic oil shales algae Tasmanites and cyanobacteria Nostocopsis are characteristic. In the Ordovician deposits of the Baltic Region so-called "dictyonemic shales" occur, in which organic matter is represented by the remains of graptolites—extinct organisms related to the phylum of coelenterates.

At one time the problem of the genesis of petroleum caused a lot of argument. However, investigations carried out by the school of petroleum scientists, headed by the Corresponding Member of the USSR Academy of Sciences N.B. Vassoyevich (1902-1981) led to a theory about the origin of petroleum from biogenic organic matter which was open to less and less doubt.

The school of Vassoyevich developed a theory of petroleum formation called "sedimentary-migrational".* According to this theory petroleum is "a child of lithogenesis". Remains of the organisms of the planktonic film of life serve as the raw material for petroleum. If the depth of the water body is not great and the conditions for burial are favourable, organic matter, comprising the remains of plankton, passes to the fossil state. The "birth" of petroleum as a liquid phase of hydrocarbons, separat-

---

* N.B. Vassoyevich, *Selected Works. Geochemistry of Organic Matter and Origin of Petroleum*, Moscow, Nauka, 1986 (in Russian).

ing from scattered organic matter, takes place in the Earth's crust within the so-called "principal zone of oil generation" located at a depth of 2 to 6 km below the Earth's surface, where temperatures range from 60 to 160 °C (it is precisely in this sense that petroleum is "the child of lithogenesis").

The isotopic composition of the carbon in petroleum provides proof that petroleum really formed from biogenic organic matter. In biogenic and abiogenic matter the ratio of carbon isotopes is not the same, and, therefore, they can be distinguished by this characteristic. Moreover, "biomolecules" have been found in petroleum, i.e., compounds which have analogues in living nature and which, thus, also bear witness to the biogenic character of the initial material of petroleum.

Vassoyevich has shown that to a considerable extent Vernadsky's views served as the basis for these conceptions. In the world literature the organic theory of the origin of petroleum is dominant.*-**

The overall reserves of caustobioliths are expressed by a figure of $n \cdot 10^{13}$ tons. However, according to the calculations of Vassoyevich, this is only 0.36% of the entire organic carbon contained in the sedimentary rocks of the continental sector of the Earth's sedimentary en-

---

* J.W. Hunt, *Petroleum Geochemistry and Geology.* Freeman a. Co., San Francisco, 1979.

** B.P. Tissot, D.H. Welte, *Petroleum Formation and Occurrence*, Springer, Berlin a.o., 1978, p. 538.

velope. Biogenic organic matter, like silica and possibly carbonates, is represented in the metabiosphere mainly in dispersed form.

Thus, the paleobiogenic organic matter of the metabiosphere has formed both on land (because of the activity of the terrestrial film of life) and in the ecosystems of inland water bodies and of the World Ocean (in the case of aquatic ecosystems, mainly because of plankton). Investigations carried out by A.V. Van demonstrated that volcanic activity strongly intensifies the accumulation of biogenic organic matter, first of all, owing to an enhancement of the productivity of living matter (discussed in Chapter Four). In the formation of caustobioliths the concentration function of living matter is manifested, but the energetic function is dominant. This very circumstance enables us, when we burn caustobioliths, to use the energy of sunbeams dating from millions of years back. It is not without reason that caustobioliths are called "tinned solar goods".

As a characteristic feature of caustobioliths Vernadsky emphasized the evolution of their composition and properties. "They (caustobioliths.—*A.L.*) display individuality and uniqueness in geological time and are a historical phenomenon, expressed in their extreme chemical diversity and can be simply explained by the fact that for every geological moment the organisms, whose bodies they represent, were unique, sharply different chemically, and as different as those microbes which had caused their formation and whose bodies enter into their composition... In caustobioliths we see a clear manifestation of the evolutionary process."* Extensive investigations in this direction are being undertaken.

Biogenic matter is not present in all sedimentary rocks in such high concentrations as are found in carbonate rocks, siliceous rocks, and in caustobioliths. In phosphatic, iron-bearing, and manganese rocks the content of biogenic matter is lower.

Phosphatic rocks usually contain at least 10% phosphorus oxide. The main minerals containing phosphorus are finely dispersed minerals of the apatite group. Phosphate rocks containing 12 to 40% phosphorus oxide are considered a mineral resource—phosphorites. Several types of phosphorites are distinguished: bedded phosphatic rocks, nodular phosphorites, coquinoid phosphorites, bone beds and guano. Ninety-five percent of all reserves of phosphorites are confined to marine sediments.

The thickness of bedded phosphatic rocks reaches 15 to 17 m. There is nothing specific in their appearance. Sometimes they are white like chalk, but more often their colour is dark, almost black. The absence of distinct macroscopic features in phosphorites is often misleading for geologists. Thus, in the thirties in Kazakhstan (Karatau) phosphorites were first mistaken for bauxites. One Siberian deposit was discovered not in the field, but on the upper floor of the Palace of Geology, in the Chernyshev Central

---

* V.I. Vernadsky, *The Chemical Structure of the Earth's Biosphere and Its Surroundings*, Nauka, Moscow, 1965, p. 269 (in Russian).

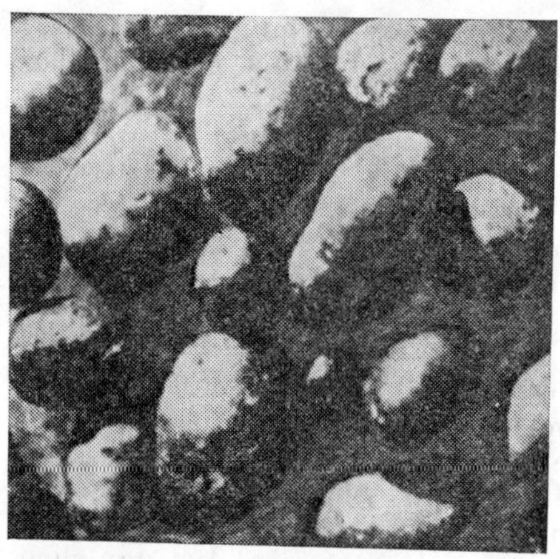

Small phosphatized coprolites. 25-fold magnification. Kazakhstan. Photographed by G.I. Bushinsky. (From: *Priroda*, 1980, 6, p. 26.)

Museum of Geological Prospecting. There, in 1949, N.A. Krasil'nikova, a prominent expert in phosphorites, while looking through the collection at the museum, came across an interesting specimen. According to the inscription on the label of the specimen, dating as far back as twenty five years, the specimen had been classified as sandstone, but in reality it turned out to be a high-quality phosphorite. Evidently, such mistakes also happened earlier: the very name "apatite" stems from the Greek "apatao", which means "I deceive".

The discovery of a large deposit of phosphorite on the small island of Nauru, lost in the expanses of the Pacific, to the southeast of Australia, is just as unusual.

They say that it all began in 1897, when an Australian sailor, who happened to be on that island, picked up a strange stone from the ground and brought it to his native land. In Sydney it was used for propping open the door of an office, until in 1900, A. Ellis, a geologist from New Zealand, noticed it. On the basis of chemical analysis Ellis came to the conclusion that the stone was top-quality phosphorite. The following year the geolo-

Sandstone with numerous shells of Obolus—so-called "obolus sandstone". The Ordovician of Estonia. (Published in the Russ. ed. of "TBB".)

gist set off for Nauru and discovered that almost the entire surface of the island was covered with a thick layer of phosphorite. The phosphorite quarry now occupies 1/3 of the territory of the island, and the annual output of phosphorite per each inhabitant of Nauru, old men, women and children included, is 250 tons. Naturally, almost all the phosphorite is exported.

Nodular phosphorites are aggregates of individual or partially fused-together nodules. The saturation of rock with nodules varies; pieces of bones and phosphatized organic remains (wood, shells of mollusks, etc.) are also encoun-

Working of guano on the Islands of Chincha (Peru). From
the photograph taken by G.E. Hutchinson in the forties.
(Published in the Russ. ed. of "TBB".)

tered. In addition, sometimes phosphatized
coprolites are present. Coquinoid phosphorites
occur mainly in Ordovician deposits. These are
sandstones or conglomerates, crammed with
shells of inarticulate brachiopods. The so-called
"Obolus sandstones" of Estonia, with a thickness of up to 11 m and including the remains of
Obolus and Schmidtia, are a typical example.

A rather rare type of phosphorite is bone
breccias. These are porous rocks, yellowish-
brown in colour, consisting of fragments of
fish skeletons or those of cave vertebrates. Finally, the last item on the list of phosphorites
is guano, which are tremendous accumulations
(up to 35 m thick) of the excrement of sea birds
(on islands and ocean coasts) or of bats (in
caves). On the Islands of Chincha, near the coast
of Latin America, the layer of guano annually
accumulated is 8 cm thick. A classical investigation of guano deposits was carried out in

the late forties by Hutchinson. His bulky (over 500-page) monograph* remains unsurpassed in its profound and thorough treatment of the material. It is usually cited in any publication dealing with the geochemistry of phosphorus.

These are the most characteristic types of phosphorites. Their origin has been the subject of discussion for many years. The difficulty of the problem resides in that the remains of the organisms which formed phosphorites are rarely preserved in them (bone breccias and Obolus sandstones are exceptions). At the same time, scientists have long suspected that living matter must play an important role in the formation of phosphorites (Fig. 25).

The biogeochemistry of phosphorus on a global scale was considered by Hutchinson**. D. McConnell*** has listed 76 phosphorus-containing minerals which are most likely formed as a result of the activity of living matter. Bones of vertebrates contain up to 60% calcium phosphate. The content of calcium phosphate is still higher in the shells of inarticulate brachiopods. It is of interest to note that the shell of brachiopods be-

---

* G.E. Hutchinson, "Survey of contemporary knowledge of biogeochemistry. 3. The biogeochemistry of vertebrate excretion". *Bull. Am. Muss. Nat. Hist.*, **96**, 554 (1950).

** G.E. Hutchinson, "The biogeochemistry of phosphorus". In: *The Biology of Phosphorus* (ed. L.F. Wolterink), St. Coll. Press, Mich., 1952, pp. 1-35.

*** D. McConnell, "Biogeochemistry of phosphate minerals". In: *Biogeochemical Cycling of Mineral-Forming Elements* (ed. P.A. Trudinger, D.J. Swaine), Elsevier, Amsterdam a.o., 1979, pp. 163-204.

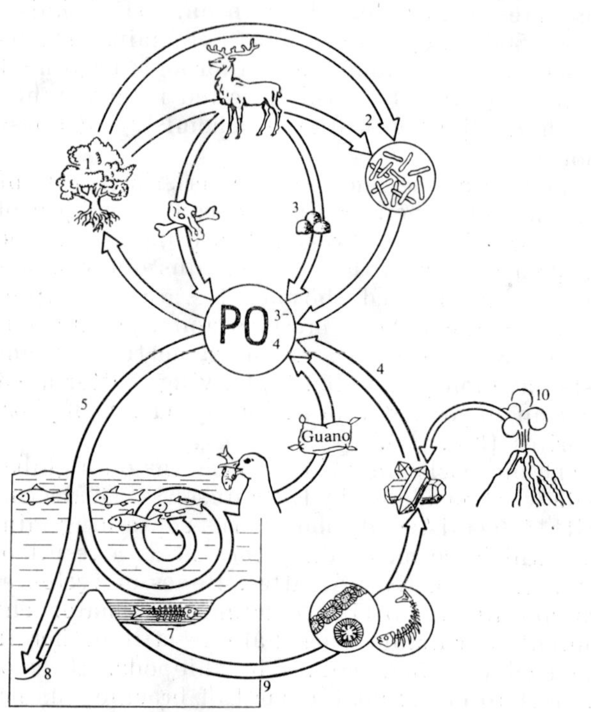

Fig. 25. The biogeochemical cycle of phosphorus (after Duvigneaud, 1974):

1—accumulation of phosphorus by higher plants; 2—decomposition of neobiogenic organic matter; 3—excrement; 4—erosion; 5—coming to the ocean; 6—volcanic apatite; 7—precipitation in bottom sediments at small depth; 8—precipitation in bottom sediments at considerable depths; 9—transition to fossil state; 10—involvement into biological cycle by diatoms

longing to a different order, to the order of articulates, consists not of phosphate, but of calcium carbonate. In plankton as a whole the content of phosphorus dioxide is many orders of magnitude higher than in seawater*. Fish scales and skeletons are also rich in phosphorus. Carapaces of crustaceans contain up to 50% calcium phosphate. If we take into account that crustaceans frequently change their "clothes" and that their lower forms occur in seas in tremendous quantities, then the role of crustaceans in the creation of phosphorites may prove to be of no small importance.

Phosphorus oxide is also concentrated in animal excrement (the first type of geological activity, effected outside of the organism). Thus, in the excrement of marine animals, the content of phosphorus oxide is 3.25 times higher than in the surrounding bottom sediments. An important piece of evidence arguing for the participation of living matter in the formation of phosphorites is also the high percentage of organic matter (up to 36% organic carbon) found in many phosphorites. Numerous examples of such phosphorite deposits were cited by V.L. Librovich in his paper read at the V Session of the All-Union Paleontological Society.

At the end of the nineteenth and beginning of the twentieth century a hypothesis was advanced that phosphorites form as a result of the mass death of organisms (J. Murray, R. Renard

---

* J. Lucas, L. Prevot, *Apatite synthesis—new data on genetic model for phosphate sedimentation*, 27 Int. Geol. Congr., Proc., Utrecht, VNU Sci. Press., 1984, v. 15

and L. Cayeux, A.D. Arkhangelsky). Bone breccias provide strong evidence in favour of this hypothesis. In modern seas, the sea floor in some areas is covered with a layer of dead fish up to 2 metres thick. The hypothesis proposed by Murray had been criticized for a long time, but it has now been shown* that mass asphyxiations of fish occur systematically at an interval of several years. This very phenomenon could lead to the accumulation of bone breccias.

Samoilov was an active supporter and promoter of the concept of the biogenic origin of phosphorites. "All deposits of phosphorites, with rare exceptions, are of organic origin; the phosphorus comprised in them has passed through the body of an animal", he wrote. Indeed, coprolites are often encountered in phosphorites. Small coprolites, of 0.2 to 1.0 mm in diameter, are frequent, but sometimes one may come across phosphatized coprolites of large animals, for instance, of ichthyosauri.

Studies of modern phosphorite nodules (concretions), which were discovered in the late sixties and early seventies on the shelves of South-West Africa, Chile, and Peru, performed by the well known geochemist G.N. Baturin, D.Sc. (geology and mineralogy)**, provided many new facts which contributed to our knowledge of the genesis of phosphorites. The modern phosphorite formations in these oceans were

---

* G.N. Baturin, "On the geological consequences of mass asphyxiations of ichthyofauna in oceans", *Oceanology*, 14, 1, 101-105 (1974).
** G.N. Baturin, "Phosphorites on the sea floor", *Devel. Sediment.*, v. 33, Amsterdam a.o., Elsevier, 1982.

found to be localized mainly in the zones of upwellings, and the dependence of the degree of
phosphate accumulation on the biological productivity can be traced quite clearly. The phosphorus in seawater is concentrated primarily by phytoplankton, while the phosphorus found in
sediment appears there chiefly in the form of
fecal pellets of zooplankton. In the course of diagenesis, the sediments become dehydrated and
gradually transform into compact phosphate grains and scirrhi. This phenomenon, first described
by Baturin, was acknowledged as a discovery in
1984 and was officially named the "Baturin
effect"*.

Living matter is likewise an important agent
for the diagenesis of neobiogenic phosphate contained in bottom sediments. In fact, the ultra-
microscopic biogenic components separated recently from modern bottom sediments on the
shelf of South-West Africa are most likely to be
the remains of bacteria that were involved in
the diagenetic production of phosphorites. Diagenetic phosphorite-forming processes run a wide
gamut, from phosphorite production by phosphatization of diatom oozes to phosphate nodules
that form in the tracks of ooze-eaters. Indeed, it
was selective phosphatization of coprolites and
the tracks of ooze-eaters that suggested to resear-
chers that enzymes have a part in the production
of phosphorites**. This had been proposed ear-

---

* *Science in USSR*, 2 (1985).
** G.I. Bushinsky, "Inhibitors and stimulators
in lithogenesis", *Lithology a. Miner. Res.*, 4, 494-497
(1967).

lier in general terms by G.I. Bushinsky (1903-1980).

Thus, one can be virtually certain today that the main bulk of phosphorite production in the contemporary biosphere develops in marine ecosystems, chiefly in upwelling concentration of life where the planktonic film is a leading factor in the accumulation of phosphorus. Ancient phosphorite accumulation that manifested itself on all the continents occurred most significantly during the late Proterozoic and early Cambrian periods. According to the Australian geologists P.J. Cook and J.H. Shergeold[*] and the Soviet geologists A.L. Yanshin, A.V. Ilyin, and E.A. Eganov[**], the environment and the conditions of phosphate accumulation at that time differed substantially from the modern circumstances. The phosphorus content in seawater was much higher than that at present. Among the living organisms which had a skeleton, the percentage of phosphate organisms was higher than at any other time in geological history. Phosphates accumulated on the shelves within the confines of the euphotic zone and were apparently not associated with upwelling (it is not for nothing that it is said that there is an exception to every rule). The formation of phosphorites of the type found in late Proterozoic and ear-

----

* P.J. Cook, J.H. Shergeold, "Late Proterozoic-Cambrian Phosphorites and Phosphogenesis", 27 Int. Geol. Congr., Proc., Utrecht, VNU Science Press, 1984, v. 15.

** A.L. Yanshin, A.V. Ilyin, A.E. Eganov, "Principal Problems on the Late Precambrian-Cambrian Phosphogenesis", *op. cit.*

A dinoflagellate Peridinium divergens. Strongly magnified. (A drawing from E. Haeckel's album *The Beauty of Forms in Nature*, St. Petersburg, 1905.)

ly Cambrian sediments never repeated itself in geological history.

Thus, the concentration function of living matter is nowhere more evident than in the formation of phosphate rocks, especially of phosphorites. And, while in the combustion of fossil fuels mankind makes use of the energy that living matter had stored millions of years ago, phosphorite fertilization of fields brings back into biotic circulation the phosphorus accumulated by the inhabitants of ancient seas. The transfer of neobiogenic substances from the sea to the con-

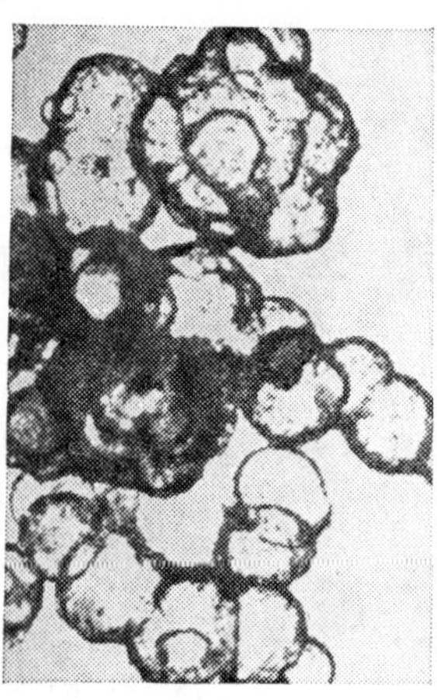

Ferrihydrite composed of remains of Gallionella. 30 000-fold magnification. Electron micrograph. (Published in the Russ. ed. of "TBB".)

tinents—the transportation function of living matter—is readily apparent in the accumulation of guano.

Next to be considered are the iron-bearing and manganese groups of sedimentary rocks. Since living matter performs similar functions in their formation, they will be discussed together. Iron-bearing sedimentary rocks occur as layers, lenses or nests. The layers sometimes extend to tens of kilometres in length and reach tens of metres in thickness. According to the mineral composition, their constituent rocks are classified into the following groups: oxidic, composed of iron oxides and hydroxides; carbonate, consisting mainly of siderite ($FeCO_3$); silicate, with dominant ferric chlorites; and mixed, involving iron-bearing rocks of oolitic texture and complex composition (hydroxides + silicates + iron carbonates, or hydroxides + iron silicates, and so on). In the Precambrian of the metabiosphere, iron-bearing quartzites and jaspilites, both iron-rich metamorphic rocks, are widespread. They are represented by banded rocks, with thin bands that are enriched with iron and silica to varying degrees. The key minerals are quartz, magnetite (Fe_3O_4) and hematite (Fe_2O_3); the percent iron content reaches 30 to 40%. Jaspilites are approximately two billion years old.

Sedimentary iron ores were produced in seas and swampy-lake locations, through interaction with minor quantities of terrigenous material. The marsh-lacustrine origin of Paleozoic and Mesozoic iron-bearing rocks was first proposed by Ya.V. Samoilov in a brief notice titled "On the genesis of iron ores in Central Russia" (1931), published posthumously*.

The main bulk of iron hydroxide entered the basins where it was transformed apparently into ferrihydrite, a recently discovered mineral from the group of iron hydroxides**. The type of transformation undergone by the iron minerals was controlled, largely, by the content of organic matter in the sediments. Where there was a low content of neobiogenic organic matter in the near-shore zone of the basins, ferrihydrite would convert to hematite resulting in the evolution of ferruginous oxidic rocks. Where there was a high content of organic matter, ferrihydrite would be reduced to ferrous-protoxide minerals (siderite, chlorites, etc.) and the ores evolved were silicates with varying siderite content. Finally, frequent changes in the

-----

* Ya.V. Samoilov, "On the genesis of iron ores in Central Russia", *Trans. of Miner. Institute. USSR Academy of Sciences*, 1, 1-3 (1931).
** F.V. Chukhrov, L.P. Yermilova, B.B. Zvyagin, A.I. Gorshkov, "Genetic System of Hypergene Iron Oxides", *Proc. Int. Clay Conf.*, Appl. Publ., Wilmette (USA), 1975, pp. 275-286.

geological environment led to the production of mixed rocks.

"There is hardly a single metal in the high concentration of which life plays such a role as it does for manganese," said Vernadsky in his address to the Conference on the Genesis of Iron, Manganese, and Aluminum Ores in April 1935. In the same way, biogenic calcium and iron masses are responsible for their greatest natural masses but along with concentrations of this origin, one is aware of equivalent concentrations related to igneous processes that are altogether independent of the biosphere. Nothing of the kind is known for manganese"*.

The sedimentary rocks which are richest in manganese contain 80% or more manganese oxide. But such high concentrations are rare, and, therefore, it is rocks with a concentration of the element's oxide greater than 10% that are usually called manganese. Similar to iron-bearing rocks, they occur as seams with thickness up to 20 m, and seams-like and lenses-like deposits. Manganese deposits are not as large in dimensions as iron-ore deposits but they may still extend to a few kilometres in length and several hundred metres in width. Oxidic and carbonate manganese rocks are known, the latter being significantly more common.

The oxidic manganese rocks are usually dark, with an earthy, sometimes coarse-grained fracture. Not infrequently, their texture is either nodular or oolitic. They accumulated in a water medium—a lake-palustrine or marine envi-

---

* V.I. Vernadsky, *Works*, v. 1, p. 537 (in Russian).

ronment. Manganese apparently entered these basins in the form of manganese hydroxide colloids and partly in ionic form. The manganese compounds precipitated by coagulation of the colloids in an oxidizing medium. The manganese ores of the weathering crust are a special facial type of oxidic manganese rocks. The major minerals of this type include manganese oxides and hydroxides, one of which has been named vernadite in honour of Vernadsky*.

Carbonate manganese rocks, which are light grey or pinkish, with a fine- or coarse-grained texture and sometimes thin-layered, resemble limestones. They are also produced in the same way that oxidic manganese rocks are produced but by the process of reduction. A.V. Khabakov, a leading Soviet lithologist, wrote the following in 1944, "It is not known in what way the manganese oozes, upon termination of their mundane terrestrial journey, could have begun new geochemical wanderings in lagoon and marine carbonate sediments. Manganiferous accumulations on land lead to finite, exceedingly stable and almost insoluble forms of tetravalent manganese (MnO_2), whereas in the lagoon and littoral-marine carbonate oozes, manganese precipitates in a bivalent form. One wonders if the very environment of life (specifically containing bacteria) along with the products of organic vital activity (humates, for example) is the cause

---

* F.V. Chukhrov, A.I. Gorshkov, V.V. Berezovskaya, A.V. Sivtsov, "Contributions of the mineralogy of antigenic manganese phases from marine manganese deposits", *Mineralium Deposita*, **14**, 3, 249-261 (1979).

Christian Gottfried Ehrenberg. (From: *Abh. Deutsch. Ak. Wiss. Berlin, Klasse für Math. u. allg. Naturwiss.*, 1954, 1.)

Alexander Grigorievich Vologdin. (Published in the Russ. ed. of "TBB".)

for the geochemical revival of manganese"*.

The question of the role of life in the formation of iron-bearing and manganese rocks has excited geologists for over a century now. And, perhaps, in no other field in the science of sedimentary rocks has the clash of opinions been so bitter and at times dramatic, as on that one issue.

Already in 1836, C.G. Ehrenberg, who was previously mentioned for his research on chalk,

---

* A.V. Khabakov, "Ulu-Telyak, a new deposit of oxidized carbonate manganese ores in the Permian deposits of Bashkiria (the western slope of the South Urals)", *Izv. AN SSSR*, *geolog. series*, 3, 19-38 (1944).

detected microbiogenic structures in the so-called "marshy", or "lake", iron ores*. Iron-concentrating bacteria were discovered at the end of the last century. The great microbiologist S.N. Vinogradsky proposed the term "iron bacteria", which is now used. Early in this century microbiogenic sedimentation was also suggested for manganese**. Later, many of the geologists active in the early half of the 20th century widely favoured a theory of the bacteriogenic origin for iron-bearing and manganese rocks.

The January 1947 Session of the Geology and Geography Section of the USSR Academy of Sciences was addressed by A.G. Vologdin*** (1896-1971), Corresponding Member of the USSR Academy of Sciences and winner of the International Paleontological Prize and the Charles Walcott Medal "For the Study of Precambrian Organisms". Vologdin gave an account of his microscopic studies covering a broad range of geological objects. Unlike the futile attempts of G. Molish, Ya.V. Samoilov, and V.S. Butkevich to discover biogenic structures in iron rusts, Vologdin was fortunate to find mineralized remains of iron bacteria in ferruginous and manganese rocks.

One man does not make a team, and A.G. Vologdin's report aroused severe criticism from the

---

* C.G. Ehrenberg, "Weitere vorläutige Nachrichten über fossile Infusorien", *Annalen der Physik u. Chemie*, **38**, 455-464 (1836).

** G.A. Thiel, "Manganese precipitated by microorganisms", *Economic Geology*, **20**, 4, 301-320 (1925).

*** A.G. Vologdin, "The geological activity of microorganisms", *Izv. AN SSSR*, *geolog. series.* 3, 19-38 (1947).

audience. The speaker was reproached for his failure to substantiate his major points, excessive enchantment with microscopy while ignoring other methods of research, unconvincing photographs of microorganisms, and other transgressions. It was over a quarter of a century later that Vologdin's work was evaluated differently.

"Vologdin's hypothesis had been turned down by the geologists of his day for being totally unfounded. In part, this was because the geological public was unprepared to appreciate the formulated ideas. Yet the main reason was, or so it seems to us, the indistinct quality of the microphotographs supplied by the author and the insufficient knowledge about iron-bacterial flora at that time. Many of the now familiar organisms of that group were yet to be described in the 1940s; therefore, the microbe-like structures discovered by the author had no living analogues that were sufficiently similar morphologically". This statement was made by the microbiologist T.V. Aristovskaya.

The major break-through in the study of iron bacteria which Aristovskaya referred to, was achieved by microbiologists when they examined modern iron- and manganese-ore formations in what might be called the laboratories of nature. One such laboratory is found in the lakes of the northwestern Soviet Union—Karelia and the Leningrad Region.

It has been known since times immemorial that the lakes of this region contain concretionary iron and manganese ores. The first iron-smelting and cannon works were built here in the

17th century. Under Peter the Great, iron-ore production was increased and the Petrovsky Plant, one of a number of new factories, was established, from which the city of Petrozavodsk arose.

Lake ores are, in effect, concretions with up to 80% iron and manganese oxides. Based on the size of the concretions the ores were classed into the following types: gunpowder, hail-like, bean, coin, plate, pancake, shield-like, and others.

In 1926, the year "The Biosphere" was published, B.V. Perfiliev, (1891-1969), later to become a professor and holder of the Lenin and State Prizes, made an outstanding discovery during the investigations on Karelia's lake ores.

He managed to uncover undisputed bacterial structures in the lake ores of the North-West and a microzonality in the bottom sediments which he ascribed to the varying intensity of activity by iron-bacteria. Perfiliev hypothesized that in the past geologic epochs, the mechanism of iron accumulation had also been bacterial*.

Perfiliev's discovery gave an impetus to further research on bacterial ore-formation**. New iron-bacterial genera and species, involved in the process, were described. In 1936 Perfiliev described a new genus of bacteria which the evi-

---

* B.V. Perfiliev, "New data on the ore-forming role of microbes", *Izv. Geolog. Comiteta*, **45**, 7, 795-819 (1926).

** B.V. Perfiliev, D.R. Gabe, et al., *Applied Capillar Microscopy. The Role of Microorganisms in the Formation of Iron-Manganese Deposits*, Consultant Bureau, New York, 1965.

Boris Vasilievich Perfiliev. (Photograph by courtesy of D.R. Grabe.)

dence today identifies as playing the major role in manganese and iron concentration in bottom sediments. Perfiliev called it "Metallogenium", or "metal-breeding". In 1949, another researcher, V.O. Kalinenko, named the newly-discovered bacterial species Leptothrix Wernadskyi, after V.I. Vernadsky. Since the late 1950s, ingenious studies into recent lacustrine iron and manganese ore formation have been initiated by G.A. Dubinina of the Institute of Microbiology of the USSR Academy of Sciences*.

Research conducted by microbiologists has revealed that some iron-bacterial species exclusively concentrate manganese oxide**, others, only iron oxide***, and a third group, both these components. Hence, today, the term "iron-manganese" is sometimes applied to describe iron bacteria. Productivity bursts in different iron-bacterial species govern the zonality of bottom sediments, or the pattern of alternating layers with varying ratios of iron-manganese oxides. The range of the physicochem-

Vernadite composed of remains of Metallogenium. 17 000-fold magnification. Electron [micrograph. (Published in the Russ. ed. of "TBB".)

---

* G.A. Dubinina, "The significance of microbiological processes in lacustrine manganese-ore formation", *Verh. int. Ver. Limnol.*, **18**, 1261-1276 (1973).

** K.H. Nealson, "The microbial manganese cycle". In: *Microbial Geochemistry* (ed. W.E. Krumbein), Oxford a.o., Blackwell Sci. Publ., 1983, pp. 191-221.

*** K.H. Nealson, "The microbial iron cycle". *Ibid*, pp. 159-190.

ical conditions of bottom-sediment environments which allow for the existence of the bacteria and its ore-forming activity proved fairly wide, with the pH ranging from 5.8 to 7.5, Eh, from + 20 to + 700 mV, and oxygen content, from trace quantities to 10 mg/litre.

Formation of iron-manganese concretions is a two-stage process. At first, the metals' oxidic compounds are reduced in the bottom sediments by sulphate-reducing and other bacteria, and the reduced iron and manganese compounds move from ooze into water. In the second stage, a reverse process occurs: iron bacteria oxidize the benthic water solutes—iron and manganese protoxidous compounds—to yield ferrihydrite, vernadite and other minerals. It has been found that vernadite can be produced only by very fast oxidation of bivalent manganese to tetravalent—so fast that it cannot be accomplished except with the participation of living matter. Under these conditions, bacteriogenic iron and manganese oxidation proceeds with sufficiently low concentrations of the solutes to exclude abiogenic precipitation. The oxides precipitate in part during mineralization of metallo-organic compounds, that are known to be rather resistant to abiogenic chemical oxidation. This provides evidence in support of Khabakov's hypothesis on the role of living matter and humates (complex-organic compounds) in manganese-ore formation.

Another natural environment where microbiologists conducted their research was the regions where iron-manganese concretions formed in the World Ocean. At depth ranging from 4 to 6.5 km

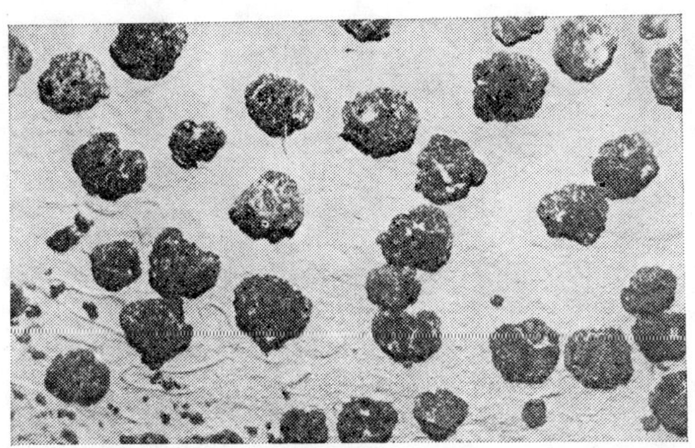

Iron-manganese nodules on the floor of the Pacific Ocean
at a depth of 5145 m. (From: B.C. Heezen, C.D. Hollister, *The Face of the Deep*, New York, 1971, p. 431.)

the concretions sometimes form a solid cover on
the ocean bed, which resembles a boulder pavement. The area covered accounts for about 10%
of the World Ocean bottom. Manganese and iron
are found in a quantity of approximately 25%
and 15%, respectively, in the concretions; the
remainder consists of nickel, cobalt, copper and
the other 35 elements of the periodic table. Like
peat, nodular phosphorites, lacustrine iron and
manganese ores these nodulars are a renewable
mineral resource. The reserves of the iron-manganese nodules increase by many million tons
per year.

Though the nodules are believed by some to be
abiogenic, the recent research findings have
shown bacteria to be an important ingredient

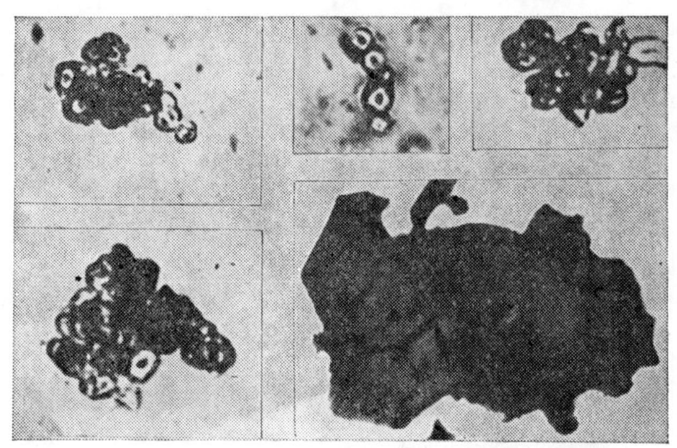

Fig. 26. Comparison of the microstructure of ferruginous minerals and bacteria:

1, 2—bacteria Siderocapsae (culture); *3, 4*—"siderocapsa-like cells" in limonite; *5*—magnetite, displaying complete absence of bacterial structure.

1000-fold magnification. Photographed by T.V. Aristovskaya. (Published in the Russ. ed. of "TBB".)

in their formation*−**. It is probable that benthic Foraminifera are also part of the process, for there are forms among them with a shell composed of various kinds of debris and cemented with iron compounds. It is more probable however that iron finds its way into the sediments with dead plankton or has an altogether different

---

* *Biogeochemical Cycling of Minerals-Forming Elements* (ed. P.A. Trudinger, D.J. Swaine), Elsevier, Amsterdam a.o., 1979, pp. 211-292.

** B.K. Dugolinsky, S.V. Margolis, W.S. Dudley, "Biogenic influence on growth of manganese nodules", *J. Sediment. Petrol.*, 47, 1, 428-445 (1977).

origin, entering the benthic seawater layers from faults in the Earth's crust.

Based on the experience of microbiologists of the past two decades, Aristovskaya revised Vologdin's conclusions. She chose as research samples a few ferruginous minerals: limonite, hematite and magnetite. The research was done microscopically, in transmitted light, following special treatment of the preparations. What was it, then, that Aristovskaya saw?

The hematite and limonite turned out to consist entirely of ferruginous deposits which duplicated the cell outlines of the iron bacteria embedded there*. By comparing the microscopic structure of the mineral masses with the growth patterns of the iron bacteria, it was possible to trace some similarities between the remains of the microorganisms comprising the minerals and fragments of the colonies of some contemporary bacteria. The magnetite, as distinct from the hematite and limonite, exhibited a total lack of bacterial structure.

Aristovskaya studied only ferruginous rocks. The manganese ores of the Paleogene in the Chiatura and Tetritzkaro deposits had been surveyed earlier by the Moscow geologist L.E. Sterenberg**. In preparations of oxalic acid-treated ores, Sterenberg detected and described biogenic structures, not unlike the colonies of the genus Metallogenium already familiar to us.

----

* T.V. Aristovskaya, "Role of microorganisms in iron mobilization and stabilization in soils", *Geoderma*, **12**, 1/2, 145-150 (1974).

** L.E. Sterenberg, "Biogenic structure in manganese ores", *Microbiology*, **36**, 710-712 (1967).

Following these studies by Aristovskaya and
Sterenberg, the biogenic origin of modern iron-
manganese ores, and their ancient analogues as
well, may be considered to be proved beyond
doubt. Many workers view as biogenic not only
Phanerozoic iron and manganese ores, but also
Precambrian iron-bearing quartzites*-**.

The formation of the biogenic matter of iron
and manganese ores follows a somewhat different
course than that of carbonate, siliceous and phosphate rocks, in that it is the benthic film of life,
and not the planktonic film that plays the leading role in the process. They have in common,
however, the conditions of their formation, as
biogenic matter keeps accumulating in aquatic
ecosystems; whether in continental water bodies
or at sea, the key factor during the stage of sedimentogenesis and diagenesis is the concentration function of living matter.

The role of life in the production of allites and
salines is a more debatable issue.

Allites are defined as being rich in free aluminum oxide (alumina). They include bauxites,
the aluminum source material—a rock consisting primarily of aluminium hydroxide minerals. Iron oxide is present in large amounts in
bauxites, ranging from 10 to 30%, while the
silica is present in small amounts in high-grade,
and up to 20% in low-grade types. Like phospho-

---

* G.L. La Berge, "Possible biological origin of Precambrian iron-formations", *Econ. geol.*, **68**, 7, 1098-1109
(1973).
    ** D.D. Klemm, "A biogenic model of the forma-
tion of the banded iron in the Transvaal Supergroup of
South Africa", *Mineral Deposits*, **14**, 3, 381-385 (1979).

rites, bauxites vary widely in external appear-
ance. They may be col-
oured black, white, yel-
low, red and cherry-like,
porous or dense, clayey
or sandy. During the
laboratory section of the
first-year general geology
course, students are
sometimes presented, as
a practical joke, a col-
lection of rocks including
crushed brick, and the
neophytes to geology
define it without hesita-
tion and assuredly as
bauxite. Once this author
also committed this sin!
The term "bauxite" ori-
ginates from Les Baux,

British oceanologist John
Murray. (From: T. Willis
a.o., *Na hraniciach Zeme*,
Bratislava, 1978, s. 354.)

a small hamlet in the south of France where
bauxites were first discovered in 1821. Bauxite
formation is usually explained in terms of a
variety of chemical processes, and as Samoilov
already mentioned in his time, almost all the
theoretically conceivable chemical agents were
cited in the hypotheses that have been suggested by geologists.

The predominant view of bauxites is as a fossilized weathering crust of aluminosilicate rocks
or products of the latter's redeposition. Early
indications that aluminosilicates could decay bio-
genically, through the action of diatom algae,
were provided by the British scientists J. Mur-

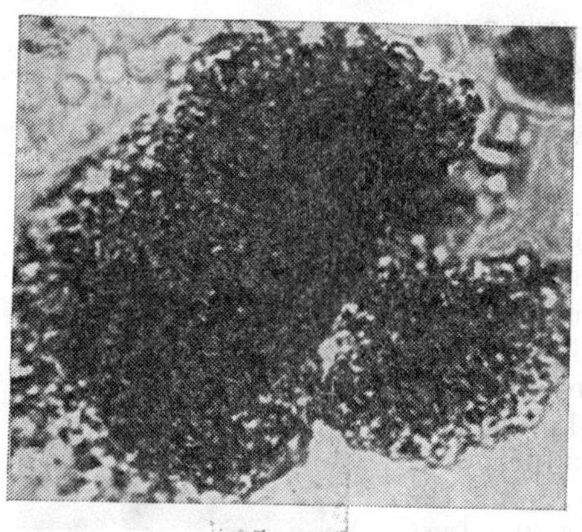

Bauxite particle consisting of microbial cells cemented together. 1000-fold magnification. Photographed by T.V. Aristovskaya. (From: T.V. Aristovskaya, *Microbiology of Soil-Formation Processes*, Leningrad, 1980, Fig. 10, *C*.)

ray and R. Irvine* as far back as the end of the last century. More recently Vernadsky and Coupin**–*** repeated these experiments and both reported their data during the same year in the same journal. Their findings left no room for doubt: diatom algae do decompose aluminosilicates

---

* J. Murray, R. Irvine, "On the silica and the siliceous remains of organisms in modern seas", *Proc. Royal Soc.*, Edinb., 18, 229-250 (1891).

** W. Vernadsky, "Sur le probléme de la décomposition du kaolin par les organismes", *C.R. Acad. Sci.* (Paris), **175**, 450-452 (1922).

*** H. Coupin, "Sur l'origine de la carapace silicense des diatomées", *C.R. Acad. Sci.* (Paris), **175**, 1226-1229 (1922).

and utilize the silica to build their tests, whereas the alumina persists in the water medium as a colloidal solution.

Bauxites were noted earlier to contain impressive quantities of iron oxide. Mindful of the fact, T. Holland* proposed in 1903 that bauxite formation might be attributed, if only in part, to the activity of iron bacteria. This remained merely a proposal, unsupported by any factual evidence, until Vologdin focused his attention on the broad distribution of iron bacteria, which are found not only in ferruginous rocks, but also in allites where they claim between 40 and 45% of the rock volume.

It was not until a few decades later that the A.P. Karpinsky All-Union Geological Research Institute came up with a set of experiments examining the biogenic decomposition of volcanic rocks by bacteria. In their own experiments, L.G. Kramarenko and O.F. Safonova** observed gabbro labradorite, on exposure to microorganisms, convert totally to alumina—the process taking either one or seven years, in an aerobic or anaerobic medium, respectively. In the anaerobic medium the biogenic decomposition of alumina slowed down to two fifths the rate in the aerobic media, and none at all occurred when microorganisms played no part in the process.

---

* T. Holland, "On the constitution, origin and dehydration of laterite", *Geol. Mag.*, *new. ser.*, decade IV, **10**, 59-69 (1903).

** L.G. Kramarenko, O.F. Safonova, "Some findings with respect to the influence of microorganisms on decomposition of gabbro labradorites", *Proc. VSEGEI*, 1976, v. 209, pp. 112-117 (in Russian).

Lev Semenovich Berg. (Published in the Russ. ed. of "TBB".)

Shortly before, G. Taylor and G. W. Hughes* had demonstrated that recent volcanic ashes, like ancient igneous rocks, were susceptible to biogenic decomposition yielding bauxites.

To sum up, one opportunity for living matter to become involved in bauxite formation is through the decomposition of abiogenic matter by the processes of the vital activity of microorganisms.

There may be another alternative though. Some of the plants are known to build up aluminium in their body**, for example, club-moss ash contains up to 30% aluminium. A detailed study of the subject was performed in the 1940s by Hutchinson in collaboration with A. Wollack***. The geological aspect of the problem was first discussed by Academician L.S. Berg (1876-1950), a man whose speciality is as hard to define

---

* G.R. Taylor, G.W. Hughes, "Biogenesis of the Rennel Bauxite", *Econ. Geol.*, 70, 3, 542-546 (1975).

** Y. Stoklasa, "Das Aluminium in Leben der Organismen", *Uonschau*, 26, 134-135 (1922).

*** G.E. Hutchinson, A. Wollack, "Biological accumulators of aluminium", *Trans. Conn. Acad. Arts. a. Sci.*, 35, 73-128 (1943).

as Vernadsky's, for he was, at once, a geographer, ichtyologist, theoretical biologist and a historian of science. Though for some reason not generally considered a geologist, among Berg's works there are the following: "On apparent periodicity in the formation of sedimentary rocks" (1944), "Life and soil formation on the Precambrian continents" (1944), "On the origin of the Ural bauxites" (1945), "Soils and aquatic sedimentary rocks" (1945), "On the origin of the iron ores of the Krivoi Rog type" (1947). With these works Berg inscribed his name in the annals of geological science.

Berg* hypothesized that bauxites might have originated from the mineralization and redeposition of the remains of higher plants containing significant amounts of alumina. Bauxites, according to Berg, were deposited on land, in marshes or in shallow waterlogged fresh water bodies.

For a long time Berg's hypothesis failed to win support among the geological community. Corroborating evidence, all of a sudden, came from where it was least expected—the experimental work of microbiologists.

Aluminium has been known for some time to form complex aluminorganic compounds in the plant body.

Aristovskaya and Zykina** examined in experiment the compounds' decomposition under the

---

* L.S. Berg, *Works*, v. 2, Izd. AN SSSR, Moscow, 1958, pp. 170-207 (in Russian).
* T.V. Aristovskaya, L.V. Zykina, "Biological factors of aluminium migration and accumulation in soil and weathering crusts". In: *Problems of Soil Sciences. Sov. pedol. XI Int. Congr. Soil Sci..*, Moscow, 1977.

action of the iron-manganese bacterium, Metallogenum, only to find that aluminium hydroxide precipitation does occur. "The metal-breeding" bacterium proved capable of breeding actually not only iron and manganese, but also aluminium. On this solid basis, the authors concluded, "We believe the phenomena discovered by us can provide a clue to the mystery of bauxite formation".

The traditional label of "chemogenic rock" for bauxite will now have to be removed, for it is no longer doubted that, at the stage of hypergenesis, the destructive role of living matter is decisive for its formation. It is not excluded either that the concentration function of living matter, responsible for the increased aluminium content in the bauxite source material, also plays an important role.

It is customary to class salines—the sedimentary rocks consisting of readily water-soluble minerals—with purely chemogenic formationsIndeed, it is no longer questioned that vaporization of saturated solutions and crystallization of salts—the spectacular process we remember from our school days—follows an abiogenic course. But where does the salt in the solution come from?

In the regions of progressive salt accumulation the plants contain a lot of mineral salts (up to 40 to 55%); the composition of their ash fraction is also quite extraordinary, with a sodium concentration reaching 65% (for ash), chlorine, as high as 48%, SO_4^{2-}, up to 36% and magnesium, 4.5%. When shedding their leaves, the plants salinize the soil; for example, saxaul litter contains 50% readily soluble salts. During decomposition of the dead organic matter, NaCl, Na_2SO_4, and $MgCl_2$ are the first salts to be leached out. Living matter does not assimilate these salts. They become toxic in large quantities and are only consumed by plants as "compulsory assortment". The remainder of the plant ash substance is composed of calcium, potassium, phosphorus, iron and silicon. Those elements are slow to free themselves during mineralization of the dead organic matter but quick to be captured by living matter.

The chlorides and sulphates of sodium and magnesium extracted from the dead organic matter, migrate in the surface and ground runoff flow, to gather in hollows without natural outlet (salt accumulation centres) or in the World Ocean. V.A. Kovda estimated* that 16 million tons of salts, or one half of the total salt supply, arrives annually at the Aral Sea from neobiogenic matter. Life dumps here the excess salts it does not need—chlorides and sulphates. The salts precipitate abiogenically from super-saturated solutions in salines or isolated sea lagoons. Soda deposits are also formed in this way, with the only difference that in this case sodium combines with atmospheric carbonic acid** as it migrates.

Yet the contribution of living matter to the production of salines is not limited to the concentration function alone. It has long been known

---

* V.A. Kovda, "Biological cycles of salt migration and accumulation", *Soil Sci. Mag.*, 4-5, 144-158 (1944).
** N.I. Bazilevich, *The Geochemistry of Soda-Saline Soils*, Nauka, Moscow, 1965 (in Russian).

Deposits of aluminium hydroxide on accretions of the iron-manganese bacteria Metallogenium. 1000-fold magnification. Photographed by T.V. Aristovskaya. (From: T.V. Aristovskaya, *Microbiology of Soil-Formation Processes*, Leningrad, 1980, Fig. 11, *E*.)

that reef-rocks frequently appear among salt deposits. Why? No plausible answer existed to that question for a long time. Only very recently three Rostov-on-the-Don scientists, V.I. Sedletsky, V.S. Derevyagin and N.I. Boiko, revealed that it is specifically the reef-rocks that most often "isolate" saliferous basins from the World Ocean. They thus become the automatic natural regulators that stabilize the latter's hydrodynamic regime. This means that in the production of salt, the medium-forming function of living matter is also manifested.

We have sequentially discussed eight groups of sedimentary rocks and everywhere found explicit signs of the activity of living matter in one form or another. Of all existing groups only two have not been discussed, detrital rocks and shales. Both these groups are known to be produced by the weathering and redeposition and further diagenesis of primary volcanic and also sedimentary rocks.

Addressing himself to the overstated role frequently assigned to mechanical weathering, Academician B.B. Polynov wrote in 1952, shortly before his death, "At this time we have to give up these habitual notions; conversely, the very concept that some sterile-abiotic weathering is occurring is, no doubt, totally unrealistic, thought-up and unconfirmed by facts. Far be it for me to deny that thermal fragmentation of massive rock is possible, as I do not deny that reactions of oxidation and carbonation are possible. What I do deny outright is that it is possible for these processes to show up in an isolated, sterile manner."* (To be more precise, one should add 'in the conditions of the biosphere'.)

Consequently, with respect to detrital rocks and shales, as in the case of allites and salts, the activity of living matter becomes obvious at the stage of hypergenesis where its main function is a destructive one, leading to the decomposition of abiogenic matter. Clay rocks, at least partially, could also have evolved, as Polynov suggested, from complete mineralization of dead organic matter. Whether this is so is still not clear. In addition to inorganic material, detrital rocks and shales contain a proportion of biogenic organic matter—an average of 0.9% in the shales

---

* B.B. Polynov, *Works*, Izd. AN SSSR, Moscow, 1956, p. 468 (in Russian).

and 0.2 to 0.5% in the detrital rocks. Negligible as these contents may seem, shales are known to contain over three-fourths and detrital rocks over 15% of all the paleobiogenic organic matter of the Earth's sedimentary crust.

Thus, the metabiosphere is composed of rocks which were formed through the participation of living matter in one form or another. Some of the rocks consist of the remains of organisms which once lived on the Earth. These include carbonate rocks, siliceous rocks and caustobioliths, and, in part, also phosphatic rocks. The metabolic products of living organisms formed iron-bearing and manganese rocks. For still other rocks, the role of living matter was limited mainly to the preparation of their source material at the stage of hypergenesis. Examples of these are detrital rocks and shales.

"While the quantity of living matter is negligible in relation to the inert and bio-inert mass of the biosphere, the biogenic rocks constitute a large part of its mass, and go far beyond the boundaries of the biosphere. Subject to the phenomena of metamorphism, they are converted, losing all traces of life, into the granitic envelope, and are no longer part of the biosphere. The granitic envelope of the Earth is the area of former biospheres"*.

Vernadsky's contemporaries found his concept of the granitic envelope as an area of former biospheres paradoxical. But it is known that "truth lies at the bottom of a well", and Vernadsky's

---

* W.I. Vernadsky, "The Biosphere and the Noösphere", *American Scientist*, **33**, 1, 6-7 (1945).

views gradually began to be assimilated by geological science. In the sixties, based on Vernadsky's ideas, the well-known Norwegian petrogra-
pher and geochemist Thomas F. W. Barth
(1899-1970) concluded that "all the rocks we see
today were once sediments... The rocks may have
been altered by plutonism, metamorphism, meta-
somatism, they may have been, at least parly,
remelted and existed in the form of magmas and
lavas, but at some time in the past they formed
from sediments". Sediments, on the other hand,
as we have established, formed with the active
participation of living matter under the conditions
of a biosphere throughout the entire geological history of the Earth.

The concept of new global tectonics that has
taken shape during the last few decades has revealed a possible mechanism for the formation
of the granite layer of the Earth's crust from sedimentary rocks. According to these concepts,
the oceanic Earth's crust moves like a conveyor
belt from the ocean ridges to the continents. It
is exactly on this belt that sediments are deposited; they gradually move forward under the
continents, where they undergo metamorphic
transformations. As a result of these processes,
all traces of the activity of living matter in the
metamorphic rocks are eradicated. It is necessary to "eliminate the metamorphism" to decipher
the initially sedimental nature of the most ancient metamorphic rocks. Geologists of the school
of Academician A. V. Sidorenko (1917-1982)
achieved great successes in this area.

The Earth's metabiosphere presents a record
documenting the development of the biosphere

by which all evolutionary stages of the planet's heterogeneous living matter can be reconstructed. The outstanding Soviet paleontologist and Honorary Member of the American Geological Society, Academician B. S. Sokolov recently stated: "It is probably easiest to determine and analyze the most ancient organisms by the concentration of the products of their vital activity, and, above all, by the accumulation of carbonaceous carbonate and iron-bearing rocks".

Conclusion

In archaeology there exists a concept of cultural stratum; it is the term applied to the layer of earth which develops on the site of human settlements and contains the artifacts of man's activity. It is underlain by the so-called subsoil—virgin soil or rock.

Similarly, the metabiosphere is the "cultural stratum" of the biosphere while the primary rocks produced outside the biosphere constitute the geologists' "subsoil". The two basically differ from each other—the massive, mostly similar, endogenetic rocks and the extremely dissimilar sedimentary and metamorphic rocks making up the Earth's metabiosphere.

Life has created this variety.

"Thereby life appears as a great, permanent and continuous infringer on the chemical diehardedness of our planet's surface... Life is not, therefore, an external and accidental development on the terrestrial surface. Rather, it is intimately related with the constitution of the Earth's crust, and forms part of its mechanism wherein it performs functions of paramount importance, without which this mechanism would not be able to exist."*

---

* W. Vernadsky, *La biosphère*, Alcan, Paris, 1929, p. 30.

Geochronological Scale and Main Events in the History of the Biosphere*

Chronological divisions			Radiometric dates, mln. years ago	Main events
Eon	Era	Period		
Phan-ero-zoic	Cenozoic	Quaternary (or Anthropogene)		Appearance of Homo sapiens, creation of noösphere
			— 2 (?) —	
		Neogenic		Hominids
			— 28 —	
		Paleogenic		Flourishing of mammals, grains
			— 63 —	Great dieing out of dinosaurs
	Mesozoic	Cretaceous		First flowering plants
			— 145 —	
		Jurassic		Flourishing of dinosaurs, first birds
			— 210 —	
		Triassic		Dinosaurs, first mammals
			255 —	

Eon	Era	Period	Age, Ma	Events
	Paleozoic	Permian		Major dieing out of marine fauna
			280	
		Carboniferous		Forests; insects, reptiles
			360	
		Devonian		Amphibians
			415	
		Silurian		Land plants and animals
			465	
		Ordovician		Primitive fish
			520	
		Cambrian		Numerous marine skeletal organisms
			590	
Cryp-to-zoic	Protero-zoic	Vendian		Ediacaric fauna of multicellular in-vertebrates
			670	
				Traces of creeping multicellular ani-mals
				Problematic pellets
			2000	First photoautotrophic eucaryotes
			2600	
	Archean		3500	Ecosystems of procaryotes
			3800	First procaryotes
				Beginning of geological history

* According to data of Flint (1973), Van Eysinga (1975), Valentyne (1981), Harland et al. (1982), and other authors.

Glossary
of Special Terms

ABIOGENIC MATTER (PROCESSES)—matter (processes) originating (proceed) without the participation of living organisms.

AEROBIC MEDIUM—a medium containing free oxygen.

ALUMINA—aluminium oxide (Al_2O_3).
ANAEROBIC MEDIUM—a medium devoid of free oxygen.

APHOTIC ZONE—the part of the ocean where photosynthesis cannot proceed because of poor illumination.

ARCHEOZOIC ERA—the earliest era in the development of the Earth.

AUTOTROPHS—living organisms which do not use ready organic compounds for synthesizing their own organic constituents; subdivided into photoautotrophs and chemoautotrophs.

BENTHIC ZONE—the bottom of lakes, seas and oceans.

BENTHOS—inhabitants of the benthic zone.

BIOCOENOSIS—a community of living organisms which has historically formed in a given ecosystem.

BIOGENIC MATTER—matter created in the course of activity of living organisms.

BIO-INERT SYSTEM—a natural system in which living and nonliving matter interact.

BIOMASS—the mass of living matter per unit area or volume.

BIOTURBATION—the stirring of sediments, conditioned by the activity of living organisms.

BLUE-GREEN ALGAE—see Cyanobacteria.

BRACHIOPODS—invertebrate animals resembling mollusks but attrributed by biologists to another phylum—Tentaculata. Brachiopods flourished in the Paleozoic Era; now they are becoming extinct.

BRYOZOANS—small aquatic animals (about 1 mm in size) of the phylum Tentaculata. Colonies of bryozoans resemble small bushes or prostrate rhizomes.

BYGONE BIOSPHERES—biospheres of the geological past; Vernadsky sometimes included the sediments formed by them in the term as well.

CAMBRIAN PERIOD—the very first period of the Paleozoic Era.

CARBONATE COMPENSATION LEVEL—the depth below which there takes place intensive dissolution of calcium carbonate in the water mass of the World Ocean.

CARBONIFEROUS PERIOD—one of the periods of the Paleozoic Era.

CENOZOIC ERA—one of the geological eras in the development of the Earth.

CHEMOAUTOTROPHS—autotrophic organisms which attain energy by oxidizing inorganic compounds, and use this energy to produce their own organic constituents.

CHEMOGENIC ROCKS (SEDIMENTS)—rocks (sediments) formed as a result of abiogenic (q.v.) chemical processes.

COPROLITES—fossil excrements of vertebrates, consisting mainly of calcium phosphate.

COQUINA—loose sediments consisting mostly or entirely of shells or fragments of sells of mollusks and brachiopods.

CRETACEOUS PERIOD—the last period of the Mesozoic Era.

CYANOBACTERIA—subkingdom of procaryotes, characterized by extreme morphological diversity. Cyanobacteria are otherwise called "blue-green algae".

DETRITUS—fine particles of any substance resulting from disintegration.

DEVONEAN PERIOD—one of the periods of the Paleozoic Era.

DIAGENESIS—one of the stages in the formation of sedimentary rocks, during which fresh sediments are transformed into dense rock.

DIATOMS—unicellular algae with siliceous cell walls, living either singly or in colonies. They are ubiquitous; are an essential component of the plankton and benthos in seas and land water bodies.

DINOFLAGELLATES (or peridinians)—microscopic algae constituting a considerable proportion of marine phytoplankton. Their mass proliferation is called "red tide".

ECHINODERMS—a phylum of multicellular invertebrates. Most echinoderms have a calcareous exoskeleton provided with diverse protrusions or spines. Echinoderms include star fish, ophiuroids, sea urchins, holothurians, crinoids—all typical inhabitants of the benthic film of life of the World Ocean.

ENDOGENETIC ROCKS—rocks which owe their origin to abyssal geological processes (these processes are called endogenic).

ENZYMES—substances that act as catalysts in biochemical processes.

EUCARYOTES—a superkingdom of living organisms characterized by the presence of a typical cell nucleus; comprises plants, fungi, and animals.

EUPHOTIC ZONE—the region of the ocean in which photosynthesis occurs.

FILTER-FEEDING ORGANISMS—aquatic animals that obtain their food by actively filtering large amounts of water in which planktonic organisms and organic detritus are suspended.

FORAMINIFERS—representatives of the Protozoa. Chiefly marine microscopic organisms which secrete chalky, many-chambered shells, the remains of which form a grey mud that is gradually transformed into chalk on the ocean bottom.

GUANO—recent accumulations of the solidified excrement of sea birds on ocean coasts (less frequently, of bats in caves).

HETEROTROPHS—living organisms which cannot independently synthesize organic substances from inorganic ones and are dependent on autotrophs for their supply of food.

HYPERGENESIS—the preparatory stage of formation of sedimentary rock. At this stage, during the weathering of various rocks, initial products of sediments originate and are transferred to various locations.

JURASSIC PERIOD—one of the periods of the Mesozoic Era.

KATAGENESIS—one of the stages of formation of sedimentary rocks, following diagenesis, during which the further densification and transformation of the rocks take place.

LITHOSPHERE—the solid outer envelope of the Earth. Its thickness probably ranges from 50 to 200 km. The upper part of the lithosphere (within the limits of the occurrence of living matter) is included in the biosphere.

LIVING MATTER—the totality of living organisms in the biosphere.

MELANOBIOSPHERE—a zone of the biosphere, where photosynthesis is not possible because of poor illumination.

MESOZOIC ERA—one of the geological eras in the development of the Earth.

METABIOSPHERE (according to Vassoyevich) —a part of the lithosphere, either generated by the living matter of past geological epochs or having been under its influence. The present-day biosphere is not included in the metabiosphere.

METABOLISM—all the chemical reactions taking place in living organisms.

MUD-EATERS—bottom-dwelling organisms which indiscriminately swallow mud and pass it through their alimentary tract.

MUSSELS—bivalve mollusks which often make up tremendous accumulation in the near-shore part of the sea (so-called "mussel banks").

NEOBIOGENIC MATTER — biogenic matter formed by the living matter of the contemporary geological epoch, or, in other epochs, by the living matter of that time. With the passing of geological time, it is transformed into paleobiogenic matter (q.v.).

NEOGENE—one of the periods of the Cenozoic Era.

NODULES—dense mineral formations, originating from the cohesion or coalescence of their constituent particles; they clearly differ from the embedding sediment (or rock.

OPAL—a mineral; solid hydrated amorphous silica ($SiO_2 \cdot nH_2O$).

ORDOVICIAN PERIOD—one of the periods of the Paleozoic Era.

PALEOBIOGENIC MATTER—fossil biogenic matter.

PALEOGENE—the first period of the Cenozoic Era.

PALEOZOIC ERA—one of the geological eras in the development of the Earth.

PELAGIC ZONE—water mass of lakes, seas, and oceans. In the World Ocean it is subdivided into two zones: neritic (the mass of water above the shelf) and oceanic (all the rest of the water mass).

PERMIAN PERIOD—the last period of the Paleozoic Era

PHANEROZOIC EON—the period of time composed of the Paleozoic, Mesozoic, and Cenozoic Eras.

PHOTOAUTOTROPHS—autotrophic organisms which use light energy for producing their organic constituents.

PLANKTON—free-floating organisms found in the upper layers of the water, incapable of active flotation.

POLYCHAETES—a class of multicellular invertebrates of the phylum Annelida (annelid worms); with the exception of a few rare cases, they are marine animals.

PROCARYOTES—superkingdom of living organisms characterized by the absence of a real cell nucleus; comprises bacteria and Cyanobacteria.

PRODUCTIVITY (of living matter)—increase of the biomass, per anum.

PROTEROZOIC ERA—one of the early geological eras in the development of the Earth.

QUATERNARY PERIOD (or Anthropogene)—the period of the Cenozoic Era, lasting up to and including the present time.

RADIOLARIANS—subclass of unicellular invertebrates with a siliceous exoskeleton; typical representatives of the zooplankton of the World Ocean.
SAPROTROPHS—living organisms which feed on degrading organic matter.

SEA URCHINS—one of the classes of echinoderms (q.v.).

SEDIMENTARY ROCKS—rocks occurring in the lithosphere strata which formed by abiogenic and biogenic sedimentation of substances, followed by transformation of the sediments during diagenesis and katagenesis (q.v.).

SEDIMENTOGENESIS—one of the stages in the formation of sedimentary rocks, during which accumulation of sediments takes place.

SHELF (or continental platform)—shallow oceanic zones around continents, extending from the shoreline to the depth at which the sea floor begins to descend steeply. Average width of the shelf is about 70 km; its average depth is about 140 m.

SILICA—silicon dioxide (SiO_2).

SILURIAN PERIOD—one of the periods of the Paleozoic Era.

SPONGES—a phylum of multicellular aquatic sessile invertebrates attached to the bottom or to other solid objects under the water. Sponges usually have the shape of a sack or a deep goblet, opened at the top.

STRATISPHERE (according to Suess)—sedimentary envelope of the Earth.

SULPHATE-REDUCING BACTERIA—heterotrophic bacteria which reduce sulphates and obtain energy by oxidizing organic substances.

THALLOME—the body of lower plants (including algae), without differentiation into stem, leaves, and root.

THIOBACTERIA—chemoautotrophic bacteria which oxidize sulphurous and ferrous compounds.

TRIASSIC PERIOD—the first period of the Mesozoic Era.

UPWELLING—the vertical motion of water in the ocean, as a result of which abyssal water rich in nitrogen, phosphorus, and other elements important for life, rises to the surface.

WEATHERING CRUST—the upper layers of the lithosphere (q.v.), transformed under the action of hypergenesis (q.v.) processes.

Bibliography

Animal-Sediment Relations. "The Biogenic Alteration of Sediments" (Eds. P.L. McCall, M.J.S. Tevesz). In: *Topics in Geobiology*, v. 2, New York, London, Plenum Press, 1982.

Biogeochemical Cycling of Mineral-Forming Elements (Eds. P.A. Trudinger, D.J. Swaine), Amsterdam a.o., Elsevier, 1979.

Biogeochemistry of Ancient and Modern Environments (Eds. P.A. Trudinger, M.R. Walter, B.J. Ralph). Berlin a. o., Springer-Verlag, 1980.

The Biosphere: Problems and Solutions. Studies in Environmental Sciences, v. 25, Amsterdam, Elsevier, 1984.

L. Carlsson, "Kemoautotrofa bakterier klarar hundragradig värme", *Kemist tidskrift*, 13, 10-15 (1984).

P. Cloud, "The biosphere", *Scientific American*, **249**, 3, 132-144 (1983).

F. Crouzel, "Action des animaux, vertébrés et invertébrés, et de la végétation sur les sédiments continentaux", *Bull. Cent. Rech. Explor.-Prod. Elf-Aquitaine*, 8, 85-95 (1984).

"Development and Interaction of the Precambrian Atmosphere, Lithosphere and Biosphere: Results and Challenges", *Precambr. Res.*, 20, 2-4, 590 (1983).

The Earth's Earliest Biosphere: Its Origin and Evolution (Ed. J.W. Schopf), Princeton Univ. Press, 1983.

A.G. Fischer, "Biological innovations and sedimentary record". In: *Patterns Change Earth Evol. Rept. Dahlem Workshop*, Berlin, May 1-6, 1983", (Eds. H.D. Holland, A.F. Trendall). Berlin a.o., Springer-Verlag, 1984, pp. 145-157.

A. Humboldt, *Kosmos. Stuttgart-Tubingen*, Gotta-Verlag, 1845-1862, Bd. 1-5.

H.W. Jannasch, *Leben in der lichtlosen Tiefe des Meeres auf der grundlage schwefelwasserstoff-oxydierender Bakterien*, Jahrb. Akad. Wiss. Gottingen (1984), 1985, pp. 61-67.

V. Jóhansson, "Athugun á uppróti botnledju vegna starfsemi kolkuskelja (Yoldia hyperborea Lonen)", *Náttúrufraedingurinn* (Reykjavik), 54, 2, 49-57 (1985).

E. Kolčinskij, "The main tendencies in the evolution of biosphere". In: *Evolution and Morphogenesis* (Eds. J. Mikovský, V.J.A. Novák), Praha, Academia, 1985, pp. 771-778.

W.E. Krumbein, B.D. Dyer, "This planet is alive—weathering and biology, a multi-facetted problem". In: *The Chemistry of Weathering* (Ed. J.I. Drever), D. Reidel Publ. Co., 1985, pp. 143-160.

J.E. Lovelock, *Gaia. A New Look at Life on Earth*. Oxford a.o., Oxford Univ. Press, 1982.

L. Margulis, D. Sagan, *Microcosmos. Four Billion Years of Evolution from our Microbial Ancestors*, New York, Summit Books, 1986.

Microbial Geochemistry (Ed. W.E. Krumbein), Oxford a.o., Blackwell Sci. Publ., 1983.

"Mineral Deposits and the Evolution of the Biosphere" (Eds. H.D. Holland, M. Schidlowski), *Dahlem Workshop Reports, Phys. and Chem. Sci. Reports*, 3, 334 (1982).

The Natural Environment and Biogeochemical Cycles.— The Handbook of Environmental Chemistry, 1985, v. 1, part D.

V. Omaljev, "Povodom 100 godišnjice rodenia A.E. Fersmana i 120 godišnjice rodenia V.I. Vernadskogo—predlog novih termina u geochemiji i biogeochemiji."—*Radovi Geoinstituta*, 1983, kn. 16, ss. 5-20.

S. Prat, *Studie o biolithogenesi*, Praha, Nakl. Česk. acad. ved a umeni, 1929.

Probleme moderne de ecologie (coord. B. Stugren), Bucuresti, Editura stiint. si enciclop., 1982.

P. Rat, "Essai sur la notion de système bio-sédimentaire," *Mem. Geol. de l'Univ. de Dijon*, 7, 491-501 (1982).

"Role of organisms and organic matter in ore deposition," GAE/MAC Symposium, May 16, 1984, London, Ontario, *Can. J. Earth Sci.*, 22, 12, 1890-1951 (1985).

S. Tagliagambe, "L'originalita e l'importanza del pensiero di Vernadskij," *Scientia*, 118, 505-535 (1983) (in Italian and English).

V.I. Vernadski, *Biosfera*, Beograd, Kultura, 1960.

R. Veski, "Kosmiline, elus—ja surnud aine," *Eesti loodus*, 12, 779-786 (1984).

E. Wada, "From biogeochemistry to global life sciences", *Protein, Nucleic Acid and Enzyme*, 30, 910-915 (1985) (in Japanese).

W.I. Wernadskij, *Geochemie in ausgewahlten Kapiteln*, Leipzig, Akad. Verlagsgessellsch., 1930.